# INVESTMENT MANAGEMENT

# INVESTMENT MANAGEMENT

**Khushboo Manoj**

CENTRUM PRESS
NEW DELHI-110002 (INDIA)

**CENTRUM PRESS**
**H.O.:** 4360/4, Ansari Road, Daryaganj,
New Delhi-110002 (India)
Tel: 23278000, 23261597, 23255577, 23286875
**B.O.:** No. 1015, Ist Main Road, BSK IIIrd Stage,
IIIrd Phase, IIIrd Block, Bangalore-560085 (INDIA)
Tel: 080-41723429
*Email:* centrumpress@gmail.com
*Visit us at:* www.centrumpress.com

*Investment Management*



First Edition, 2011

ISBN 978-93-80921-05-1

PRINTED IN INDIA

*Printed at* Balaji Offset, Delhi.

# Contents

# Preface

All the material is soundly grounded in scientific theory, the book strongly emphasizes applied methods for evaluating investments. This book is very useful for investment professionals as a textbook book. It can also be utilized as a review guide for analysts seeking to update or refresh their skills. It can serve as an excellent supplement to existing texts for investment courses. For the students of Punjab Technical University, the book is an excellent stand-alone investment text for post -graduate courses at all levels.

The book fills an important gap in comprehensive books on investments as it focuses on state-of-the-art theories that can be applied in real-life situations, and it provides actual examples of such applications. As a result of the practical orientation, the book is more rigorous and uses more advanced models than existing investment texts. However, it is easier to understand and learn than alternatives because it supplies an integrated theory of investments that is consistently applied throughout the book and that is concentrated on the concepts which are necessary for real-world applications. The book thus contrasts with typical investment texts that ramble on about useless descriptions of theories without practical significance.

***Author***

# 1

# Introduction

Investment management is the professional management of various securities (shares, bonds and other securities) and assets (e.g., real estate), to meet specified investment goals for the benefit of the investors. Investors may be institutions (insurance companies, pension funds, corporations etc.) or private investors (both directly via investment contracts and more commonly via collective investment schemes e.g. mutual funds or exchange-traded funds).

The term asset management is often used to refer to the investment management of collective investments, (not necessarily) whilst the more generic fund management may refer to all forms of institutional investment as well as investment management for private investors. Investment managers who specialize in advisory or discretionary management on behalf of (normally wealthy) private investors may often refer to their services as wealth management or portfolio management often within the context of so-called "private banking".

The provision of 'investment management services' includes elements of financial statement analysis, asset selection, stock selection, plan implementation and ongoing monitoring of investments. Investment management is a large and important global industry in its own right responsible for caretaking of trillions of dollars, euro, pounds and yen. Coming under the remit of financial services many of the world's largest companies are at least in part investment managers and employ millions of staff and create billions in revenue.

Fund manager (or investment adviser in the United States) refers to both a firm that provides investment management services and an individual who directs fund management decisions.

## TYPES OF INVESTMENTS

*The various types of investment are*:

- *Cash investments*: These include savings bank accounts, certificates of deposit (CDs) and treasury bills. These investments pay a low rate of interest and are risky options in periods of inflation.
- *Debt securities*: This form of investment provides returns in the form of fixed periodic payments and possible capital appreciation at maturity. It is a safer and more'risk-free' investment tool than equities. However, the returns are also generally lower than other securities.
- *Stocks*: Buying stocks (also called equities) makes you a part-owner of the business and entitles you to a share of the profits generated by the company. Stocks are more volatile and riskier than bonds.
- *Mutual funds*: This is a collection of stocks and bonds and involves paying a professional manager to select specific securities for you. The prime advantage of this investment is that you do not have to bother with tracking the investment. There may be bond, stock- or index-based mutual funds.
- *Derivatives*: These are financial contracts the values of which are derived from the value of the underlying assets, such as equities, commodities and bonds, on which they are based. Derivatives can be in the form of futures, options and swaps. Derivatives are used to minimize the risk of loss resulting from fluctuations in the value of the underlying assets (hedging).
- *Commodities*: The items that are traded on the commodities market are agricultural and industrial commodities. These items need to be standardized

and must be in a basic, raw and unprocessed state. The trading of commodities is associated with high risk and high reward. Trading in commodity futures requires specialized knowledge and in-depth analysis.

- *Real estate*: This investment involves a long-term commitment of funds and gains that are generated through rental or lease income as well as capital appreciation. This includes investments into residential or commercial properties.

## CAPITAL ACCUMULATION

Capital is wealth that may be in the form of money or property (including real estate, stocks and bonds) owned by an entity (a person or business). In the world of investing, the term capital can be used for assets that are invested in order to gain from a rise in their value. Capital accumulation is the growth in the total value of the capital.

## CAPITAL: RELATED TERMS

*Here are some terms associated with the concept of capital*:

- *Capital Asset*: Any asset used for wealth creation.
- *Capital Gains*: The profits made on selling an asset.
- *Capital Market*: This is the marketplace for securities, such as shares and bonds, where businesses try to raise long term funds.
- *Financial Instruments*: Contracts of various combinations of capital assets, serving as a store of value, unit of account, medium of exchange or standard of deferred payment.
- *Capital Budgeting*: Also known as investment appraisal, it is the planning process that determines the profitability of long term investments.
- *Cost of Capital*: The cost to a borrower when they are loaned money, or the interest rate on a principal amount that has been loaned.
- *Capital Appreciation*: The rise in the market value of an asset the original investment in it.

- *Capital Risk*: The risk of losing the whole or part of the principal amount spent on an investment.

## CONNOTATIONS OF CAPITAL ACCUMULATION

*The term capital accumulation can have various connotations in different contexts*:

- Spending less than what one earns (accumulation in the form of savings).
- Making investments in physical assets such as plants, equipment, machinery and raw materials.
- Investing in contracts of assets on paper.
- Training human capital and increasing its skill base.

There is always a possibility that the return on an investment will differ from expectations. The amount of risk that investors are willing to take is directly proportional to the potential returns on their investments. This is because investors have to be rewarded for taking additional risk. For example, US Treasury bonds are one of the safest and lowest yielding investments. The capital appreciation on stocks is much higher, since they are much more risky (a corporation is more likely to declare bankruptcy than the US government).

## COST OF CAPITAL

Cost of capital is the minimal return that investors intend to earn on their investments. For shareholders, the cost of capital is the dividend and capital gains on the share value, while for bondholders it is the interest rate quoted on a bond.

While investing, it is essential to consider the opportunity cost of the invested capital, as it represents the return that is foregone by investors by choosing an alternative investment opportunity that has similar or comparable risk. So, this factor may be considered while calculating the cost of capital.

## CALCULATING COST OF CAPITAL

*There are two ways to calculate the cost of capital*:

Weighted Average Cost of Capital (WACC)- This is the minimum return that a company must realise from an existing asset base in order to fulfill the needs of its creditors, owners and investors.

Weighted average cost of capital (WACC) for the invested capital contains equal proportions of equity and debt, which is calculated as:

- WACC = (E/F) Re + (D/F) Rb (1-tc)
- Where Total capital invested (F) = D + E and,
- Re = Expected rate of return on equity or cost of equity (%)
- Rb = Expected rate of return on borrowings or cost of debt (%)
- tC = Corporate tax rate (%)
- D = Current value of the firm's total debt and leases
- E = Total market value of equity and equity equivalents

However, if a part of the capital comprises of a preferred stock or an asset with a different cost of invested equity, then the formula may be modified as follows:

- WACC = Wd (1-T) Rd + We Re
- Wd = Debt portion of value
- T = Tax rate
- Rd = Cost of debt (rate)
- We = Equity portion of the total value of a firm
- Re = Rate (Cost) of internal equity

Capital Asset Pricing Model (CAPM) – This model states that investors must be compensated for the risks associated with an investment and time value of money. So, the CAPM calculates the expected return from a security (Es) as follows:

$$Es = Rf + ßs (Rm-Rf)$$

*Where*:

- Rf = Expected risk-free return from the security
- ßs = Sensitivity of the security to market risk
- Rm = Historical returns from financial markets
- (Rm-Rf) = Risk premium of market assets over risk-free assets

Investors are advised to refrain from investing when the expected return falls short of the required return.

## INVESTING RISK

In investing parlance, risk refers to the probability of a monetary loss or actual returns from an investment being lower than the expected returns. There is an inverse relationship between investing risk and return. Investment options that are risky need to offer higher returns than those that are less risky in order to attract investors and make it worthwhile to take on the additional risk.

## TYPES OF RISKS

A US Treasury bond is considered to be among the safest investments and equities are associated with higher risks. However, every investment involves risk, the difference being in the degree and the type.

- *Capital risk*: This refers to the risk of losing the capital invested.
- *Currency risk*: If one holds assets in a foreign currency, changes in the exchange rate can cause fluctuations in the asset value. A decline in the value of the foreign currency vis-à-vis the investor's domestic currency will result in a reduction in the value of the asset in terms of the home currency. This is known as currency risk or exchange rate risk.
- *Liquidity risk*: The risk associated with a delay in the trade of an asset is known as liquidity risk. An asset sale may be difficult due to the small size of the market or low demand, preventing the owner from converting the asset into cash.
- *Credit risk*: The risk associated with the inability of the borrower to repay the principal is known as credit risk. For instance, the owner of a corporate bond could suffer losses in case the issuing company declares bankruptcy and is unable to redeem the bond.
- *Inflation risk:* Inflation erodes the value of a currency. The possibility of the value of an asset declining due to contraction in the purchasing power of a currency is called inflation risk.

- *Interest rate risk*: The possibility of devaluation of an interest-baring asset (such as bonds, stocks and loans) due to a change in the interest rate is known as interest rate risk.
- Market risk: This refers to the possibility of a decline in the value of an investment due to a change in price. Price fluctuations may be caused by changes in the interest rate, foreign exchange rate, inflation or demand and supply situation.
- *Legal risk*: The risk associated with changes in laws and regulations is called legal risk.
- *Counterparty risk*: This refers to the risk of the other party in an agreement defaulting. For instance, the risk faced by an option owner of the other party not selling the underlying asset as agreed is called their counterparty risk.

There are a number of other risks that an investor may be exposed to. Before making a choice of investment, it is critical to understand the risk involved and ways in which one can minimize risk exposure.

## INVESTOR

An investor is a person or entity who invests money in various asset classes for financial gain. Investors can be individuals or companies that purchase equity, debt securities, currency, real estate and commodity derivatives to generate income streams, capital appreciation or both.

## INVESTOR TYPES

*Investors can be categorized as*:

- *Individual investors*: These can be anybody looking to invest in shares, bonds, foreign exchange or other securities. Trusts acting on behalf of individuals also come under this category.
- *Investment banks*: These are financial institutions that assist companies in raising funds by issuing equity. These banks perform other financial services, such as trading in equities, foreign exchange, commodities

and derivatives, on behalf of their clients. Apart from providing consultancy services to businesses, these banks facilitate corporate restructuring and mergers and acquisitions. Investment banks earn profits by issuing and selling stocks and bonds.

- *Businesses*: These are organizations that make investments in companies requiring funds to either expand into new markets or for new product development. These businesses fund the capital requirements of such companies in exchange for a stake in the company or for a share of profits generated through these new ventures. The risk is shared equally by the investors and the company that receives the funds.
- *Funds:* These may be hedge funds or mutual funds, in which investors pool in money to invest in securities, such as shares, bonds or commodities. The ownership of these funds may not be publicly tradable.
- *Venture capital funds*: These funds collect money from high net worth individuals (HNWIs) or institutional investors to invest primarily in early-stage, high-potential companies. The pooled money, called venture capital, is invested in such growth companies in exchange for a stake in these firms. The aim of venture capital funds is to realise huge profits during the invested company's IPO (initial public offering) or sale. However, investments in growth firms are inherently risky.
- *Angel investors*: These are either individuals or a group of affluent investors who provide starting capital for a business in exchange for a part ownership or convertible debt. These investors sometimes also provide specific expertise to these new firms. The sole investment purpose of these investors is to generate high returns. Other types of investors are those who collect valuable objects, such as antiques and works of art.

## ASSET

An asset is anything of value owned by a person or company. Assets can be converted into cash depending on demand conditions. In accounting, the term "asset" in a balance sheet includes cash, inventories, property rights and goodwill. Assets can be used to generate cash flows.

## TYPES OF ASSETS: TANGIBLE

*The various types of assets are*:

- *Tangible assets*: These assets have a physical existence, such as equipment, building and real estate. It has two sub-classes:
- *Current assets*: These are cash as well as assets that can be converted into cash, or consumed within a year or within an operating cycle.

*These assets include*:

- *Cash and its equivalents*: Including currency, deposit accounts, money orders, checks and bank drafts.
- Inventory: Stock of goods held by an organization.
- *Accounts receivable*: The amount owed to an asset holder in exchange for goods and services provided.
- *Short term investments*: Securities bought to be sold in the near future. These investments are aimed at generating income on short-term price movements.
- *Prepaid expenses*: Operating costs paid for services or products to be used in the future.
- *Long-term investments*: These assets are often bought to be held for long term and can include land, special funds, bonds, long-term notes and stocks.

*Fixed assets*: These assets, such as tools, machinery, land, buildings and furniture, are purchased with the sole aim of generating profits. Fixed assets, also called PPE (property, plant and equipment), are purchased for long term use.

## TYPES OF ASSETS: INTANGIBLE

### Intangible Assets

Are not present in the physical form, which makes it very

difficult to evaluate the m. Thus, these assets cannot be bought and sold at fair value.

*These assets include*:

- *Patents*: Exclusive rights granted to a person for an invention or a discovery for a specific timeframe.
- *Copyrights*: Legal rights granted to the owner of an intellectual property, granting him/her exclusive rights. No one can use that intellectual property without obtaining permission from the copyright owner.
- *Goodwill*: This is the difference between the current and fair market price of the net asset value (NAV) of a company.
- *Trademark:* A distinguishing attribute by which a company is readily identified.
- *Trade name*: It is a name under which a business trades. This name could be different from the registered or legal name and can be considered as the company's brand.

## APPRECIATION

Appreciation is an increase in the value of an asset, such as stocks, options, currency, bonds and real estate, over a specific period of time. It is the amount by which the selling price of an asset is higher than the initial price. This term also encompasses a rise in the value of an asset held in a company's accounting book.

Appreciation may be driven by a sudden spurt in the demand for an asset, the scarcity of supply of the asset or changes in the inflation rate or the interest rate.

## HOW TO MEASURE APPRECIATION?

*Appreciation in the value of an investment option includes*:

- Capital appreciation: This is the difference between the actual sale and the purchase price of a financial asset, such as stocks, options, currency and bonds. For example, if an investor purchases 100 shares of a company for $10 per share and sells the same after

12 months for $10.50 per share, then the capital appreciation is $50 ($0.50 per share).

- Interest amount: Interest is generally paid on capital invested in debt instruments, such as bonds and mutual funds, as well as cash investments, such as savings accounts and certificates of deposit (CD). Interest can be either simple or compound. Simple interest is the interest calculated on the principal amount and does not take into account the time value of money (which refers to inflation/deflation and increases or decreases in the purchasing power of the invested capital). Compound interest is calculated on both the principal and the interest accrued over 12 months.

Interest and capital appreciation together form the total return on investment (ROI). For instance, if a bond is purchased at $20 and pays $2 as interest annually and the bondholder sells the bond for $25 after 12 months, then the ROI is $7 ($5 of capital appreciation and $2 as interest).

*Different methods are used to calculate interest in varies types of securities*:

- *Stock dividends, US mortgages and GIC*: Simple interest is calculated.
- *Bond yields*: Compounds interest every six months.
- *Bond coupons*: Are accrued daily and measured as simple rate.
- *Stock indexes*: Interest compounds annually on the price alone.
- *Stocks and mutual funds*: Compound every time cash flows to/from investors.
- *US normal mortgage*: Interest is measured as simple rate.

## RETURN ON INVESTMENT

Return on investment (ROI) is also called the rate of return (ROR) and is a measure of the performance of any investment. It is the ratio between the financial benefit or loss of an investment and the amount of money invested.

## RETURN ON INVESTMENT: CALCULATION

*The return on investment can be calculated by the following formula*:

ROI = (Net Income/Cost of Investment) × 100,

where,

ROI = Return on Investment

Net Income = Income from investment - Cost of Investment

The return on investment is always expressed as a percentage.

For instance, if the cost of investment is $20,000 and the gain from the investment is $22,000, then the net income will be $22,000-$20,000, or $2,000, and the ROI will be ($2,000/$20,000) × 100 = 0.1 × 100, or 10%.

In case the ROI is negative, it means the cost of investment is higher than the benefits (income) from that investment. This indicates a loss and this investment should not be considered.

## ROI AND TIME

The calculation of ROI does not indicate the duration of the investment. It does not reveal the gestation period.

## ROI AND THE RULE OF THUMB

There are certain rules of thumb that make it easy to introduce the concept of time in ROI. These rules assume that the annual rate of return is constant and that the ROI is compounded once a year.

- *Rule of* 72: This indicates how long it would take to double your investment. To calculate this, divide 72 by the ROI. For instance, if the ROI is 10, then the time it would take to double this investment is 7.2 (72/10) years.
- *Rule of* 114: This indicates how long it would take to triple your money. To calculate this, divide 114 by the rate of return. It would take 11.4 (114/10) years to grow your money threefold.
- *Rule* of 144: This calculates how long it will take to grow your money four times. In the example

considered, the time taken to quadruple your money is 14.4 (144/10) years.

While these are fairly good estimates, they are by no means accurate. A proper understanding of ROI is a prerequisite for investing wisely. So, don't forget to calculate and compare the ROI of the various investments you are considering.

## INVESTMENT COMPANY

An investment company is one that is in the business of investing in securities. Its core business is to hold securities of other companies only for investment purposes. The profits and losses are shared among those who invest in an investment firm as per their portfolio. The performance of the securities is the major factor determining the performance of investment companies.

## TYPES OF INVESTMENT COMPANIES

*The following are the main types of investment companies*:

Management Investment Company: Most investment companies are management investment companies, which are engaged in managing portfolios of securities. Management investment companies can be divided into two categories depending upon the types of securities they offer:

- *Open-End Investment Company*: This type of investment company issues new shares on a continuous basis. The shares may be bought from and sold back to the investment company. Open-end investment companies may also be referred to as mutual funds.
- *Closed-End Investment Company*: This type of investment company sells shares in a onetime public offering. The shares are not offered on a continuous basis. Investors can buy and sell the shares in the open market. The demand and supply of the shares of these closed-end funds determine their market value.
- *Unit Investment Trusts (UITs): These investment companies have the following features*:

- A trustee supervises the management of a UIT investment company.
- A predetermined number of shares are sold to unit holders, who become eligible for a share of net income that the main trust generates.
- The securities of UITs are redeemable.
- The portfolio of securities is not managed on a daily basis.

Exchange-Traded Funds (ETFs): These investment companies can be either UITs or open-end investment companies. The goal of ETFs is to attain a return equal to a particular market index.

- *Hedge Funds*: These are investment pools that are private and unregistered. They are not subject to the numerous regulations that protect investors of mutual funds.
- *Face Amount Certificates*: These investment companies are engaged in issuing debt certificates at a fixed interest rate. Such investment companies are rare today. Face amount certificate holders can covert them into cash on a predetermined date before maturity. Buyers can pay either a lump-sum or periodic installments.

## REAL ESTATE INVESTMENT

Real estate investment involves the commitment of funds to property with an aim to generate income through rental or lease and to achieve capital appreciation. Real estate refers to immovable property, such as land, and everything else that is permanently attached to it, such as buildings. When a person acquires real estate, s/he also acquires a set of rights, including possession, control and transfer rights.

Understanding real estate investment is crucial because it usually involves a substantial investment and a long-term one. Moreover, the real estate market can be unpredictable. This is particularly important when one goes beyond buying a home to actually 'investing' in real estate. There are a number of ways in which an investor can participate in the real estate market.

## REAL ESTATE INVESTMENT: RENTAL

One can opt for real estate investment with an aim to rent the property out to a tenant. The owner (landlord) earns a continuous stream of rent from the tenant, but is responsible for paying the mortgage, taxes and any costs associated with maintaining the property. The owner also benefits from capital appreciation (a rise in the value of the property over time). The landlord runs the risk of not finding a tenant and could suffer negative monthly cash flows, with mortgage payments and maintenance expenses still to be borne. As compared to owning stocks and bonds, rental real estate requires a significant amount time and effort to be devoted by the landlord.

## REAL ESTATE INVESTMENT GROUPS

Real estate investment groups are similar to small mutual funds. They are set up for rental properties. While an investor may own one or more units, a professionally managed company acquires, builds, maintains and lets out all the units on the properties in exchange for a percentage of the monthly rent.

## REAL ESTATE TRADING

Real estate traders hold properties for only a short span of time (less than four months), aiming to sell them at a profit. This process is called flipping properties. Investors aim at purchasing significantly undervalued or very hot properties. Such owners may or may not invest money into improving the property before putting it back on sale. A bear market could result in substantial losses for a real estate trader, since the investment is large.

## INVESTMENT FUND

An investment fund is a firm that pools funds from a number of retail investors and invests the same for a fee. Thus, an investment fund enables investors to gain exposure to a broad range of options. Moreover, the investment fund is able to achieve economies of scale, bringing down the trading costs.

Investment funds are suitable for investors who wish to invest in securities without studying the characteristics of the various options. Private bankers, trust managers or other advisers often direct some or all of the assets of their clients towards fund investments.

In terms of risk and reward, an investment fund can range from being ultra-safe, low-yielding bond funds to being highly-leveraged derivative hedge funds.

## TYPES OF INVESTMENT FUNDS

Investment funds can be open-ended or closed-ended. An open-ended fund is an investment fund that allows investors to sell their share in the fund whenever they want, whereas closed-ended investment funds require the investment to be kept locked up for a fixed period.

*Investment funds can be either of the two types*:

- *Private funds*: This type of fund involves up to 50 investors, with each contributing a significant amount of money (not less than $1 million per investor). The money is then invested into a particular class of assets. Private funds are usually closed-ended funds and are selected by people who have a long-term investment horizon. In this type of investment fund, money managers use their specialized knowledge of the selected asset class to obtain higher returns than that expected from public funds.
- *Public funds*: Public funds offer high flexibility, liquidity and transparency. These funds are required by law to declare their net asset value (NAV) on a regular basis. Most of these funds have an open-ended structure.

## INVESTMENT FUNDS IN EMERGING MARKETS

The contribution of investment funds in emerging markets has risen dramatically over the past several years. Only a few investment funds, with a total cash flow of $700 million, were investing in listed securities in the emerging markets in 1984.

However, within a decade, the capital targeted at emerging markets had risen to more than $100 billion, with close to a thousand funds participating in the change.

## EXAMPLES OF INVESTMENT FUNDS

*Some of the high-yielding investment funds are:*

- Melchior Japan Opportunities.
- Jupiter Emerging Markets.
- Invesco Perpetual Latin American.
- New Star UK Strategic Income.
- Old Mutual UK Smaller Companies.
- Old Mutual UK Select Mid-cap.
- JPMF UK Dynamic.
- Allianz RCM UK Mid-cap.

## INVESTOR RELATIONS

Investor relations refers to communication between a company and the investing community regarding developments that could have a bearing on the company's stock valuation. Investor relations is considered a management responsibility and several disclosures are required by law. Such disclosures may include quarterly or annual financial reports, change in the top management of a company or strategic alliances. These days, most public traded financial entities and corporations have departments dedicated to investor relations. This department also addresses and resolves queries from potential investors. The investor relations department may be headed by a treasurer or the chief financial officer. Effective investor relations contributes towards a company's stock achieving fair valuation.

## HISTORY OF INVESTOR RELATIONS

The evolution of investor relations covers three eras, namely 1945 to 1970 (the communication era), 1970 to 2000 (the financial era) and from 2000 onwards (the synergy era).

In the communication era, investor relations and issues were handled by press agents or other publicists. The lack of financial expertise and strategic management were the weak areas of this era. In 1953, it was Ralph Cordiner, the chairman of General Electric, who created a new position for handling shareholder communications, which is today known as 'investor relations.'

In the financial era, professional investors became important. Finance professionals and accountants handled tasks related to investor relations.

In the synergy (current) era, an effective combination of communication and financial skills are utilized to contribute to investor relations.

This two-way communication enables the company and investors to share information and helps to improve understanding on both sides.

## CURRENT TRENDS IN INVESTOR RELATIONS

The current trends in investor relations involve the easy flow of information to support investor meets. The Securities and Exchange Commission (SEC) favours the use of electronic communication tools by companies and investors. Popular tools include blogs, electronic shareholder forums and proxies.

Travel budgets have begun to shrink, thanks to conference calls and new web tools that have made shareholder interactions smoother than before. Companies are also eager to let investors access valuable information and provide instant feedback. Increased awareness of transparency requirements and the introduction of XBRL (Extensible Business Related Language) have remarkably impacted the possibilities for further growth and expansion in investor relations.

## INVESTMENT SECURITIES

Investment securities refer to certificates or documents that indicate that you have an interest in a business or have lent money to a company or a government entity. Investment securities are of two types, namely equity securities (such as common stocks) and debt securities (such as bank notes, Treasury bills and bonds). An entity or corporation that issues securities is known as the issuer.

## WHAT ARE THE TYPES OF INVESTMENT SECURITIES?

*Here is a list of the main types of investment securities*:

*Bond*: A bond is a type of loan or debt security for a certain period for which the issuer pays interest at a predetermined rate. Bonds can be issued by credit institutions, government agencies, corporations and public authorities. The principal amount is paid back at a later date – the maturity date or maturity.

The issuer can pay the interest on bonds in intervals or as a lump-sum after maturity. Bonds generate fixed income in the form of interest.

*Underwriting is the most common method of issuing bonds. Bonds are categorised as follows*:

- Bearer and Registered Bonds
- Treasury Bonds
- Treasury Bills
- Treasury Notes
- General Obligation and Revenue Bonds
- Participating Bonds
- Zero Coupon Bonds
- Convertible Bonds
- High Yield (Junk) Bonds
- Indexed Bonds
- Warrant Bond (Bonds with warrants)
- Mortgaged backed Securities
- Commercial Paper
- Sinking Bond Funds

*Equities*: Also known as shares, this pertains to the amount of ownership you buy in a company. The general public usually opts for equities.

*Consider investing in the following*:

- Common Stock
- Preferred Stock
- Par Value
- Book Value
- Classes of Stock
- Dividends

- Ex-Dividend
- Stock Splits
- Treasury Stock
- Depository Receipts
- DRIPS

*Commodities*: Commodities are those goods which are supplied by a number of suppliers irrespective of differentiation in quality. Tea, coffee, petroleum, milk, copper, rice, wheat, and coal are commodities. So, a contract for buying or selling these commodities can be termed as a security.

*Derivatives*: These are financial instruments that drive their value from direct securities, such as equities and bonds. Derivatives were called as hedging instruments earlier.

*Consider the following options*:

- Futures
- Swaps
- Index options
- Covered calls
- Uncovered calls
- Warrants
- Repurchase Agreements

## INVESTMENT SERVICES

Financial institutions and professional financial advisers offer a host of investment services that are focused on helping their clients meet predetermined financial goals. These investment services may be customised to a client's income levels, circumstances and objectives and focus on wealth creation and protection. Investment services include making, organizing and managing investments and may also encompass financial planning, accounting, life insurance and tax planning.

## TYPES OF INVESTMENT SERVICES

Prior to the late 1990s, US commercial banks were forbidden by law to offer investment services. The Gramm-Leach-Bliley Act of 1999 made it legal for a bank to offer both commercial and investment services. Over the years, the distinction between commercial and investment banks has blurred.

*The types of investment services offered by banks include*:

- *Money management*: The first step for any investor is to ascertain the amount of money he has at his disposal for investing and the various financial options available to maximize returns and tax rebates and minimize risks.
- *Portfolio management services*: These services are aimed at investors achieving the right mix of investments, such as stocks, bonds, commodities, derivatives and CDs, depending upon their financial goals and risk appetite. Portfolio management encompasses making a choice between equity and debt, domestic and international investments as well as growth and safety.
- *Retirement planning services*: Once the retirement goals have been laid down, appropriate investments need to be made into pension plans, 401(k) plans and profit sharing plans. One may also need to invest into the financial and money markets to ensure a steady stream of income post retirement.
- *Collective investment portfolio management*: Banks offer advice on collective investments, such as mutual funds, ETFs and managed funds. One may also need professional advice for investing in hedge funds. Such funds hedge their risks via methods like short selling.
- *Brokerage services*: Investors need brokers to trade in bonds, stocks, foreign currency and derivatives. The brokerage services offered by banks are considered more reliable and are preferred to those offered by individual brokers.

Apart from financial goals, investors may have other priorities that financial institutions providing investment services can take into account. Such priorities may include socially responsible investing, green investing and sustainable investing.

## SPECULATION

Speculation refers to making financial decisions by assuming the risk of loss for the potential for increased returns. There is really a very thin line of difference between speculation and investment and between a speculator and an investor. While all investors must speculate (albeit at different degrees), all speculators must invest in order to make profits.

## THE DIFFERENCE BETWEEN INVESTMENT AND SPECULATION

*The difference between an investor and a speculator can be seen vis-à-vis the following parametres:*

- *Holding period*: While an investor usually has a longer planning horizon and holds the investment for at least a year, a speculator holds the investment for a few days or months.
- *Risk disposition*: While an investor takes on moderate risks, a speculator assumes significantly higher risk.
- *Expectation of returns*: An investor expects moderate returns, while a speculator makes investments that promise high returns.
- *Decision making*: An investor would carefully evaluate the factors impacting the investment. A speculator would depend more on tips and market sentiments.

## HOW SPECULATION YIELDS RETURNS

The degree of speculation tends to rise when the economy is bullish and the markets are buoyant. This is how bubbles are created. A bubble is a phenomenon during which the value of an investment (such as real estate, stock, foreign exchange and petroleum futures) rises substantially. Most of the investments are overpriced in such a scenario, yielding high returns.

## SPECULATION: DANGERS

A speculative buying spree, devoid of analytical calculation, aggravates the element of risk. Any downturn in prices can cause panic and excessive selling, resulting in a dramatic plummeting of prices and eventually a market crash. The stock market crisis of 2008 can be attributed to consecutive periods of speculative buying, followed by panic and speculative selling.

## HOW SPECULATION HELPS THE MARKET

Speculation can be a blessing for the economy. This is because speculators inject capital in the market, thereby increasing liquidity. Speculative investments also minimize the risk for arbitrageurs and hedgers.

Benjamin Graham (author of the classic books Security Analysis and The Intelligent Investor and mentor to Warren Buffett) urged people to ignore the market as a whole and focus on the true "value" represented by an investment.

## CAPITAL INVESTMENT

A business needs cash to purchase fixed assets, such as land, building, equipment and machinery, as well as to take care of day-to-day operating expenses. The money invested in a business for the purchase of fixed or large assets is called capital investment.

Capital investment decisions are crucial as their impact on a business is long term. Thus, it is important to evaluate the economic feasibility of the investment.

## POINTS TO CONSIDER WHILE MAKING A CAPITAL INVESTMENT

While making a capital investment, one must consider its impact on the profitability of the business in the long term. When estimating profitability, one needs to consider the time value of money. This concept is based on the fact that cash in hand is worth more than cash receivable at a future date. This is because currently-available cash can be invested to generate earnings, while the value of cash to be received in future can decline due to inflation.

A capital investment may result in an increase in revenues. However, revenue growth does not necessarily mean positive returns from the investment, since several factors, such as inflation, interest rates on loans and opportunity cost of money, need to be taken into consideration while calculating the returns.

## DETERMINING THE FEASIBILITY OF A CAPITAL INVESTMENT

*One can determine the economic feasibility of a capital investment through the following steps*:

- Discount the cash returns from the investment to reflect the time value of money. Adjusting the future flow of income to the present value would help in judging whether the returns are at least equal to the cost of the debt and equity funds that need to be committed by your business to purchase the asset.
- Calculate the present value of cash required to buy the asset. This value is equal to the purchase price of the asset in most cases. However, this value can be higher in case you wish to build in additional capital to replace or maintain equipment within the facility.
- Calculate the annual benefits or net cash flows within the asset's useful lifetime. The benefits would be the increased net cash flows from the specific investment on an after-tax basis.
- Compute the present value of the annual net cash flows. This will give you an estimate of the amount of net cash flows you would be able to generate through the capital investment.
- The last computation required is the subtraction of the present value of investment derived in step 2 from the net present value of the investment returns calculated in step.
- A capital investment should be approved only if the value in step 5 is positive. A negative figure reflects that the capital investment will result in losses.

## INVESTMENT PROPERTIES

A property that you buy with the purpose of generating financial returns is called an investment property. This property could be land, a single apartment or house, a block of flats, a commercial or industrial building. Investment properties generate profitsthrough rental income, capital growth or both. Investment properties are generally not used for residential purposes. You can also generate rental income from your residential home by renting out spare rooms, but this is finding compatible and reliable tenants can be tough. So, buying a separate investment property and using this to generate rental income is usually a better option.

## BENEFITS OF BUYING INVESTMENT PROPERTIES

- Investment in property is usually prone to less volatility than shares. The investment in this sector is relatively a safe form of investment.
- The value of your property rises in the long term.
- You become eligible to receive tax deductions. You can include depreciation in the value of the investment property due to wear, tear and obsolescence as deductions in your tax returns.
- You can obtain tax variations and enhance your cash flows.
- You can earn from the rental income.
- You can make use of negative gearing. A negatively geared investment property is one in which the interest on the property loan is higher than the rental income derived from the property. By indicating the difference between the interest and the rental income as losses incurred on the investment, you can get deductions in your tax returns. This is the legal remedy to reduce your taxes.

By seeking proper advice from qualified experts such as accountants, financiers and quantity surveyors, it is possible to maximize the benefits you receive from your investment property.

## INVESTMENT PORTFOLIO

An investment portfolio refers to a collection of investments held by an institution or an individual. This mix of investments may include stocks, bonds, options, futures, gold certificates, currency, real estate or any other instrument that generates returns.

## HOW TO CREATE AN INVESTMENT PORTFOLIO?

Investment portfolio, as this will determine your overall returns and risk exposure.

- *Set your financial goals*: Financial goals would have to be set taking into account several factors, including your present income, an estimate of your future income, the number of years left for your retirement, your financial responsibilities (such as child's education or aging parents) and the prospects of the economy.
- *Asset allocation*: Any portfolio must include a mix of investments. This is because each financial instrument entails a different combination of risks and rewards. The various financial instruments can be broadly classified into four financial investment vehicles.

| Asset | Return | Risk |
|---|---|---|
| Cash Investments (like bank accounts | Low | Low |
| Debt Investments (like bonds) | Moderate | Moderate |
| Equities (stocks) | High | High |
| Mutual Funds | Low to High | Low to High |

An investment portfolio should be balanced and spread over the broad investment classes with varying risk and reward levels. Diversifying the investment portfolio helps to minimize risk exposure, while maximizing potential return. Hence, one would need to have a basic knowledge of the various instruments available for investing.

Avoid rebalancing your portfolio regularly: It is not a good idea to rebalance the investment portfolio too often. This is because risks are lower in the longer term and asset values may be volatile in the short term. So it is better to set an annual or long term rebalancing schedule.

## THINGS TO CONSIDER WHILE CREATING AN INVESTMENT PORTFOLIO

*Here are a few things you need to keep in mind while building your investment portfolio:*

- Take full advantage of your company's investment plans. This may include 401(k), profit sharing and stock options.
- Ensure that you are adequately covered against unforeseen losses through insurance.
- In case you do not have the time to study the various investment vehicles or to stay in touch with changes in regulations and the developments in the economy, consider seeking the services of a financial advisor.
- A good place to begin for a novice investor is a mutual fund, which pools money from several investors and spreads them over various investment vehicles.

## BUSINESS INVESTMENT

Business investment refers to the commitment of funds to a business either in an active capacity or as a passive investor. An active investor would provide seed capital or startup capital, pre-IPO funds or franchising finance. However, most people seek business investment opportunities as passive investors, purchasing stocks and bonds. Business investment decisions require a risk-return tradeoff analysis.

## BUSINESS INVESTMENT: RETURNS

Business investment opportunities are largely contingent on the prospective rate of return or profit of a proposed business venture. The return on investment (ROI) is the ratio of money gained to the amount of funds invested. In case of passive investing (into shares and bonds), the ROI (or rate of return) includes a stream of income (dividends for shares and interest for bonds) as well as capital gains (appreciation in share or bond prices over time). The rate of return from a business investment is more than a function of the expected cash flows and capital appreciation. Since inflation erodes the value of money, it is important to consider the time value of money. The annual percentage return realised on an investment and adjusted for changes in prices on account of inflation or other external effects is known as the real rate of return.

## CREATION OF BUSINESS INVESTMENT OPPORTUNITIES

At the international level, the World Bank Group lends around $15-20 billion every year to finance developmental projects in the third world countries. The International Bank for Rural Development (IBRD), International Finance Corporation (IFC) and Multilateral Investment Guarantee Agency (MIGA) offer specific products, such as bonds, loans and guarantees, to potential investors for financing development in the emerging and underdeveloped economies. The IFC aids small and medium enterprises (SMEs) in the developing world by providing capital, equipment, technical assistance and guidance to fund these projects.

The European Bank for Reconstruction and Development (EBRD) and European Investment Bank (EIB) promote the basic and infrastructural sectors in Southeastern Europe in countries like Bosnia and Serbia. The Clean Development Mechanism (CDM) of the Kyoto Protocol, which has been put into operation by the United Nations Conference on Trade and Development (UNCTAD) in the developing countries, also promotes a greener and cleaner world for sustainable development.

## IMPORTANT BUSINESS INVESTMENT DESTINATIONS

Business investment opportunities have been on good ground in India, China, Vietnam, Singapore and the Gulf region. Also, a few African and Latin American countries have been doing well over the past few years. There exist huge business opportunities in Tanzania in Africa in the field of manufacturing, mining and agriculture. In India, the state of Gujarat offers excellent business investment opportunities. The

Indian government can be credited with the surge in investment opportunities in the country. Liberalization of the economy since 1991 has opened up sectors such as food processing, chemicals, automobiles, oil and natural gas and telecommunications. Besides, a slew of incentives are being offered to promote investments in the country, including the relaxation of norms for external borrowing, capital goods imports and customs duty reduction and tax deductions for certain sectors.

Investment opportunities in the infrastructural sector, such as roads, ports and civil aviation, are huge in countries like India, as is in the power, coal and renewable energy sectors. With the government allowing most of the Foreign Direct Investment (FDI) via the automatic route in these sectors, business investment opportunities have emerged enabling foreign investors to garnering good returns. An FDI cap in the telecommunications sector has been raised to 100% in case of Internet service providers according to the latest investment policy followed by the Indian government.

The development of the non-oil sector in the Gulf countries entails attractive inward investments. Countries such as Bahrain have various sectors that are attractive for business investment. These include the finance industry, manufacturing and tourism. The government of Bahrain has been actively involved with the private sector for creating investment avenues for investors from across the world. Most of the GCC countries that attract business investment offer a tax-free environment. Investors are permitted to own 100% of the enterprise and there are no restrictions on the movement of capital.

## FINANCIAL INVESTMENT

Financial investment is the commitment of funds into financial instruments, such as securities, bonds, real estate and currencies. The term "investment" is closely related to the disciplines of finance and economics and essentially refers to "savings" or "deferred consumption," which involves purchasing an asset or making a deposit in a bank in the hope of future returns. The term "investment" is used differently in economics and finance. By the term investment, an economist refers to real investment, such as in a machine or a house. On the other hand, a finance professional would refer to a financial asset as an investment. Such financial assets could be money that is deposited in a bank or invested in the money market.

## TYPES OF FINANCIAL INVESTMENT

Financial investments are of several types, including equities, debt instruments, derivatives, currencies and real estate. These financial assets are acquired with the expectation of future cash flows and may increase or decrease in value resulting in capital gains or losses to investors.

## HOW IS FINANCIAL INVESTMENT MADE?

People invest spare money to offset the effect of inflation on idle cash as well as to benefit from an additional source of income and capital appreciation. Financial investments are typically made indirectly via intermediaries such as banks, insurance companies, mutual funds, pension funds, collective investment schemes and investment clubs. An intermediary generally makes investments using the money from many individuals.

## FINANCIAL INVESTMENT AND EXCHANGES

Exchanges are financial markets where financial products are traded. There are various kinds of exchanges, such as stock exchanges, futures exchanges and commodity exchanges. These exchanges formulate their own rules and procedures for smooth transactions and ensuring fairness for all investors.

The exchanges are guided by regulating agencies. For instance, the Securities and Exchange Commission (SEC) is the watchdog of the American stock market, while the Securities and Exchange Board of India (SEBI) regulates the Indian stock market.

*The various markets for financial investment are*:

*Bond Market – The following products trade in this market*:

- Fixed income

- Corporate bond
- Government bond
- Municipal bond
- Bond valuation
- High-yield debt

*Stock (Equities) Market – The following financial instruments trade in this market*:

- Stock
- Preferred stock
- Common stock
- Registered share
- Voting share

*Forex Market – The following financial instruments trade in this market*:

- Currency
- Currency futures
- Non-deliverable forward
- Forex swap
- Currency swap
- Foreign exchange options

*Derivatives Market - The following financial products trade in this market*:

- Credit derivative
- Hybrid security
- Options
- Futures
- Forwards
- Swaps

The broad range of investment opportunities represents varied levels of risks and rewards. Success in financial investment requires good knowledge of investing. Instead, one could seek the help of financial advisors, who use various technical and fundamental analysis tools to manage portfolios.

## INVESTMENT STRATEGY

A well-planned investment strategy is essential before having any investment decisions. A business strategy is generally based upon long run period. Formation of business strategy largely dependent upon the factors such as long-term goals and risk on the investment. As the return on investment is not always clear, so the investors prepare the strategy so as to face the ongoing challenges in investment. A balanced investment strategy is generally required in the process of investment, which possesses long time period and some risk tolerance. In the case, when a strategy is aggressive the chance of attaining a higher goal is higher.

An efficient strategy can be obtained from portfolio theory, which shows good estimates on risk and return. Investment Strategy is usually considered to be more of a branch of finance than economics. It is defined as set of rules, a definite behaviour or procedure guiding an investor to choose his investment portfolio. For example, investing in mutual funds has recently emerged as a very favourable investment strategy. An investment strategy is centered on a risk-return tradeoff for a potential investor. High return investment instruments such as real estate and mutual funds usually have more risks associated with it than low return-low risk investment opportunities. Return on investment can be calculated on past or current investment or on the estimated return on future investment.

*Symbolically, it can be expressed as*:

- Vf/Vi -1 where Vf denotes final investment value and Vi is the initial investment value. ("f" and "i" should be noted as subscripts)

Return on investment (ROI) is profitable when Vf/Vi-1>0 and the investment is deemed to be unprofitable when the value of final investment is less than that of the initial investment. ROI is calculated to be 1 or 100% when the value of the final investment is twice the value of the initial investment.

## TYPES OF INVESTMENT STRATEGIES

A passive investment strategy attempted to minimize transaction costs. An active investment strategy guide used to maximize returns based on moves such as proper market timing. This usually mean, "buying in the lows and selling in the highs" or buying investment instruments when they are cheap and selling them off when their price appreciates. This strategy, however, is not very beneficial for small time investors. Small time investors can adopt the buy and hold investment strategy to invest in equities, which although volatile in nature, give favourable long run returns. Investing in equity markets for small time investors is associated with the investors holding on for very long periods. In the case of real estate, the holding period extends the lifespan of the mortgage. Notably, in case of this strategy, indexing or buying a small proportion of all the shares in market index or a mutual fund is a purely passive variant of the strategy.

The strategy of value investing, a classic investment strategy propagated by Benjamin Graham simply concentrates on the strategy that an investor buys shares of a company as if he was buying off the whole company without paying any attention to the stock market scenario or any exterior conditions such as the political climate. At the end of the day, if he can buy the stock at less than that its actual future worth to the buyer, the person is said to have discovered a "value investment." Investment strategies can also denote the investment strategies a national or federal government should follow to bring about economic growth in a country. This can only be achieved by domestic investment as well as significant FDI (Foreign Direct Investment) flows to particular sectors of countries, especially the less developed ones of Asia and Africa. In case of India, infrastructural problems, excessive government intervention, rigid labour laws and corruption are stifling the flow of FDI in the critical sectors. Less developed countries such as those in the Asia- Pacific region and Africa can bring about much needed development in these economies.

An investment strategy in mutual funds is probably the best bet for a profitable investment. Mutual funds is defined as a pool of money supplied by different investors and in turn used by the mutual fund company to invest in various assets such as stocks and bonds. However, a detailed research has to be conducted for choosing the mutual fund companies and only those should be considered which have a professional investment manger.

This will ensure that the funds get channeled towards the right investments. This also applies for investing in stock markets where a decision to invest should follow a through research about the past and current trends of the stock prices and their Net Asset Values (NAV).

Analyses from market researchers about the predicted future trends should also be considered otherwise gains from capital appreciation; capital gain distribution (in case of mutual funds) and dividends might not be realised. Lastly, investment strategies leading to green investments or investments in renewable sources of energy will be the next big thing in the investment spectrum.

## INVESTMENT PLANNING

Investment planning focuses on identifying effective investment strategies according to an investor's risk appetite and financial goals. There is a wide variety of investment options, including shares, bonds, mutual funds, bank deposits, real estate and futures and options. Through investment planning, one can identify the most appropriate portfolio mix.

## INVESTMENT PLANNING: HOW IT WORKS

Investment planning begins after you have taken into account your current and expected income level and have laid down your financial goals. The important aspects of investment planning are:

Investors aiming at long-term goals focus on capital growth. A long-term investment will allow you to tide over rough times without changing your plans. Stocks, mutual funds and real estate represent investment options for capital growth. On the other hand, if you're investing to meet a short-term goal or to give you a regular flow of funds to complement your present salary, you should opt for income investments. These investments generate a regular flow of income in the form of dividends and interest and include fixed-income investments, such as bonds and certificates of deposit (CDs).

While making a selection, you should consider the tax implications and associated risks.

*Risk*: Every investment option represents a unique risk-return trade-off. Typically, more risky investments offer higher returns in order to make it worthwhile for investors to take on the additional risk. Investment planning should take into account an investor's risk appetite, which dependents on your current income level, savings, lifestyle and responsibilities.

*Determine your investment profile*: This can be done by considering your risk appetite.

*There are mainly four types of investment profiles*:

- *Conservative (Low Risk Tolerance)*: Such portfolios comprise mainly (about 70%) of income assets, such as fixed interest and cash.
- *Balanced (Average Risk Tolerance)*: This refers to portfolios with an equal emphasis on growth and income assets.
- *Growth (High Risk Tolerance)*: Such portfolios comprise mainly (up to 80%) of growth investments, such as stocks and foreign currencies.
- *High Growth or Aggressive (Very High Risk Tolerance)*: This refers to portfolios with more than 90% of the funds in growth investments

*Review your investment plan regularly*: This helps in fine-tuning a portfolio to suit your current financial situation and a change in risk preference.

## BENEFITS OF INVESTMENT PLANNING

*Investment planning helps you*:

- Generate income and/or capital gains.
- Enhance your future wealth.
- Strengthen your investment portfolio.
- Save on taxes

# 2

# Security Analysis

## INTRODUCTION

Security analysis is a pre-requisite for making investments. In the present day financial markets, investment has become complicated. One makes investments for a return higher than what he can get by keeping the money in a commercial or cooperative bank or even in an investment bank. In the finance field, it is a common knowledge that money or finance is scarce and that investors try to maximize their return. But the finance theory states that the return is higher, if the risk is also higher. Return and risk go together and they have a trade off. Most of the investments are risky to some degree. The art of investment is to see that the return is maximised with the minimum of risk, which is inherent in investments. If the investor keeps his money in a bank in savings account, he takes the least risk, as the money is safe and he will get back when he wants it. But he runs the risk that the return in real terms, adjusted for inflation is negative or small and even if positive, it may not come up to his expectations or needs.

In the discussion, we concentrated on the word'Investment'. But for making investment, we need to make security analysis. It then becomes necessary to define properly investment and security analysis at the outset.

## INVESTMENTS: MEANING, TYPES AND CHARACTERISTICS

Financial markets have the basic function of mobilising the investments needed by corporate entities. They also performance as market places for investors who are attracted by the returns offered by the investment opportunities in the market. In this context there is a need to understand the meaning of investment and the motives of investment.

Investment may be defined as an activity that commits funds in any financial/physical form in the present with an expectation of receiving additional return in the future. The expectation brings with it a probability that the quantum of return may vary from a minimum to a maximum. This possibility of variation in the actual return is known as investment risk. Thus every investment involves a return and risk.

Investment is an activity that is undertaken by those who have savings. Savings can be defined as the excess of income over expenditure. However, all savers need not be investors. For example, an individual who sets aside some money in a box for a birthday present is a saver, but cannot be considered an investor. On the other hand, an individual who opens a savings bank account and deposits some money regularly for a birthday present would be called an investor. The motive of savings does not make a saver an investor. However, expectations distinguish the investor from a saver. The saver who puts aside money in a box does not expect excess returns from the savings. However, the saver who opens a savings bank account expects a return from the bank and hence is differentiated as an investor. The expectation of return is hence an essential characteristic of investment.

An investor earns/expects to earn additional monetary value from the mode of investment that could be in the form of physical/financial assets. A bank deposit is a financial asset. The purchase of gold would be a physical asset. Investment activity is recognised when an asset is purchased with an intention to earn an expected fund flow or an appreciation in value.

An individual may have purchased a house with an expectation of price appreciation and may consider it as an investment. However, investment need not necessarily represent purchase of a physical asset. If a bank has advanced some money to a customer, the loan can be considered as an investment for the bank. The loan instrument is expected to give back the money along with interest at a future date. The purchase of an insurance plan for its benefits such as protection against risk, tax benefits, and so on, indicates an expectation in the future and hence may be considered as an investment.

From the examples it can be seen that investment involves employment of funds with the aim of achieving additional income or growth in value. The essential quality of an investment is that it involves the expectation of a reward. Investment, hence, involves the commitment of resources at present that have been saved in the hope that some benefits will accrue from them in the future.

## TYPES OF INVESTMENTS

Investments may be classified as financial investments or economic investments. In the financial sense, investment is the commitment of funds to derive future income in the form of interest, dividend, premium, pension benefits, or appreciation in the value of the initial investment. Hence, the purchase of shares, debentures, post office savings certificates, and insurance policies are all financial investments. Such investments generate financial assets. These activities are undertaken by anyone who desires a return and is willing to accept the risk from the financial instrument.

Economic investments are undertaken with an expectation of increasing the current economy's capital stock that consists of goods and services. Capital stock is used in the production of other goods and services desired by the society. Investment in this sense implies the expectation of formation of new and productive capital in the form of new constructions, plant and machinery, inventories, and so on. Such investments generate physical assets and also industrial activity. These activities are undertaken by corporate entities that participate in the capital market. Financial investments and economic investments are, however, related and dependent. The money invested in financial investments is ultimately converted into physical assets. Thus, all investments result in the acquisition of some asset, either financial or physical. In this sense, markets are also closely related to each other. Hence, the perfect financial market should reflect the progress pattern of the real market since, in reality, financial markets exist only as a support to the real market.

**Characteristics of Investment**

The features of economic and financial investments can be summarised as return, risk, safety, and liquidity.

Return: All investments are characterised by the expectation of a return. In fact, investments are made with the primary objective of deriving a return. The expectation of a return may be from income (yield) as well as through capital appreciation. Capital appreciation is the difference between the sale price and the purchase price of the investment. The dividend or interest from the investment is the yield. Different types of investments promise different rates of return. The expectation of return from an investment depends upon the nature of investment, maturity period, market demand, and so on. The purpose for which the investment is put to use influences, to a large extent, the expectation of return of the investors. Investment in high growth potential sectors would certainly increase such expectations. The longer the maturity period, the longer is the duration for which the investor parts with the value of the investment. Hence, the investor would expect a higher return from such investments.

**Risk**

Risk is inherent in any investment. Risk may relate to loss of capital, delay in repayment of capital, non-payment of interest, or variability of returns. While some investments such as government securities and bank deposits are almost without risk, others are more risky. The risk of an investment is determined by the investment's maturity period repayment capacity, nature of return commitment, and so on.

The longer the maturity period, greater is the risk. When the expected time in which the investment has to be returned is a long duration, say 10 years, instead of five years, the uncertainty surrounding the return flow from the investment increases. This uncertainty leads to a higher risk level for the investment with longer maturity rather than on an investment with shorter maturity.

**Safety**

The safety of investment is identified with the certainty of return of capital without loss of money or time. Safety is another feature that an investor desires from investments. Every investor expects to get back the initial capital on maturity without loss and without delay. Investment safety is gauged through the reputation established by the borrower of funds. A highly reputed and successful corporate entity assures the investors of their initial capital. For example, investment is considered safe especially when it is made in securities issued by the government of a developed nation.

**Liquidity**

investment that is easily saleable or marketable without loss of money and without loss of time is said to possess the characteristic of liquidity. Some investments such as deposits in unknown corporate entities, bank deposits, post office deposits, national savings certificate, and so on are not marketable. There is no well-established trading mechanism that helps the investors of these instruments to subsequently buy/sell them frequently from a market. Investment instruments such as preference shares and debentures are marketable. The extent of trading, however, depends on the demand and supply of such instruments in the market for the investors. Equity shares of companies listed on recognised stock exchanges are easily marketable. A well-developed secondary market for securities increases the liquidity of the instruments traded therein. An investor tends to prefer maximisation of expected return, minimisation of risk, safety of funds, and liquidity of investments.

## OBJECTIVES OF INVESTMENT

A prudent and consistent saving habit lets income earners

to set aside a certain amount of current ncome for future consumption. Savings kept as cash do not result in an incremental return. Hence, savings are invested in assets with the desired risk -return characteristics. The main objective of an investment process is to minimise risk while simultaneously maximising the expected returns from the investment and assuring safety and liquidity of the invested assets. Investors look for growth/increase in current wealth through investment opportunities. Given an investment environment, an investor's preference will be for investment opportunities that give the highest return.

Investors desire to earn as large returns as possible but with the minimum of risk. Risk can also be stated as the probability that the actual return realised from an investment may be different from the expected return. Financial assets can be grouped into different classes of risk based on the return. Government securities constitute the low risk category as there is very little deviation from expectations and hence are riskless. Shares of corporate entities would form the high-risk category of financial assets as their returns depend on many uncontrollable factors. An investor would be prepared to assume a higher risk only if the expected return is proportionately higher. Hence, there is a trade-off between risk and return.

The objective of safety and liquidity helps an investor to design a retirement plan. This is done to substantiate an investor's earnings beyond the employment tenure. With this in mind, the investor sets aside a part of the current income in growth/income-yielding assets that would give an assured return after a period of time.

Savings kept as idle cash do not become investments since it loses its value over time due to rise in prices. This rise in prices, or inflation, invariably erodes the value of money. Investments are, hence, made with the objective to provide a hedge or protection against inflation over the investment duration. This time value concept necessitates investors to choose asset types that will enable them to retain at least the cash value held at present over a future period. In effect, the real rate of return would be negative if the investment cannot earn a higher return than the inflation rate. For example, if inflation is at an average annual rate of 4 per cent, then the expected return from an investment should be 4 per cent to help savings funds to flow into investment avenues. The objective of investment hence can be stated as giving an expected return from the asset that is higher than the prevalent inflation rate in the economy.

The third objective of investment is the utilisation of tax incentive plans offered by the government. In order to foster investment habits, many economies offer incentives in the form of tax-saving plans. Tax rates are applicable for a fiscal year; therefore, to cut down on immediate tax expenditures as investor would invest in tax- saving investment plans offered by the government. This objective of the investor to reduce present tax payments and hence invest in tax-saving plans can be considered as a short-term investment objective. Tax-saving plans also offer a marginal return to the investors. Based on the tax policies of the country, investment criteria could solely depend on this factor also.

## Types of Investors

Investors can be classified on the basis of their risk bearing capacity. Investors in the financial market have different attitudes towards risk and hence varying levels of risk-bearing capacity. Some investors are risk averse, while some may have an affinity for risk. The risk bearing capacity of an investor is a function of personal, economic, environmental, and situational factors such as income, family size, expenditure pattern, and age. A person with a higher income is assumed to have a higher risk-bearing capacity. Thus investor can be classified as risk seekers, risk avoiders, or risk bearers. A risk seeker is capable of assuming a higher risk while a risk avoider choose instruments that do not show much variation in returns. Risk bearers fall in between these two categories. They assume moderate levels of risk.

Investors can also be classified on the basis of groups as individuals or institutions. Individual investors operate alongside institutional investors in the investment market. However, their characteristics are different. Individual investors in any financial market are large in number, but in terms of value of investment they are comparatively smaller. Institutional investors, on the other hand, are organisations with surplus funds beyond immediate business needs or organisation whose business objective is investment. Mutual funds, investment companies, banking and non-banking companies, insurance corporations, and so on are organisations with large surplus funds to be invested in various profitable avenues. While these institutional investors are fewer in number compared to individual investors, their resources are much larger. Institutional investors engage professional fund managers to carry out extensive analysis. Institutional investors and individual investors combine to make the investment market dynamic.

## Investment Vs Speculation

Investment and speculation both involve the purchase of assets such as shares and securities, with an expectation of return. However, investment can be distinguished from speculation by risk bearing capacity, return expectations, and duration of trade.

The capacity to bear risk distinguishes an investor from a speculator. An investor prefers low risk investments, whereas a speculator is prepared to take higher risks for higher returns. Speculation focuses more on returns than safety, thereby encouraging frequent trading without any intention of owning the investment. The speculator's motive is to achieve profits through price change, that is, capital gains are more important than the direct income from an investment. Thus, speculation is associated with buying low and selling high with the hope of making large capital gains. Investors are careful while selecting securities for trading. Investments, in most instances, expect an income in addition to the capital gains that may accrue when the securities are traded in the market.

Investment is long term in nature. An investor commits funds for a longer period in the expectation of holding period gains. However, a speculator trades frequently; hence, the holding period of securities is very short.

The identification of these distinctions helps to define the role of the investor and the speculator in the market. The investor can be said to be interested in a good rate of return on a consistent basis over a relatively longer duration. For this purpose the investor computes the real worth of the security before investing in it. The speculator seeks very large returns from the market quickly. For a speculator, market expectations and price movements are the main factors influencing a buy or sell decision. Speculation, thus, is more risky than investment.

In any stock exchange, there are two main categories of speculators called the bulls and bears. A bull buys shares in the expectation of selling them at a higher price. When there is a bullish tendency in the market, share prices tend to go up since the demand for the shares is high. A bear sells shares in the expectation of a fall in price with the intention of buying the shares at a lower price at a future date. These bearish tendencies result in a fall in the price of shares.

A share market needs both investment and speculative activities. Speculative activity adds to the market liquidity. A wider distribution of shareholders makes it necessary for a market to exist.

## Investment Vs Gambling

Investment can also to be distinguished from gambling. Examples of gambling are horse race, card games, lotteries, and so on. Gambling involves high risk not only for high returns but also for the associated excitement. Gambling is unplanned and unscientific, without the knowledge of the nature of the risk involved. It is surrounded by uncertainty and a gambling decision is taken on unfounded market tips and rumours. In gambling, artificial and unnecessary risks are created for increasing the returns.

Investment is an attempt to carefully plan, evaluate, and allocate funds to various investment outlets that offer safety of principal and expected returns over a long period of time.

Hence, gambling is quite the opposite of investment even though the stock market has been euphemistically referred to as a"gambling den".

## Meaning of Security Analysis

Investment is commitment of funds in the expectation of some positive rate of return. These funds are to be used by another party, user of fund, for productive activity. It can be giving an advance or loan or contributing to the equity or debt capital of a corporate or non-corporate business unit. In other words, investment means conversion of cash or money into a monetary asset or a claim on future money for a return. This return is for saving, parting with saving or liquidity and lastly for taking a risk involving the uncertainty about the actual return, time of waiting and cost of getting back funds, safety of funds, and risk of the variability of the return.

Investment in capital market is made in various financial instruments, which are all claims on money. These instruments may be of various categories with different characteristics. These are all called securities in the market parlance. In a legal sense also, the Securities Contracts Regulation Act, (1956) has defined the security as inclusive of shares, scrips, stocks, bonds, debentures or any other marketable securities of a like nature or of any debentures of a company or body corporate, the Government and semi-Government body etc. It includes all rights and interests in them including warrants, and loyalty coupons etc., issued by any of the bodies, organisations or the Government. The derivatives of securities and Security Index are also included as securities in the definition in 1998.

In the strict sense of the word, a security is an instrument of promissory note or a method of borrowing or lending or a source of contributing to the funds needed by a corporate body or non-corporate body. Private security for example is also a security as it is a promissory note of an individual or firm and gives rise to a claim on money. But such private securities or even securities of private companies or promissory notes of individuals, partnerships or firms to the extent that their marketability is poor or nil, are not part of the capital market and do not constitute part of the security analysis. In nutshell, securities are financial instruments that have been created to represent a legal obligation to pay a sum in future in return for the current receipt of value. Securities thus represent the cash equivalent received from another person.

## DEFINITION OF SECURITY ANALYSIS

For making proper investment involving both risk and return, the investor has to make a study of the alternative avenues of investment- their risk and return characteristics and make proper projection or expectation of the risk and return of the alternative investments under consideration. He has to tune the expectations to his preferences of the risk and return for making a proper investment choice.

The process of analysing the individual securities and the market as a whole and estimating the risk and return expected from each of the investments with a view to identifying undervalued securities for buying and overvalued securities for selling is both an art and a science and this is what is called security analysis.

Security Analysis in both traditional sense and modern sense involves the projection of future dividend, or earnings flows, forecast of the share price in the future and estimating the intrinsic value of a security based on the forecast of earnings or dividends. Thus, security analysis in traditional sense is essentially an analysis of the fundamental value of a share and its forecast for the future through the calculation of its intrinsic worth of the share.

Security Analysis stands for the proposition that a well-disciplined investor can determine a rough value for a company from all of its financial statements, make purchases when the market inevitably under-prices some of them, earn a satisfactory return, and never be in real danger of permanent loss. They encouraged investors to take an entirely different approach by gauging the rough value of the operating business that lay behind the security.

Modern security analysis relies on the fundamental analysis of the security, leading to its intrinsic worth and also risk-return analysis depending on the variability of the returns, covariance, safety of funds and the projections of the future returns. If the security analysis is based on fundamental factors of the company, then the forecast of the share price has to take into account inevitably the trends and the scenario in the economy, in the industry to which the company belongs and finally the strengths and weaknesses of the company itself- its management, promoters' track record, financial results, projections of expansion, diversification, tax planning etc. all these studies are only a part of the total security analysis that the investor should aim at.

Fundamental analysis is about using real data to evaluate a security's value. Although most analysts use fundamental analysis to value stocks, this method of valuation can be used for just about any type of security.

For example, an investor can perform fundamental analysis on a bond's value by looking at economic factors, such as interest rates and the overall state of the economy, and information about the bond issuer, such as potential changes in credit ratings. For assessing stocks, this method uses revenues, earnings, future growth, return on equity, profit margins and other data to determine a company's underlying value and potential for future growth. In terms of stocks, fundamental analysis focuses on the financial statements of a the company being evaluated.

*Meaning of portfolio management:* A combination of such securities with different risk -return characteristics will constitute the portfolio of the investor. Thus, a portfolio is a combination of various assets and/or instruments of investments. The combination may have different features of risk and return, separate from those of the components. The portfolio is also built up out of the wealth or income of the investor over a period of time, with a view to suit his risk or return preferences to that of the portfolio that he holds. The portfolio analysis is thus an analysis of the risk-return characteristics of individual securities in the portfolio and changes that may take place in combination with other securities due to interaction among themselves and impact of each one of them on others. As referred earlier, portfolios are combinations of assets held by the investors. These combinations may be of various asset classes like equity and debt and of different issuers like Government bonds and corporate debt or of various instruments like discount bonds, warrants, debentures and Blue chip equity or scrip of emerging blue chip companies.

The traditional Portfolio Theory aims at the selection of such securities that would fit in well with the asset preferences, needs and choices of the investor. Thus, a retired executive invests in fixed income Investment management is the professional management of various securities (shares, bonds etc) assets (e.g. real estate), to meet specified investment goals for the benefit of the investors.

Investors may be institutions (insurance companies, pension funds, corporations etc.) or private investors (both directly via investment contracts and more commonly via collective investment plans e.g. mutual funds). The term asset management is often used to refer to the investment management of collective investments, whilst the more generic fund management may refer to all forms of institutional investment as well as investment management for private investors. Investment managers who specialize in advisory or discretionary management on behalf of (normally wealthy) private investors may often refer to their services as wealth management or portfolio management often within the context of so-called"private banking".

The provision of investment management services includes elements of financial analysis, asset selection, stock selection, plan implementation and ongoing monitoring of investments. Investment management is a large and important global industry in its own right responsible for caretaking of trillions of dollars, euro, pounds and yen. Coming under the remit of financial services many of the world's largest companies are at least in part investment managers and employ millions of staff and create billions in revenue.

Securities for a regular and fixed return. A business executive or a young aggressive investor on the other hand invests in new and growing companies and in risky ventures. Modern Portfolio Theory postulates that maximisation of return and or minimisation of risk will yield optimal returns and the choice and attitudes of investors are only a starting point for investment decision and that rigorous risk return analysis is necessary for optimisation of returns.

In risk return analysis, the attitudes and preferences of investors are taken into account as also their risk-return trade off stemming from the analysis of individual securities. The return on portfolio is a weighted average of returns of the individual stocks; and the weights are proportional to each stock's percentage in the total portfolio. Besides the stocks when put together in a basket may not give a total risk which is the mathematical equivalent of total of risks of all the individual stocks, due to the simple reason that the risks of some stocks may be compensated by the risks of other stocks or vice versa.

The risks of some stocks can also be accentuated by those of others in the portfolio. The modern portfolio theory states that the combined risk of a portfolio may be greater or lesser than the sum of the risks of the components of individual securities.

*Asset allocation:* The different asset classes and the exercise of allocating funds among these assets (and among individual securities within each asset class) is what investment management firms are paid for. Asset classes exhibit different market dynamics, and different interaction effects; thus, the allocation of monies among asset classes will have a significant effect on the performance of the fund. Some research suggested that allocation among asset classes have more predictive power than the choice of individual holdings in determining portfolio return. Arguably, the skill of a successful investment manager resides in constructing the asset allocation, and separately the individual holdings, so as to outperform certain benchmarks (e.g., the peer group of competing funds, bond and stock indices).

*Long-term returns:* It is important to look at the evidence on the long-term returns to different assets, and to holding period returns (the returns that accrue on average over different lengths of investment). For example, over very long holding periods (eg. 10+ years) in most countries, equities have generated higher returns than bonds, and bonds have generated higher returns than cash. to financial theory, this is because equities are riskier (more volatile) than bonds which are themselves more risky than cash.

*Diversification:* Against the background of the asset allocation, fund managers consider the degree of diversification that makes sense for a given client (given its risk preferences) and construct a list of planned holdings accordingly. The list will indicate what percentage of the fund should be invested in each particular stock or bond. The theory of portfolio diversification was originated by Markowitz and effective diversification requires management of the correlation between the asset returns and the liability returns, issues internal to the portfolio (individual holdings volatility), and cross-correlations between the returns.

Portfolio analysis includes selection of securities, portfolio construction, revision of portfolio, evaluation and monitoring of the performance of the portfolio.

## Financial Assets

Conducive economic environment attracts investment, which in turn influences the development of the economy. One of the essential criteria for the assessment of economic development is the quality and quantity of assets in a nation at a specific time. There are two broad types of assets:

- Real assets,
- Financial assets.

Real assets comprise the physical and intangible items available to a society. Physical assets are used to generate activity and result in positive or negative contribution to the owner of the asset. Intangible assets also result in a positive or negative contribution to the owner, but are different in that they do not have a physical shape or form. Besides real assets, the economy is supported by another group of assets called financial assets. The major component of the financial assets is cash, also called money. Financial assets help the physical assets to generate activity. Some examples of financial assets besides cash are deposits, debt instruments, shares, and foreign currency reserves.

Assets in any economy can thus be broadly grouped into physical, financial, and tangible assets, based on their distinct characteristics.

Physical assets can be classified into fixed assets and working capital assets, based on the length of their life. Fixed assets, such as land, building, machinery and other infrastructure facilities, are utilised by the society over a long period of time when compared with working capital assets. Movable/circulating capital assets are produced and consumed by the society within a financial year. Examples of movable/ circulating capital assets include materials, merchandise, durable goods, jewellery (gold), and similar items. Intangible assets are goodwill, patents, copyrights, and royalties.

In a macro sense, financial assets are regulated by the government of a country. Financial assets smoothen the trade and transaction of an economy and give the society a standard measure of valuation. Money or cash is the basic financial asset created by the government of an economy. The extent of flow of this financial asset has to be regulated in a country for the demand for and supply of funds to match the macro level, financial assets also represent the current/ future value of physical and intangible assets.

The current/future value of financial assets depends on the current/future return expectations from these financial instruments. All the financial assets in an economy represent a real asset either in the present context or in the context of the future.

Their dependence on real assets requires the financial assets to be valued differently. The distinctive value determination of financial instruments also requires a specific market to patronise them. Financial assets have specific properties that distinguish them from physical and intangible assets. These properties are monetary value, divisibility, convertibility, reversibility, liquidity, and cash flow.

## Financial Markets

A financial market is a place/system where financial instruments are exchanged. Such markets enhance the unique characteristics of the financial instruments. Financial markets can be classified on the basis of the nature of instruments exchanged in the economy.

The instruments can be broadly divided into claim instruments and currency instruments. Claim instruments are subdivided into those that are fixed claims and those instruments that get a residual or equity claim. Fixed claim markets that have very short durations, that is, less than a year are traded in the money market while the fixed claims that have a maturity of more than a year and equity claim instruments are traded in the capital markets.

Financial market is a mechanism that allows people to easily buy and sell (trade) financial securities (such as stocks and bonds), commodities (such as precious metals or agricultural goods), and other fungible items of value at low transaction costs and at prices that reflect the efficient market hypothesis.

Financial markets have evolved significantly over several hundred years and are undergoing constant innovation to improve liquidity.

Both general markets (where many commodities are traded) and specialized markets (where only one commodity is traded) exist. Markets work by placing many interested buyers and sellers in one"place", thus making it easier for them to find each other. An economy which relies primarily on interactions between buyers and sellers to allocate resources is known as a market economy in contrast either to a command economy or to a non-market economy such as a gift economy.

Money markets are also referred to as a wholesale financial market while capital markets are referred to as retail markets since the size of the transactions in the money market is quite large when compared to that in the capital markets. The trading of currency instruments among different countries is conducted through the foreign exchange market. The subdivisions of the major markets are shown in,

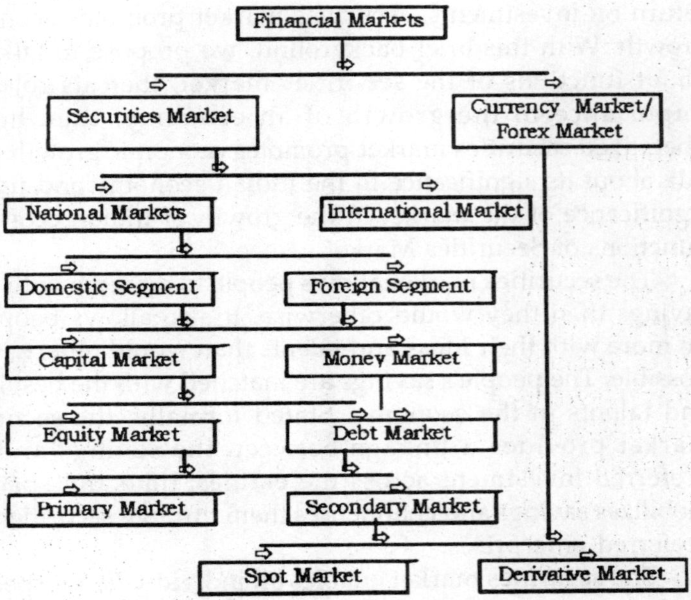


**Fig.** Financial Markets

## Securities Market

It is needless to say that the financial markets (banks and the securities markets) finance economic growth. They channelise savings to investments and thereby decouple these two activities. As a result, savers and investors are not constrained by their individual abilities, but by the economy's ability to invest and save respectively, which inevitably enhances savings and investment in the economy. To the extent the growth of an economy depends on the rate of savings and investment, financial markets promote economic growth.

The banks and securities markets are two competing mechanisms to channel savings to investment. The securities markets score over banks in the allocational efficiency, as it allocates savings to those investments which have potential to yield higher returns.

This inevitably leads to higher returns to savers on their savings and higher productivity on investments to enterprises. Hence to the extent economic growth depends on the rate of return on investments, securities market promotes economic growth. With this brief background, we propose to talk first about functions of the securities market, then its role and importance in the growth of an economy, then how a liberalized securities market promotes economic growth, then talk about its significance in the Indian economy and finally, significance of the market in the growth of Indian economy.

Functions of Securities Market

The securities market allows people to do more with their savings than they would otherwise. It also allows people to do more with their ideas and talents than would otherwise be possible. The people's savings are matched with the best ideas and talents in the economy. Stated formally, the securities market provides a linkage between the savings and the preferred investment across the entities, time and space. It mobilizes savings and channelises them through securities into preferred enterprises.

The securities market enables all individuals, irrespective of their means, to share the increased wealth provided by competitive enterprises. The securities market allows individuals who can not carry an activity in its entirety within their resources to invest whatever is individually possible and preferred in that activity carried on by an enterprise. Conversely, individuals who can not begin an enterprise they like can attract enough investment form others to make a start and continue to progress and prosper. In either case, individuals who contribute to the investment share the fruits The securities market also provides a market place for purchase and sale of securities and thereby ensures transferability of securities, which is the basis for the joint stock enterprise system.

The liquidity available to investors does not inconvenience the enterprises that originally issued the securities to raise funds. The existence of the securities market makes it possible to satisfy simultaneously the needs of the enterprises for capital and of investors for liquidity. The liquidity the market confers and the yield promised or anticipated on security encourages people to make additional savings out of current income. In the absence of the securities market, the additional savings would have been consumed otherwise. Thus the provision of securities market results in net savings. The securities market enables a person to allocate his savings among a number of investments.

This helps him to diversify risks among many enterprises, which increases the likelihood of long term overall gains. Securities are financial instruments that have been created to represent a legal obligation to pay a sum in future in return for the current receipt of value. Securities thus represent the cash or cash equivalent received from another person. The creation of a security is situation and need specific, and many innovative instruments have been floated in the market. The existence of such financial instruments is, however, within the legal regulations governing the market in which they are floated. The securities market, hence, is place-sensitive. The immediate classification of the securities market can be in terms of national boundaries due to the legal environment. The securities market can be subdivided into national and international markets. However, with technological innovations, international agreements and standards, the line distinguishing a national from an international market is fast disappearing.

## National Market

National markets are markets within the boundary of a nation. National markets cater to the financial requirements of the local players. Players from foreign countries are permitted to bring their financial instruments into the national market, subject to their following the rules and regulations imposed by the nation.

There are vast differences in the rules and regulations of the securities market among nations. Each nation has a regulatory authority under whose scrutiny financial instruments are exchanged in that country. The regulatory authority imposes the overall procedure and guidelines to be followed by the players in the national market. National markets sometimes make a difference between pure domestic players and the participation of international players. Hence, there can be a further subdivision of the national market into a domestic segment and a foreign segment.

**International Market**

International markets are usually referred to as offshore markets. Certain national markets, due to their policy regulations, do not discriminate between the securities issued in its country vis-à-vis other countries. A precise example of an international market is the Euromarket, where the representation of several countries is viewed together. A firm in any one member nation in the European subcontinent could list its securities simultaneously in other countries of the European Union. For example, firm with its headquarters in France, could simultaneously trade its securities in France, Spain, and Germany. This concept of opening the national market to other group countries came to be known as international market.

*Domestic Segment:* The domestic market caters exclusively to firms registered in a country. The country's regulatory authority controls the domestic market. In India, the Reserve Bank of India along with the Securities Exchange Board of India (SEBI) regulates the functioning of the money market and the capital market, the two types of markets within the umbrella of the domestic market. Based on the economic performance of the country, the domestic markets are also called advanced markets and emerging markets. Advanced markets are usually markets in nations that are economically sound and have also progressed technologically. The US and UK markets are termed as advanced markets. Emerging markets are those in developing nations whose economic progress is forward looking. The Indian market is termed as an emerging market. The domestic markets can be further subdivided into money market and capital market.

*Money market:* Short-term debt markets are known as money markets. Debt is a fixed income security and represents the borrowing of a market player. Money markets are mostly wholesale markets for financial instruments. Small values are not exchanged in the money market. The minimum value that is exchanged in the Indian money market, for instance, is Rs. 1 million. The large quantum of trade essentially limits the players in the money market to institutional investors such as banks, other financial institutions, government, and large business firms. Here, the players exchange surplus funds at the prevailing interest rates (call rates) for a short duration. The duration could be a day, a week, a month, six months, or a year. This duration indicates the maturity of the instrument. At the time of the issue of the money market instrument as well as at the time of maturity of the instrument, the account transfer of the initial amount along with the interest charges takes place between the players in the money market.

Money market has accommodated within its fold several types of trades. The money market can be differentiated into the call market, treasury bill market, inter-bank market, certificate of deposit market, repo market, commercial paper market, intercorporate deposit market, and commercial bills market

**Capital Market**

Capital markets exchange both long-term fixed claim securities and residual/equity claim securities. The main economic role of a capital market is to match players who have excess funds to players who are in need of funds. Capital markets also provide liquidity to financial instruments. In this exchange process, there is a valuation of the instruments done by the market for the specific risk assumed by the investors. Risk is prevalent in the capital market since the market valuation process is subject to change. For example, deviation in return is one type of risk prevalent in the instruments traded in the capital market. Besides, the instruments could also have economic risk, liquidity risk, default risk, trading risk, and so on. There are two forms of returns from instruments.

One is the claim on the instrument; the other form of return is due to trade. The claim on the instrument could be fixed or residual. The return through claim is either nil or positive. While fixed claim instruments hardly show any variation in returns, residual claim instruments display fluctuating returns thus exposing the holders to greater risk.

Capital market is the market for securities, where companies and governments can raise long-term funds. The capital market includes the stock market and the bond market. Financial regulators, such as the U.S. Securities and Exchange Commission, oversee the capital markets in their designated countries to ensure that investors are protected against fraud. The capital markets consist of the primary market, where new issues are distributed to investors, and the secondary market, where existing securities are traded.

The capital gain/loss in buying/selling the security is the trade return from the security. Given the risk-return characteristic of the capital market, the expectations of the market participants play a major role in the market price determination of the securities traded. This riskreturn characteristic of the instruments necessitates a subdivision of the capital market into debt market and equity market.

## Debt Market

Financial instruments that have a fixed income claim and have a maturity of more than one year are traded in the debt market. Debentures or bonds are examples of debt instruments in the capital market.

Debt instruments may have several distinguishing features. They can be secured or unsecured debt. A secured debt has assets to fall back on while an unsecured debt is subject to more risk. Since an unsecured debt does not have an asset backing, the repayment risk is more. Mortgaged debt refers to a mortgage lien on a group of assets or on a specific asset category. Such a debt is also a secured debt.

Debt can also be categorised as redeemable debt or irredeemable debt. Based on the redemption (repayment) characteristic, it will be stated at the time of issue itself whether the debt will be repaid at maturity. Unless otherwise stated, all debt is usually redeemable debt. Irredeemable debt is a rollover debt, is renewed after maturity. Debt can also be classified as convertible debt or non-convertible debt.

Convertible debt implies that the original debt instrument would be converted into another financial instrument at the time of maturity. A non-convertible debt is repaid at the end of the maturity period.

Based on the type of claim on the instrument, debt can be classified as regular interest debt, flexi debt, and zero coupon debt. A debt will bear a fixed claim, which is usually the interest payment made by the issuer to the debt holder. The nominal fixed percentage of interest is specified at the time of issue and the instruments. A flexi debt has the characteristic of changing its interest rate with the prevailing economic environment. The flexible debt is usually associated with inter-bank offer rates. For example, LIBOR (London Inter-bank Offer Rate) is a popular base rate for flexi debt instruments. A zero coupon debt, on the other hand, does not pay regular interest, but issues a document at an offer price and repays the document with value additions that compensates for the regular income through the duration of debt. The debt market distinguishes fresh issues from the subsequent trading of the securities and hence can be further subdivided into primary and secondary markets.

## Equity Market

Equity instruments bestow ownership on the holder of the security. Equity hence implies ownership rights in the corporate entity that has issued the instruments to the public. The claim of the owners of these instruments is residual in nature, that is the owners will have a claim in the distribution of profits and not a fixed interest as in the case of debt instruments. The distribution of dividend out of the profits after payment to debt holders will be decided in the general body meeting of the corporate entity. The corporate will announce the dividend rates. Dividends can be annual or quarterly or extraordinary. Sometimes equity owners also claim additional returns from the firm in the form of bonus shares. Dividend can be distributed either in the form of cash or as new shares.

A stock market, or (equity market), is a private or public

market for the trading of company stock and derivatives of company stock at an agreed price; these are securities listed on a stock exchange as well as those only traded privately.

The expression"stock market" refers to the market that enables the trading of company stocks collective shares, other Security finance|securities, and Derivative finance| derivatives. Bonds are still traditionally traded in an informal, Over-the-counter finance|over-the-counter market known as the bond market. Commodities are traded in commodities markets, and derivatives are traded in a variety of markets but, like bonds, mostly'over-the-counter.

The size of the worldwide"bond market" is estimated at Rs45 trillion. The size of the stock market is estimated at about Rs51 trillion. The world derivatives market has been estimated at about Rs480 trillion face or nominal value, 30 times the size of the U.S. economy…and 12 times the size of the entire world economy. It must be noted though that the value of the derivatives market, because it is stated in terms of Notional amount|notional values, cannot be directly compared to a stock or a fixed income security, which traditionally refers to an Actual cash value|actual value. Many such relatively illiquid securities are valued as mark to model|marked to model, rather than an actual market price.

The stocks are listed and traded on stock exchanges which are entities a corporation or mutual organization specialized in the business of bringing buyers and sellers of stocks and securities together.

The stock market is one of the most important sources for companies to raise money. This allows businesses to be publicly traded, or raise additional capital for expansion by selling shares of ownership of the company in a public market. The liquidity that an exchange provides affords investors the ability to quickly and easily sell securities. This is an attractive feature of investing in stocks, compared to other less liquid investments such as real estate.

History has shown that the price of shares and other assets is an important part of the dynamics of economic activity, and can influence or be an indicator of social mood. Rising share prices, for instance, tend to be associated with increased business investment and vice versa. Share prices also affect the wealth of households and their consumption. Therefore, central banks tend to keep an eye on the control and behaviour of the stock market and, in general, on the smooth operation of financial system functions. Financial stability is the raison d'être of central banks.

Exchanges also performance as the clearinghouse for each transaction, meaning that they collect and deliver the shares, and guarantee payment to the seller of a security. This eliminates the risk to an individual buyer or seller that the counterparty could default on the transaction.

The smooth functioning of all these activities facilitates economic growth in that lower costs and enterprise risks promote the production of goods and services as well as employment. In this way the financial system contributes to increased prosperity

Equity instruments can also be of several types. The most distinguishable types of equity are preference equity and common/ or ordinary equity. Preference equity has a preferential claim over dividend payment and/or payment of face value at the time of liquidation (closure) of a corporate. Sometimes a preferential equity may also have a claim for a minimum percentage of dividends when the corporate declares dividend. Common equity instruments do not have such preferential rights. The equity market is also subdivided into the primary market and secondary market.

**Primary Market**

The primary market is the doorway for corporate enterprises to enter the capital market. The issues of new securities are offered to the public through the primary market. The issue is thus an open public offer to sell the securities. The sale is made at a value predetermined by the firm issuing the security. Sometimes a road show is conducted to feel the pulse of the public in fixing the value for a security. The securities have a face value, which is the denomination in which it is divided. For instance, an instrument could have a face value of Re 1, Rs. 5, Rs. 10, or Rs. 100 in India. This denomination determines the number of units of the security that are offered to the public. The price at which the security is offered to the public is the offer price of the instrument. This price could be equal to or greater or lesser than the face value. When the offer price is greater than the face value, the offer is said to be at a premium. When the offer price is less than the face value, the offer is at a discount. When the two prices are equal, the offer is at par.

The primary is that part of the capital markets that deals with the issuance of new securities. Companies, governments or public sector institutions can obtain funding through the sale of a new stock or bond issue. This is typically done through a syndicate of securities dealers. The process of selling new issues to investors is called underwriting. In the case of a new stock issue, this sale is an initial public offering (IPO). Dealers earn a commission that is built into the price of the security offering, though it can be found in the prospectus. Features Of Primary Market are:-

- This is the market for new long term capital. The primary market is the market where the securities are sold for the first time. Therefore it is also called New Issue Market (NIM).
- In a primary issue, the securities are issued by the company directly to investors.
- The company receives the money and issue new security certificates to the investors.
- Primary issues are used by companies for the purpose of setting up new business or for expanding or modernizing the existing business.
- The primary market performs the crucial function of facilitating capital formation in the economy.
- The new issue market does not include certain other sources of new long term external finance, such as loans from financial institutions. Borrowers in the new issue market may be raising capital for converting private capital into public capital; this is known as'going public'.

*Methods of issuing securities in the Primary Market*:

- Initial Public Offer;
- Rights Issue (For existing Companies); and
- Preferential Issue.

Several intermediaries have sprung up to help corporate entities to offer their debt and equity instruments to the public. Merchant bankers and underwriters are the major intermediaries who help to match the fund requirement of corporate entities with the surplus fund position of public. The public is re both individual investors and institutional investors. Sometimes, when the market is dominated by institutions, the market is said to be institutionalised. Once the offer process of the securities to the public is complete, the securities are listed in the markets. The corporate then has to comply with the specific regulations of each local market in which its securities are listed.

## Secondary Market

The secondary market refers to the exchange of securities that have been listed through the primary market. The price at which it is traded in the capital market is the market price of the instrument. It is the secondary market that offers tradability to the financial instruments. The number of financial instruments participating in the secondary market hence, cannot exceed the number of financial instruments recorded through the primary market. The secondary market also comes under the regulatory authorities of the market and the main role of the regulator in the secondary market is to safeguard the interest of players in the market. Both individuals and institutions can take part in the secondary market. Brokers and depositories are the main intermediaries in this market, who transact business on behalf of the investors. The brokers can appoint a network of sub- brokers to mobilise investors participation in the market. Depositories help in scripless trading by holding investor accounts in electronic media.

The secondary market is the financial market for trading of securities that have already been issued in an initial private or public offering.[1] Alternatively, secondary market can refer to the market for any kind of used goods. The market that exists in a new security just after the new issue, is often referred to as the aftermarket. Once a newly issued stock is listed on a stock exchange, investors and speculators can easily trade on the exchange, as market makers provide bids and offers in the new stock.

Over a period of time, the secondary market has grown in size and in terms of efficiency. The secondary market may be further sub-divided into the spot market and derivative market.

## Spot Market

Spot market denotes the current trading price of financial instruments. The spot market or cash market is a commodities or securities market in which goods are sold for cash and delivered immediately. Contracts bought and sold on these markets are immediately effective. Spot markets can operate wherever the infrastructure exists to conduct the transaction. The spot market for most securities exists primarily on the internet. In the context of time, the spot market may range between one day, two days, or a week. The transactions in the spot market are settled immediately, that is, on the immediate settlement date. Each market specifies the type of settlement to be made- a rolling settlement or a fixed day settlement. The rolling settlement, to the specific exchange, will be T+1, T+3, or T+5. A T+1 rolling settlement indicates that trading entered on day T will be settled for cash on day T + 1. On the other hand, the fixed day settlement will be on a specific day of a week, say the working Thursday or Friday of a week.

## Derivative Market

Unlike the spot market, the derivative market is a futures market. Trade takes place here with the intention to settle it at a later date. The derivative market has forward, futures, options, or other derivative instruments trading. Forward trade helps in the exchange of instruments in the future at prices or rates determined in the present. Forward contracts involve an obligation and are legally binding on the parties who have entered into a forward agreement. However, forward contracts have the disadvantage of inflexibility of timing. They are conducted on a one-to-one basis between parties who initially entered into the agreement. A forward contact cannot be surrendered or liquidated as easily as the other derivative instruments.

A future contract is an agreement by one participant to either buy or sell a financial instrument at a predetermined date in the future at a predetermined price. The basic function of the futures trade is to enable the market participants to hedge against the risk of adverse price movement/volatility in the market. A contract to buy 100 shares of Ranbaxy Laboratories three months later, at Rs. 859.97 per share is a futures contract. The price at which the financial instrument is transferred at a later date (in this case, Rs. 859.97) is called the futures price. The time stated in the contract in which the contract will be enforced (three months hence) is called the delivery date/expiry date. Futures contacts are derivatives since they are based on financial instruments that are traded in the capital market.

Derivatives are financial instruments whose value changes in response to the changes in underlying variables. The main types of derivatives are futures, forwards, options, and swaps.

*Insurance and Hedging*: One use of derivatives is as a tool to transfer risk by taking the opposite position in the underlying asset. For example, a wheat farmer and a wheat miller could enter into a futures contract to exchange cash for wheat in the future. Both parties have reduced a future risk: for the wheat farmer, the uncertainty of the price, and for the wheat miller, the availability of wheat.

Stock index futures and options are sometimes referred to as derivative products because they derive their existence from actual market indexes, but have no intrinsic characteristics of their own. The reason some believe they lead to greater market volatility is that enormous amounts of securities can be controlled by relatively small amounts of margin or option premiums.

*Speculation and arbitrage:* Speculators may trade with other speculators as well as with hedgers. In most financial derivatives markets, the value of speculative trading is far higher than the value of true hedge trading. As well as outright speculation, derivatives traders may also look for arbitrage opportunities between different derivatives on identical or closely related underlying securities.

In addition to directional plays (i.e. simply betting on the direction of the underlying security), speculators can use derivatives to place bets on the volatility of the underlying security.

This technique is commonly used when speculating with traded options. Speculative trading in derivatives gained a great deal of notoriety in 1995 when Nick Leeson, a trader at Barings Bank, made poor and unauthorized investments in index futures. Through a combination of poor judgement on his part, lack of oversight by management, a naive regulatory environment and unfortunate outside events like the Kobe earthquake, Leeson incurred a Rs1.3 billion loss that bankrupted the centuries-old financial institution.

The main use of derivatives is to reduce risk for one party. The diverse range of potential underlying assets and pay-off alternatives leads to a huge range of derivatives contracts available to be traded in the market. Derivatives can be based on different types of assets such as commodities, equities (stocks), bonds, interest rates, exchange rates, or indexes (such as a stock market index, consumer price index (CPI)—or even an index of weather conditions, or other derivatives). Their performance can determine both the amount and the timing of the pay-offs.

Options are the other forms of derivatives that give the holder of the contract the choice to buy or sell a financial asset. Options can take the form of equity options or index options. Equity options such as Infosys call options may have a strike price of Rs. 3,900 at a premium of Rs. 190 with the expiry date of one month. The premium is the amount that is given to the writer of the contract for giving the buyer the right to sell the Infosys share at the future date for the agreed price.

Derivative instruments are called so because these financial instruments derive their value from the price of the underlying asset. These instruments are traded in a physical stock exchange through brokers. Derivative instruments are used to a large extent to reduce the risk in the underlying asset price.

Investment is commitment of funds in the expectation of some positive rate of return. Investment in capital market is made in various financial instruments, which are all claims on money. These instruments may be of various categories with different characteristics. These are all called securities in the market parlance. Modern security analysis relies on the fundamental analysis of the security, leading to its intrinsic worth and also risk-return analysis depending on the variability of the returns, covariance, safety of funds and the projections of the future returns.

A financial market is a place/system where the exchange of financial instruments takes place. Financial markets are broadly classified into money market and capital market. Capital market deals with both debt and equity instruments through the primary and secondary market segments. Money market, on the other hand, deals mostly in debt instruments of shorter duration. Another market existing in the financial structure of an economy is the forex market. This market enables the exchange of foreign currency.

# 3

# Risk and Return in Investment

## INTRODUCTION

Investors have many motives for investing. Some investors invest in order to gain a sense of power or prestige. The control of corporate empires, thus, is an important motive. For most investors, however, the prime interest in investments is largely to earn a return on their money. However, selecting stocks exclusively on the basis of maximization of return is not enough. The most investors do not place available funds into the one, two, or even three stocks promising the greatest returns suggests that other factors must be considered besides return in the selection process. Investors not only like return, they dislike risk.

To facilitate our job of analysing securities and portfolios within a return-risk context, we must begin with a clear understanding of what risk and return are, what creates them, and how these should be measured. In fact, we find the answer to the following two questions while taking investment decisions:

- What securities should be held, and
- How many rupees should be allocated to each.

These decisions are normally made in two steps. First, estimates are made of the return and risk associated with available securities over a forward holding period. This step is known as security analysis. Second, return-risk estimates must be compared in order to decide how to allocate available funds among these securities on a continuing basis. This step comprises portfolio analysis, selection, and management. In fact, security analysis provides the necessary inputs for analysing and selecting portfolios..

## Returns on Financial Assets

People want to maximize expected returns subject to their tolerance for risk. Return is the principal reward in the investment process, and it provides the basis to investors in comparing alternative investments. Measuring historical returns allows investors to assess how well they have done, and it plays a part in the estimation of future, unknown returns.

We often use two terms regarding return from investments, realised return and expected return. Realised return is after the fact return- return that was earned (or could have been earned).

Realised return is history. For example, a deposit of Rs. 5,00,000 in the Punjab National Bank on January 1 in a certificate of deposit at a stated annual interest rate of 5 per cent will be worth Rs. 525000 one year later. The realised return for the year is Rs. 25000 or 5 per cent.

Expected return is the return from an asset that investors anticipate they will earn over some future period. It is a predicted return, and it may or may not occur.

### *Components of Return*

Return on a financial asset, generally, consists of two components. The principal component of return is the periodic income on the investment, either in the form of interest or dividends. The second component is the change in the price of the asset- commonly called the capital gain or loss. This element of return is the difference between the purchase price and the price at which the asset can be or is sold.

The price change may bring a gain or a loss as it may be in any side. The income from an investment consists of one or more cash payments made at specified intervals of time. Interest payments on most bonds are paid either semi-annually or yearly, whereas dividends on common stocks are usually paid on yearly basis. The distinguishing feature of these payments is that they are paid in cash by the issuer to the holder of the asset.

We often use the term yield to express return. Yield refers to the income component in relation to some price for a security. For our purposes, the price that is relevant is the purchase price of the security. The yield on a Rs. 1,000 par value, 6 per cent coupon bond purchased for Rs. 950 is 6.31 per cent (Rs. 1,000 par value, 6 per cent coupon bond purchased for Rs. 950 is 6.31 per cent (Rs. 60/Rs. 950). However, we need to remember that yield is not, for most purposes, the proper measure of return from a security. The capital gain or loss must also be considered.

Equation is a conceptual statement for total return.

Total return = Income + Price change (+/-)

Note that either component of return can be zero for a given security over any given time period.

A bond purchased for Rs. 800 and held to maturity provides both type of income: interest payments and a price change. The purchase of a non-dividend-paying stock that is sold four months later produces either a capital gain or a capital loss, but no income.

Thus, a measure of return must consider both dividend/ interest income and price change.

Returns over time or from different securities can be measured and compared using the total return concept. The total return for a given holding period relates all the cash flows received by an investor during any designated time period to the amount of money invested in the asset. Total return is defined as,

$$r = \frac{(P_{t-1} - P_{t-1}) + D}{P_{t-1}} \times 100$$

where, r = total return, Pt = price of an asset at time,

(t), $P_{t-1}$ = price of an asset at time (t-1), D = dividend or interest income in simple terms.

*Example:* Tata Steels share's price on June29, 2004 is Rs. 900 (Pt-1) and the price on June 28, 2005 (Pt), is Rs. 950. Dividend received is Rs. 76 (D). Determine the rate of return.

$$r = \frac{(P_{t-1} - P_{t-1}) + D}{P_{t-1}} \times 100$$

$$= \frac{(950 - 900) + 76}{900} \times 100$$

$$= \frac{50 + 76}{900} \times 100$$

$$= 14\%$$

### *Calculation of Average Returns*

The total return is an acceptable measure of return for a specified period of time. But we also need statistics to describe a series of returns. For example, investing in a particular stock for ten years or a different stock in each of ten years could result in 10 total returns, which must be described mathematically.

There are two generally used methods of calculating the average return, namely, the arithmetic average and geometric average. The statistics familiar to most people is the arithmetic average. The arithmetic average, customarily designated by the symbol X = X n, or the sum of each of the values being considered divided by the total number of values.

*Example:* The return of stock A for four quarters is as follows:

Quarter-I = 10%; Quarter-II= 8%; Quarter-III= -4%; and Quarter IV= 20%. The average return is,

X = {10 + 8 + (-4)} + 20/ 4 = 8.5%

The arithmetic average return is appropriate as a measure of the central tendency of a number of returns calculated for a particular time, such as a year. However, when percentage changes in value over time are involved, the arithmetic mean of these changes can be misleading. For example, suppose an investor purchased a stock in Year 1 for Rs. 50 and it rose to Rs. 100 by year-end. This is a 100 per cent return [(100-50)/50]. Then the stock went from Rs. 100 at the start of Year 2 to Rs. 50 at the end of that year. The return for year 2 is -50 per cent [(50-100)/100)]. The arithmetic average return is 25 per cent

[(+100-50)/2)]. But, realistically, if an investor bought a stock for Rs. 50 and held it two years and it was still at Rs. 50, clearly there is no return at all.

From the it is obvious that an analyst should use a different average to describe accurately the true rate of return over multiple periods. The geometric average return measures compound, cumulative returns over time. It is used in investments to reflect the realised change in wealth over multiple periods.

The geometric average is defined as the nth root of the product resulting from multiplying a series of returns together, as in Equation,

$$G = [(1 + r_1)(1 + r_2) \ldots (1 + r_n)]^{1/n} - 1$$

where, r = total return, n = number of periods.

*Return relative*: On adding 1.0 to each return (r), we shall get a return relative. If the return for a period is 10 per cent (.10), then the return relative is 1.10. The investor has received Rs. 1.10 relative to each Rs. 1 invested. If the return for a period is -15 per cent (-.15) then the return relative is.85 (1-.15). Return relatives are used in calculating geometric average returns because negative total returns cannot be used in the math.

For our stock that started at Rs. 50, rose to Rs. 100, and then dropped to Rs. 50 over a two-year period, the geometric return would be calculated as follows:

Return relative, Year 1 = 1.00 + 1.00 = 2.00

Year 2 = –.50 + 1.00 =.50

$$\text{Geometric average (G)} = [(2.0)^*(.5)]^{1/2} - 1 = [1.0]^{1/2} - 1 = 0.00$$

Here, we also need to note that the geometric average rate of return would be lower than the arithmetic average rate of return because it reflects compounding rather than simple averaging.

## Risk in Holding Securities

Risk is generally associated with the possibility that realised returns of securities will be less than the returns that were expected. The source of such risk is the failure of dividends (interest) and/or the security's price to materialize as expected.

There are numerous forces that contribute to variations in return- price or dividend (interest). These forces are termed as elements of risk. Some factors are external to the firm and cannot be controlled.

These factors affect large numbers of securities. In investments, those forces that are uncontrollable, external, and broad in their effect are called sources of systematic risk. Other forces are internal to the firm and are controllable to a large degree.

The controllable, internal factors somewhat peculiar to industries and/or firms are referred to as sources of unsystematic risk. That portion of total variability in return caused by factors affecting the prices of all securities is known as systematic risk. Economic, political, and sociological changes are sources of systematic risk.

Their effect is to cause prices of nearly all individual common stocks and/or all individual bonds to move together in the same manner. For example, if the economy is moving towards inflation and corporate profits shift upward, stock prices may rise across a broad front. Nearly all stocks listed on the National Stock Exchange (NSE) move in the same direction as the S & P Nifty index of NSE. that on the average, 50 per cent of the variation in a stock's price can be explained by variation in the market index. Conversely, the portion of total risk that is unique to a firm or industry is called unsystematic risk. Factors such as management capability, consumer preferences, and labour strikes cause unsystematic variability of returns in a firm. Unsystematic factors are largely independent of factors affecting securities markets in general. Because these factors affect one firm, they must be examined for each firm.

## Sources of Systematic Risk

As discussed, the main constituents of systematic risk include- market risk, interest rate risk and purchasing power risk.

### *Market Risk*

The price of a stock may fluctuate widely within a short span of time even though earnings remain unchanged. The causes of this phenomenon are varied, but it is mainly due to a change in investors' attitudes towards equities in general, or towards certain types or groups of securities in particular. Variability in return on most common stocks that is due to basic sweeping changes in investor expectations is referred to as market risk.

Risk which is common to an entire class of assets or liabilities. The value of investments may decline over a given time period simply because of economic changes or other events that impact large portions of the market. Asset allocation and diversification can protect against market risk because different portions of the market tend to underperform at different times. also called systematic risk.

The reaction of investors to tangible as well as intangible events causes market risk. Expectations of lower corporate profits in general may cause the larger body of common stocks to fall in price. Investors are expressing their judgement that too much is being paid for earnings in the light of anticipated events. The basis for the reaction is a set of real, tangible events-political, social, or economic.

Intangible events are related to market psychology. Market risk is usually touched off by a reaction to real events, but the emotional unstability of investors acting collectively leads to a snowballing overreaction. The initial decline in the market can cause the fear of loss to grip investors, and a kind of herd instinct builds as all investors make for the exit. These reactions to reactions frequently culminate in excessive selling, pushing prices down far out of line with fundamental value. With a trigger mechanism such as the threat of war, or an oil shortage, virtually all stocks are adversely affected.

Interest-rate risk: The risk of variations in future market values and the size of income, caused by fluctuations in the general level of interest rates is referred to as interest-rate risk. The basic cause of interest-rate risk lies in the fact that, as the rate of interest paid on Indian government securities rises or falls, the rates of return demanded on alternative investment vehicles, such as stocks and bonds issued in the private sector, rise or fall. In other words, as the cost of money changes for risk-free securities, the cost of money to risk-prone issuers will also change.

People normally regard government securities like treasury bills risk- free. The interest rates demanded on these securities are thought to approximate the"pure" rate of interest, or the cost of hiring money at no risk. Interest rates on gilts shift with changes in the supply and demand for government securities. For example, a large operating deficit experienced by the Indian government will require financing. Issuance of added amounts of Indian government securities will increase the available supply. Potential buyers of this new supply may be induced to buy only if interest rates are somewhat higher than those currently prevailing on outstanding issues. If rates on gilts advance from 8 per cent to 8¼ per cent, investors holding outstanding issues that yield 8 per cent will notice a decline in the price of their securities. Because the 8 per cent rate is fixed by contract on these"old" gilts, a potential buyer would be able to realise the competitive 8¼ per cent rate only if the current holder"marked down" the price. As the rate on guilts advances, they become relatively more attractive and other securities become less attractive. Consequently,bond purchasers will buy governments instead of corporates. This will cause the price of corporates to fall and the rate on corporates to rise. Rising corporate bond rates will eventually cause preferred and inturn common stock prices to adjust downward as the chain reaction is felt throughout the system of security yields. Thus the direct effect of increases in the level of interest rates is to cause security prices to fall across a wide span of investment vehicles.

Also there are indirect effects on common stocks. First, lower or higher interest rates make the purchase of stocks on margin (using borrowed funds) more or less attractive. Higher interest rates, for example, may lead to lower stock prices because of a diminished demand for equities by speculators who use margin. Second, many firms, such as public utilities finance their operations quite heavily with borrowed funds. Others, such as financial institutions, are principally in the business of lending money. Advancing interest rates can bring higher earnings to lending institutions whose principal revenue source is interest received on loans. For these firms, higher earnings could lead to increased dividends and stock prices.

Purchasing-power risk: Purchasing-power risk refers to the uncertainty of the purchasing power of the money to be received. In simple terms, purchasing-power risk is the impact of inflation or deflation on an investment. When we think of investment as the postponement of consumption, we can see that when a person purchases a stock, he has foregone the opportunity to buy some goods or service for as long as he owns the stock.

If, during the holding period, prices on desired goods and services rise, the investor actually loses purchasing power. Rising prices on goods and services are normally associated with what is referred to as inflation. Falling prices on goods and services are termed deflation. Both inflation and deflation are covered in the all-encompassing term purchasing-power risk.

Generally, purchasing-power risk has come to be identified with inflation (rising prices); the incidence of declining prices in most countries has been slight. The anticipated purchasing power changes manifest themselves on both bond and stocks.

### *Unsystematic Risk*

Market, purchasing-power, and interest-rate risks are the principal sources of systematic risk in securities; but we should also consider another important category of security risks- unsystematic risks.

- Specific risk is a risk that affects a very small number of assets. This is sometimes referred to as"unsystematic risk". In a balanced portfolio of assets there'd be a spread between general market risk and risks specific to individual components of that portfolio. Determination of the extent of exposure to individual risks is made using models such as Treynor-Black in which the optimal share of a security is inversely proportional to the square of its specific risk.

An example would be news that is specific to either one stock or a group of companies, such as the loss of a patent or a major natural disaster affecting the company's operation. The portion of total risk that is unique or peculiar to a firm or an industry, and beyond that affecting securities markets in general is called unsystematic risk. Factors such as management capability, consumer preferences, and labour strikes can cause unsystematic variability of returns for a company's stock.

### Examples of Unsystematic Risks

- *Business risk:* Business risk relates to the variability of the sales, income, profits etc., which in turn depend on the market conditions for the product mix, input supplies, strength of competitors, etc. The business risk is sometimes external to the company due to changes in government policy or strategies of competitors or unforeseen market conditions. They may be internal due to fall in production, labour problems, raw material problems or inadequate supply of electricity etc. The internal business risk leads to fall in revenues and in profit of the company, but can be corrected by certain changes in the company's policies.
- *Financial Risk:* This relates to the method of financing, adopted by the company; high leverage leading to larger debt servicing problems or short-term liquidity problems due to bad debts, delayed receivables and fall in current assets or rise in current liabilities. These problems could no doubt be solved, but they may lead to fluctuations in earnings, profits and dividends to share holders. Sometimes, if the company runs into losses or reduced profits, these may lead to fall in returns to investors or negative returns. Proper financial planning and other financial

adjustments can be used to correct this risk and as such it is controllable.

- Default or insolvency risk: The borrower or issuer of securities may become insolvent or may default, or delay the payments due, such as interest instalments or principal repayments. The borrower's credit rating might have fallen suddenly and he became default prone and in its extreme form it may lead to insolvency or bankruptcies. In such cases, the investor may get no return or negative returns. An investment in a healthy company's share might turn out to be a waste paper, if within a short span, by the deliberate mistakes of Management or acts of God, the company became sick and its share price tumbled its face value. Other Risks Besides the described risks, there are many more risks, which can be listed, but in actual practice, they may vary in form, size and effect.

Some of such identifiable risks are the Political Risks, Management Risks and Liquidity Risks etc. Political risk may occur due to the changes in the government, or its policy shown in fiscal or budgetary aspects, changes in tax rates, imposition of controls or administrative regulations etc.

Management risks arise due to errors or inefficiencies of management, causing losses to the company. Marketability liquidity risks involve loss of liquidity or loss of value in conversions from one asset to another say, from stocks to bonds, or vice versa. Such risks may arise due to some features of securities, such as callability; or lack of sinking fund or Debenture Redemption Reserve fund, for repayment of principal or due to conversion terms, attached to the security, which may go adverse to the investor. All the types of risks are of varying degrees, resulting in uncertainty or variability of return, loss of income, and capital losses, or erosion of real value of income and wealth of the investor. Normally the higher the risk taken, the higher is the return.

### *Risk Measurement*

Understanding the nature and types of risk is not

adequate unless the investor or analyst is capable of measuring it in some quantitative terms. The quantitative expression of the risk of a stock would make it comparable with other stocks. However, the risk measurements cannot be considered fully accurate as it is caused by multiplicity of factors such as social, political, economic and managerial aspects.

Risk is measured by the variability of returns. The statistical tool often used to measure risk is the standard deviation. We know, standard deviation is a measure of the values of the variables around its mean or it is the square root of the sum of the squared deviations from the mean divided by the number of observations. This can be emphasised with an example.

The concepts of variance, standard deviation, covariance and beta coefficients etc., are also used to explain the measure of risk. In the context of portfolio of assets, or investment in any assets risk is inherent in all such dealings. This risk primarily arises first out of parting of your funds or loss of liquidity. Money lent or parted is always having an element of risk. This element is the same as the concept of total risk.

## *Capital Asset Pricing Model (CAPM)*

CAPM uses the concept of Beta to link risk with return. Using CAPM, investors can assess the risk return trade off involved in any investment decision. Beta is a measure of non-diversifiable risk (Systematic Risk). It shows how the price of a security responds to changes in market prices.

The equation for calculation of Beta is,

$R_i = \alpha_i + \beta_i R_m + e_i$

$R_i$ = Estimated return on ith stock

$\alpha$ = Expected return when market return is zero (intercept)

$\beta_i$ = Beta, a measure of stock's sensitivity to the market index

$R_m$ = Return on market index

$e_i$ = the error term

Using the Beta concept the Capital Asset Pricing Model will help to define the required return on a security. Normally the higher is the risk we take, the higher should be the return as otherwise we avoid risk. So, the higher the, the higher should be the return.

The equation for CAPM is,

$R_i = Rf + \beta\, i\, (R_m - Rf)$

Ri is the required return

Rf is the risk free return

$R_m$ is the average market return

$B_i$ is the measure of systematic risk which is non-diversifiable.

Presently, the risk free return is 6% as the Treasury Bill rate and market return is expected to vary with the chosen. Let us take as and expected market return is 18%, then the return on the stock i is as follows:

$R_i$ = 6% + 1.2 (18 - 6)
= 0.06 + 1.2 (0.12)
= 0.06 +.144
= 20.4%

If the investor is risk taker and chooses a Beta of 1.8, then the expected return will be higher as shown.

$R_i$ = 6 + 18 (18-12)
=.06 + 1.8 (.12)
=.06 +.216 =.276 = 27.6%

### *Security Market Line (SML)*

When the Capital Asset Pricing Model is drawn graphically, we get the S.M.L. If the investor wants to decide on an investment with an expected return he would know the level of risk he has to take or alternatively given the level of risk, he has preferred to take. The investor has to assess whether it is worth taking a level of risk, if he has a target return which involves that risk, as he is assumed to be generally risk averse.

Thus, CAPM and SML help the investor in evaluating risk for a return, in making any investment decision. The principle of the higher the risk, the higher is the return is embodied in this Model.

*Concept of portfolio Models:* Risks in relation to portfolios are also to be understood in the present discussion. Therefore, the concept of Risk in two Major Models used in valuation is related to systematic, unsystematic and total risk. The two models are those of Markowitz and Sharpe which go by the name of Modern Portfolio Theory.

The return on investments in financial assets takes the form of dividend and/or interest income and appreciation in the price of the asset held.

The risk associated with holding common stocks is really the likelihood that expected returns will not materialize. If dividends or price appreciation fall short of expectations, the investor is disappointed. The principal sources behind dividend and priceappreciation uncertainties are factors that are either controllable or not subject to control by the firm.

The sources of systematic risk, include market, interest-rate, and purchasing-power risks. Market risk reflects changes in investor attitudes towards equities in general that stem from tangible and intangible events.

Interest-rate risk and purchasing-power risk are associated with changes in the price of money and other goods and services. Increases in interest rates cause the prices of all types of securities to be marked down. Rising prices of goods and services (inflation or purchasing-power changes) have an adverse effect on security prices because the postponement of consumption through any form of investment means less'real' buying power in the future.

The major sources of unsystematic risk affecting the holding of common stocks are business risk and financial risk. Business risk refers to changes in the operating environment of the firm and how the firm adapts to them. Financial risk is related to the debt-andequity mix of financing in the firm. Operating profits can be magnified up or down, depending upon the extent to which debt financing is employed and under what terms.

The various sources of risk in holding common stocks must be quantified so that the analyst can examine risk in relationship to measures of return. A reasonable surrogate of risk is the variability of return.

This proxy measure in statistics is commonly the variance or standard deviation of the returns on a stock around the expected return. Total risk of an investment consists of two components: diversifiable and non-diversifiable risk. The former risk can be almost entirely by holding a large enough mix of carefully selected securities.

The only risk an investor is compensated for taking is thus non-diversifiable risk. Beta measures this risk and can be used to determine the appropriate required return on a security. Conversely, the market risk is considered as non-diversifiable risk.

# 4

# Valuation of Fixed Income Securities and Bonds

## INTRODUCTION

Fixed income financial instruments which, traditionally, have been identified as a long-term source of funds for a corporate enterprise are the cherished conduit for investor's money. An assured return and high interest rate are responsible for the preference of bonds over equities.

The year 1996-97 witnessed hectic trading in the debt market, as resource mobilisation reached a record level of almost Rs. 25,000 crores which was much the equity segment. In the first seven months of the fiscal year 1998-99, the funds mobilised by ICICI (Four debt issues) and IDBI have accounted for 90 per cent of Rs. 3,175 crores mopped in the primary market.

Financial institutions, banks and corporate bodies are offering attractive bonds like retirement bonds, education bonds, deep discount bonds, encash bonds, money multiplier bonds and index bonds. Knowing how to value fixed income securities (bonds) is important both for investors and managers. Such knowledge is helpful to the former in deciding whether they should buy or sell or hold securities at prices prevailing in the market.

## BOND VALUATION-TERMINOLOGY

A bond or debenture is a debt instrument issued by the government or a government agency or a business enterprise.

**Table. Debt Instruments**

| Type | Typical Features |
|---|---|
| Central Government Securities | Medium- to long-term bonds issued by RBI on behalf of GOI. Coupon payments are semi-annual. |
| State Government Securities | Medium- to long-term bonds issued by RBI on behalf of the state government. Coupon payments are semi-annual. |
| Government-Guaranteed Bonds | Medium - to long -term bonds issued by government agencies and guaranteed by the central government or a state government. Coupon payments are semi-annual. |
| PSU Bonds | Medium- to long-term bonds issued by public sector companies in which the central or state government has an equity stake of 51 per cent or more. |
| Corporate | Short-to medium-term debt issued by Debentures private and public sector companies. |
| Money Market Instruments | Debt instruments like Treasury Bills (issued by GOI),Commercial Paper (issued by corporates) and Certificates of deposits (issued by banks and financial institutions) that have a maturity of less than a year. |

In order to understand the valuation of bonds, we need to be familiar with certain bond-related terms. Par Value- It is the value stated on the face of the bond. It represents the amount the firm borrows and promises to repay at the time of maturity. Usually the par or face value of bonds issued by business firms is Rs. 100. Sometimes it can be Rs. 1000.

Coupon Rate and Interest- A bond carries a specific interest rate which is called the coupon rate. The interest payable to the bond holder is simply par value of the bond × coupon rate. Most bonds pay interest semi-annually. For example, a GOI security which has a par value of Rs. 1000 and a coupon rate of 11 per cent pays an interest of Rs. 55 every six months. Maturity Period- Typically, bonds have a maturity period of 1-10 years; sometimes they have a longer maturity. At the time of maturity the par (face) value plus perhaps a nominal premium is payable to the bondholder.

***The Time Value Concept***

The time value concept of money is that the rupee received today is more valuable than a rupee received tomorrow. The investor will postpone current consumption only if he could earn more future consumption opportunities through investment. Individuals generally prefer current consumption to future consumption. If there is inflation in the economy, a rupee today will represent more purchasing power than a rupee at a future date.

Interest is the rent paid to the owners to part their money. The interest that the borrower pays to the lender causes the money to have a future value different from its present value. The time value of money makes the rupee invested today grow more than a rupee in the future. To quantify this concept mathematically compounding and discounting principles are used. The one period future time value of money is given by the equation: Future Value = present value (1 + interest rate). If hundred rupees are put in a savings bank account in a bank for one year, the future value of money will be:

Future Value = Rs. 100 (1.0 + 6%)

= 100 × 1.06 = Rs. 106.

If the deposited money is allowed to cumulate for more than one time, the period exponent is added to the equation.

Future value = (Present Value) (1 + interest rate)t

t- the number of time periods the deposited money accumulates as interest. Suppose Rs. 100 is put for two years at the 6% rate of interest, money will grow to be Rs. 112.36.

Future Value = Present value (1 + interest rate)2

= 100 (1 + 0.06)2

= 100 (1.1236)

= 112.36.

### *The Present Value*

The present value of money can be found simply by reversing the earlier equation.

Present value × (1 + interest rate) = Future value,

$$\text{Persent value} = \frac{\text{Future value}}{1 + \text{Interest rate}}$$

Here, the discounting principle is used. Today's worth of Rs. 100 to be received after a year at 10 per cent interest would be:

$$\text{Persent value} = \frac{\text{Future value}}{(1 + \text{Interest rate})}$$

$$= \text{Rs.} \frac{100}{1+0.10} = \frac{100}{1.1} = \text{Rs. } 90.90.$$

The multiple period of present value equation takes into account of the multiple periods.

$$\text{Persent value} = \frac{\text{Future value}}{(1 + \text{Interest rate})}$$

### Valuation Model

The value of a bond- or any asset, real or financial- is equal to the present value of the cash flows expected from it. Hence, determining the value of a bond requires:

- An estimate of expected cash flows
- An estimate of the required return.

To simplify the analysis of bond valuation as suggested, make the following assumptions: The coupon interest rate is fixed for the term of the bond. The coupon payments are made every year and the next coupon payment is receivable exactly a year from now. The bond will be redeemed at par on maturity.

Given these assumptions, the cash flow for a non-callable bond comprises an annuity of a fixed coupon interest payable annually and the principal amount payable at maturity. Hence the value of a bond is:

$$P = \sum_{t=1}^{n} \frac{C}{(1+r)^t} + \frac{M}{(1+r)^n}$$

Where P = value (in rupees),

N = number of years

C = annual coupon payment (in rupees)

R = periodic required return

M = maturity value

T = time period when the payment is received.

Since the stream of semi-annual coupon payments is an ordinary annuity, we can apply the formula for the present value of an ordinary annuity.

*Hence the bond value is given by the formula*:

P = C × PVIFAr, n + M × PVIFr, n (10.1 a)

To emphasise how to compute the value of a bond, consider a 10-year, 12 per cent coupon bond with a par value of Rs. 1000. Let us assume that the required yield on this bond is 13 per cent.

*The cash flows for this bond are as follows*:

10 annual coupon payments of Rs. 120.

Rs. 1000 principal repayment 10 years from now.

The value of the bond is:

P = 120 × PVIFA13%, 10 yr + 1,000 × PVIF13%, 10yr

= 120 × 5.426 + 1000 × 0.295

= 651.1 + 295 = Rs. 946.1

*Bond Values with Semi-Annual Interest*

Most bonds pay interest semi-annually. To value such bonds, we have to work with a unit period of six months, and not one year. This means that the bond valuation equation has to be modified along the following lines: The annual interest payment, C, must be divided by 2 to obtain the semi-annual interest payment. The number of years to maturity must be multiplied by two to get the number of half-yearly periods.

The discount rate has to be divided by two to get the discount rate applicable to half-yearly periods.

With the modifications, the basic bond valuation becomes:

$$P = \sum_{t=1} \frac{C/2}{(1+t/2)^t} + \frac{M}{(1+r/2)^{2n}}$$

$$= C/2\left(PVIFA_{r/2}2n\right) + M\left(PVIF_{r/2,2n}\right)$$

Where P = value of the bond

C/2 = semi-annual interest payment

R/2 = discount rate applicable to a half-year period

M = maturity value

2n = matutrity period expressed in terms of half-yearly periods.

Illustration Consider a 8-year, 12 per cent coupon bond with a par value of Rs. 100 on which Interest is payable semi-annually. The required retrun on this bond is 14 per cent.

*Solution:*

*Applying the value of the bond is:*

$$P = \sum_{t=1} \frac{6}{(1.07)^t} + \frac{100}{(1.07)^{16}}$$

$$= 6\,(PVIFA_{7\%,\,16\,yr}) + 100\,(PVIF_{7\%,\,16\,yr})$$

= Rs. 6 (9.447) + Rs. 100 (0.388) = Rs. 95.5.

Illustration At an annual rate of compounding of 9 per cent, how long does it take for a given sum to become double and triple its original value?

*Solution:*

$P_t = P_0\,(1 + r)^n$

When the n value is not given it can be solved by using log ln,

$n \ln (1 + r) = \ln P_t$

$n \ln (1 + 0.09) = \ln 2$

n. ln 0.0862 = ln 0.6931 n = 8.04 years

To triple

$n \ln (1 + 09) = \ln 3$

n. ln 0.0862 = ln 1.0986

$= 12.74$ years $\frac{2100}{(1+r)^n}$

*Illustration:* following whic0 amount is worth more at 16 per cent; Rs. 1000 today or Rs. 2100 after five years.

*Solution:*

The present worth of Rs. 2100,

$$= \frac{2100}{(1+0.16)^5}$$

$$= 2100 \times 0.476 = 999.60$$

The present worth of Rs. 2100 is Rs. 999.60 which is less than Rs. 1,000. Hence Rs. 2100 after five years is not worthful.

Illustration Determine the price of Rs. 1,000 zero coupon bond with yield to maturity of 18 per cent and 10 years to maturity. What is YTM of this bond if its price is Rs. 220 ?

*Solution.*

$$\text{Price} = \frac{\text{Face value}}{(1+\text{YTM})^n}$$

$$= \frac{1{,}000}{(1+0.18)^{10}} = \frac{1{,}000}{5.2338}$$

$$= \text{Rs. } 191.07$$

$$\left(\frac{\text{Face value}}{\text{Bond Value}}\right)^{1/T} -1 = \text{YTM}$$

$$\left(\frac{\text{Rs. } 1000}{\text{Rs. } 200}\right)^{1/W} -1 = \text{YTM}$$

$$(4.55)\ 0.1 - 1 = \text{YTM}$$

$$1.163 - 1 = 16.3$$

Illustration Arvind considers Rs. 1000 par value bond bearing a coupon rate of 11% that matures after 5 years. He wants a minimum yield to maturity of 15%. The bond is currently sold at Rs. 870. Should he buy the bond?

*Solution:*

$$P_0 = \frac{\text{Coupon}}{(1+Y)} + \ldots + \frac{\text{Coupon} + \text{Face value}}{(1+Y)^5}$$

Or

$P_0$ = (Coupon) (PVIFA, n) + (Principal amount) (PVIF/k,n)
$P_0$ = 110 (PVIFA 15%, 5 years) + 1000 (PVIF/15%, 5 yrs)
= 110 (3.352) + 1000 (0.497)
= 368.7 + 497 = 865.7.

At Arvind's anticipated minimum yield of 15% the price should be Rs. 865.70 but the market price is higher. Hence, he should not buy.

Illustration 10.6. Anand owns Rs. 1,000 face value bond with five years to maturity. The bond has an annual coupon of Rs. 75.

The bond is currently priced at Rs. 970. Given an appropriate discount rate of 10%, should Anand hold or sell the bond?

*Solution.*

$$\begin{aligned} P_0 &= \text{Coupon (PVIFA k, n)} + \text{Principal amount (PVIF k, n)} \\ &= 75 \text{ (PVIFA 10\%, 5 yrs)} + 1000 \text{ (PVIF 10\%, 5 yrs)} \\ &= 75 \times 3.7908 + 1000\ (0.6209) \\ &= \text{Rs. } 284.31 + 620.9 \\ &= \text{Rs. } 905.21. \end{aligned}$$

The market price Rs. 970 is higher than the estimated price Rs. 905.2. It is better for Anand to sell the bond.

*Bond return*: Holding period return- An investor buys a bond and sells it after holding for a period.

*The rate of return in that holding period is*:

$$\text{Holding period return} = \frac{\text{Price gain or loss during the holding Period + Coupon interest rate, if any}}{\text{Price at the begining of the holding period}}$$

The holding period rate of return is also called the one period rate of return.

This holding period return can be calculated daily or monthly or annually. If the fall in the bond price is greater than the coupon payment the holding period return will turn to be negative.

*Illustration:*

- An investor'A' purchased a bond at a price of Rs. 900 with Rs. 100 as coupon payment and sold it at Rs. 1000. What is his holding period return ?
- If the bond is sold for Rs. 750 after receiving Rs. 100 as coupon payment, then what is the holding period return?

*Solution.*

- $$\text{Holding period return} = \frac{\text{Price gain} + \text{Coupon payment}}{\text{Purchase Price}}$$

$$= \frac{100+100}{900} = \frac{200}{900} = 0.2222$$

Holding period return = 22.22%

- $$\text{Holding period return} = \frac{\text{Gain or loss} + \text{Coupon payment}}{\text{Purchase price}}$$

$$= \frac{150+100}{900} = \frac{-50}{900} = 0.0555$$

Holding period return = 5.5%

With this measure the investors can find out the rate of cashflow from their investments every year. The current yield differs from the coupon rate, since the market price differs from the face value of the bond.

When the bond's face value and market price are same, the coupon rate and the current yield would be the same. For example, when the coupon payment is 8% for Rs. 100 bond with the same market price, the current yield is 8%. If the current market price is Rs. 80 then the current yield would be 10%.

### *Yield to Maturity*

The concept of yield-to-maturity (YTM) is one of the widely used tools in bond investment management. Arithmetically, YTM is the single discount factor that makes present value of future cashflows from a bond equal to the current price of the bond. Intuitively, YTM is the rate of return, which an investor can expect to earn if the bond is held till maturity. The yield to maturity is calculated based on certain assumptions. They are:

- There should not be any default. Coupon and principal amount should be paid as per schedule.
- The investor has to hold the bond till maturity.
- All the coupon payments should be reinvested immediately at the same interest rate as the same yield to maturity of the bond.

Understanding this, is crucial for better investment decisions. For example, if an 11 per cent coupon paying bond with four years to mature has a TYM, of say 13 per cent it would be realised only if two conditions are met: One, the bond is held till maturity (for four years), and two, the interest received from the bond is reinvested for the rest of the period at 13 per cent. Otherwise actual or realised rate of return of the investor will be different from the expected return.

In the example, if coupon receipts are re-invested at say, 10 per cent for the rest of the period then the realised rate of return will be less than the YTM. Conversely, if the coupon receipts are reinvested at 14 per cent, the realised rate of return will be higher than the YTM. Any difference in the re-investment rate will cause a difference between the actual return and the YTM.

In this sense, the YTM is only a measure of yield. It cannot be regarded as a measure of return from a coupon-paying bond. The YTM concept has a slightly different meaning for Zero Coupon Bonds (ZCB), popularly known as Deep Discount Bonds (DDB). ZCBs do not carry any coupon but are issued at a price discounted to the face value. On maturity, these bonds are redeemed at face value. Since thee bonds do not have any coupon payments during the life of the bond, the question of re-investment of coupon payments does nto arise at all. There is no re-investment risk for ZCBs. To find out the yield to maturity the present value technique is adopted. The formula is,

$$\text{Present value} = \frac{\text{Coupon}_1}{(1+y)^1} + \frac{\text{Coupon}_2}{(1+y)^2} + \ldots + \frac{(\text{Coupon}_n + \text{face value})}{(1+y)^n}$$

Y = The yield to maturity.

Illustration A four-year bond with the 7% coupon rate and maturity value of Rs. 1000 is currently selling at Rs. 905. What is its yield to maturity? Solution. Since all the three values are known out of the four values, it can be found out by using trial and error procedure. Let us try ten per cent.

| Cash flow | PV for 10% | PV of CF |
|---|---|---|
| 70 | 0.9091 | 63.64 |
| 70 | 0.8264 | 57.85 |
| 70 | 0.7513 | 52.59 |
| 1070 | 0.6830 | 730.82 |
| | | **Rs. 904.90** |

The yield to maturity is 10 per cent

The approximate yield to maturity can be found out by using the following formula too.

$$Y = \frac{C + (P \text{ or } D/\text{years to maturity})}{(P_0 + F)/2}$$

Y= Yield to matrurity

C= Coupon interest

$P_0$or D = Premium or discount

$P_0$ = Present value

F = Face value

In the case of sum,

$$= \frac{70+(95/4)}{(905+1000)/2} = \frac{93.75}{952.5} = 0.098$$

$$Y = 9.8\%$$

Yield to maturity is 9.8%.

### *Price-Yield Relationship*

A basic property of a bond is that its price varies inversely with yield. The reason is simple. As the required yield increases, the present value of the cash flow decreases; hence the price decreases. Conversely, when the required yield decreases, the present value of the cash flow increases; hence the price increases. The graph of the price-yield relationship for any callable bond has a convex shape

Relationship between bond price and time. Bond prices, generally, change with time as the price of a bond must equal its par value at maturity (assuming that there is no risk of default). For example, a bond that is redeemable for Rs. 1000 (which is its par value) after 5 years when it matures, will have a price of Rs. 1000 at maturity, no matter what the current price is. If its current price is Rs. 1100, it is said to be a premium bond. If the required yield does not change between now and the maturity date, the premium will decline over time. On the other hand, if the bond has a current price of say Rs. 900, it is said to be a discount bond. Only when the current price is equal to par value-in such a case the bond is said to be a par bond-there is no change in price as time passes, assuming that the required yield does not change between now and the maturity date.

Relationship between coupon rate, required yield, and price As yields change in the marketplace, prices of bonds change to reflect the new required yield. When the required yield on a bond rises its coupon rate, the bond sells at a discount. When the required yield on a bond equals its coupon rate, the bond sells at par. When the required yield on a bond falls its coupon rate, the bond sells at a premium. We can summarise the relationship between coupon rate, required yield, and price as follows:

Coupon rate < Required yield ⇔ Price < Par(Discount bond)
Coupon rate = Required yield ⇔ Price = Par
Coupon rate > Required yield ⇔ Price > Par (Premium bond)

### *Realised Yield to Maturity*

The YTM calculation assumes that the cash flows received through the life of a bond are reinvested at a rate equal to the yield to maturity. This assumption may not be valid as reinvestment rate/s applicable to future cash flows may be different. It is necessary to define the future reinvestment rates and figure out the realised yield to maturity. How this is done may be emphasised by an example.

Consider a Rs. 1000 par value bond, carrying an interest rate of 15 per cent (payable annually) and maturing after 5 years. The present market price of this bond is Rs. 850. The reinvestment rate applicable to the future cash flows of this bond is 16 per cent. The future value of the benefits receivable from this bond. The realised yield to maturity is the value of $r^*$ in the following equation.

$$\text{Present market price } (1+r^*)^5 = \text{Future value}$$

$$850(1+r^*)^5 = 2033$$

$$(1+r^*)^5 = 2033/850 = 2.391$$

$$1+r = (2.391)^{1/5}$$

$$r^* = 0.19 \text{ or } 19\%$$

***Exhibit:Future Value of Benefits***

| | 0 | 1 | 2 | 3 | 4 | 5 |
|---|---|---|---|---|---|---|
| Investment | 850 | | | | | |
| Annual interest | | 150 | 150 | 150 | 150 | 150 |
| Re-investment period (in years) | | 4 | 3 | 2 | 1 | 0 |
| Compound factor (at 16%) | | 1.81 | 1.56 | 1.35 | 1.16 | 1.00 |
| Future value of intermediate cash flows | | 271.5 | 234.0 | 202.5 | 174.0 | 150.0 |
| Maturity value | | | | | | 1000 |
| Total future value = 271.5 + 234.0 + 202.5 + 174.0 + 150.0 + 1000 = 2032 | | | | | | |

## Bond Market

Bonds are bought and sold in large quantities. Most trading in bonds, however, takes place over the counter. This means that the transactions are privately negotiated and they do not take place through the process of matching of orders on an organised exchange. This is a characteristic of bond markets all over the world, not just in India. Because the bond market is largely over the counter, it lacks transparency. A financial market is transparent if you can easily observe its prices and volumes. The National Stock Exchange has a Wholesale Debt Market (WDM) segment. The WDM segment is a market for high value transactions in government securities, PSU bonds, commercial papers, and other debt instruments. The quotations of this segment mostly reflect over- the-counter transactions that are privately negotiated over the phone or computer and registered with the exchange for reporting purposes.

### *The Term Structure of Interest Rate (Yield Curve)*

The bond portfolio manager is often concerned with two aspects of interest rates; the level fo interest rate and the term structure of interest rate. The relationship between the yield and time or years to maturity is called term structure. The term structure is also known as yield curve. In analysing the effect of maturity on yield all other influences are held constant. Usually pure discount instruments are selected to eliminate the effect of coupon payments. The bonds chosen do not have early redemption features. The maturity dates are different but the risks, tax liabilities and redemption possibilities are similar.

The general reception is that the curve will be upward moving up to a point then it becomes flat. There are at least three competing theories that attempt to explain the term structure of the interest rates viz., the expectation theory, liquidity preference theory and preferred habitat or segment theory. Expectation theory- The theory was developed by J.. Hicks (1939), F. Lutz (1940) and B. Malkiel (1966). The expectation theory, the shape of the curve can be explained by the expectations of the investors about the future interest rates. If the short term rates are expected to be relatively low in the future, then the long term rate will be the short term rate. There are three reasons for the investors to anticipate the fall in the interest rate.

- Anticipation of the fall in the inflation rate and reduction in the inflation premium.
- Anticipation of balanced budget or cut in the fiscal deficit.
- Anticipation of recession in the economy, and a fall in the demand for funds by the private corporate.

The long term rates will exceed the current short term rates if there is an expectation that the market rates would be higher in the future. Thus the yield curve depends upon the expectations of the investors.

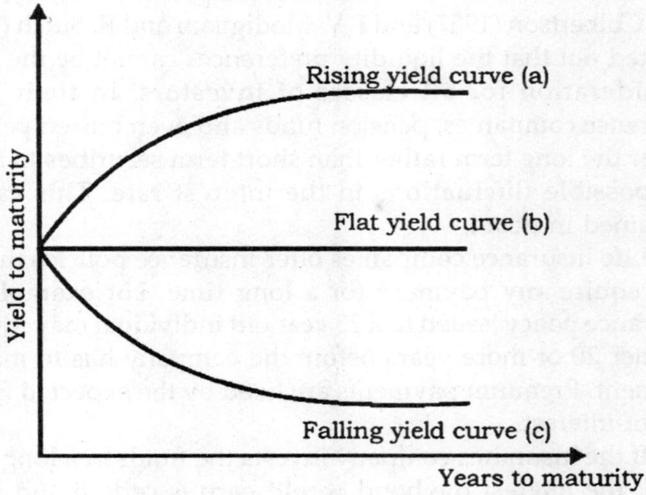


A rising yield curve (a) indicates that the investors' expectation of a continuous rise in interest rate. The flat yield curve (b) means that the investors expect the interest rate to remain constant. The declining yield curve (c) shows that the investor expects the interest rate to decline.

*Liquidity preference theory*: Keynes' liquidity preference theory as advocated by J.R. Hicks (1939) accepts that expectations influence the shape of the yield curve. In a world of uncertainty, it would be more desirable for the investors to invest in short term bonds than on long term bonds because of their liquidity property.

If no premium exists for holding the long term instruments, investors would prefer to hold short term bonds to minimise the possible variation in the nominal value of their portfolio.

The exponents of the liquidity preference theory believe that the investors prefer short term rather than long term. Hence they must be motivated to buy the long term bonds or lengthen the investment horizon. The bond issuing corporate or contributor pay premium to motivate the investors to buy. This liquidity premium theory indicates that in years time the forward rates are actually higher than the projected interest rate.

*Sementation theory*: Critics of the expectation theory, such as, J. Culbertson (1957) and F.V. Modigliani and R. Sutch (1966) pointed out that the liquidity preferences cannot be the main consideration for all classes of investors. In their view insurance companies, pension funds and even retired persons prefer the long term rather than short term securities to avoid the possible fluctuations in the interest rate. This can be explained in detail.

Life insurance companies offer insurance policies that do not require any payment for a long time. For example, an insurance policy issued to a 25 year old individual may involve another 20 or more years before the company has to make a payment. Premium payments are fixed by the expected future rate of interest.

If the insurance company invests the funds in a long term bond, the interest the bond would earn is certain and if the earned interest rate is higher than the promised interest rate, the company stands to gain and its risk is also reduced. If it invests in one year bonds, the risk of re-investment is there and if there is a fall in the market interest rate, the insurance company stands to lose and it would be difficult for the company to meet its obligation. This leads the insurance companies to prefer the long term bonds rather than short term bonds.

On the other hand, commercial banks and corporates may prefer liquidity to meet their short term requirements and therefore, they prefer short-term issues. Supply and demand for fund are segmented in sub markets because of the preferred habitats of the individuals. Thus the yield is determined by the demand and supply of the funds.

### *Riding the Yield Curve*

When the long term coupon rates are higher than the short term rates, the yield curve would have an upward sloping shape. Bond portfolio manager tries to exploit this to his advantage and tries to increase the yield by purchasing the long term bonds. This strategy is known as riding the yield curve. When the long term bond approaches to maturity, the interest rate may get closer to the short term bond but, there would be capital gain.

The bond portfolio manager may maintain the long term bond to utilise the capital gains as the bond moves to maturity date and"rides down the yield curve" to the lower interest rate, which will be appropriate when it becomes shorter term bond. Riding the yield curve would be successful only if the market interest rate does not rise.

Sometimes the market interest rate may increase or short term end of the yield curve may slope upwards causing capital losses to the bond portfolio manager. To manage the situation efficiently the bond portfolio manager should be continuously watchful about the shape of the yield curve and the shifts that occur in the market interest rates.

## *Duration*

Duration measures the time structure of a bond and the bond's interest rate risk. The time structure ways. The common way to state is how many years until the bond matures and the principal money is paid back.

This is known as asset time to maturity or its years to maturity. The other way is to measure the average time until all interest coupons and the principal is recovered. This is called Macaulay's duration.

Duration is defined as the weighted average of time periods to maturity, weights being present values of the cash flow in each time period. The formula for duration is,

$$D=\frac{\frac{C_1}{(1+r)}}{P_o}+\frac{\frac{C_2}{(1+r)^2}}{P_o}2+\ldots+\frac{\frac{C_t}{(1+r)^t}}{P_0}\times T$$

This can be summarised as,

$$D=\sum_{t=1}^{T}\frac{P_v(C_t)}{P_o}\times t$$

D = Duration

C = Cash flow

R = Current yield to maturity

T = Number of Years

PV (C) = Present value of the Cash flow

P = Sum of the present values of cash flow.

Illustration Calculate the duration for bond A and Bond B with 7 per cent add 8 per cent coupons having maturity period of 4 years. The face value is Rs. 1000. Both the bonds are currently yielding 6 per cent.

*Solution:*

$$D = \frac{\frac{C_1}{(1+r)}}{P_o}1 + \frac{\frac{C_2}{(1+r)^2}}{P_o}2 + \frac{\frac{C_3}{(1+r)^3}}{P_o}3 + \frac{\frac{C_4}{(1+r)^4}}{P_o}4$$

$C_4$ includes principal repayment

**Bond 'A' with 7% coupon rate.**

| Year | Cash flow Ct | $\frac{1}{(1+r)^t}$ | PV × CT | $\frac{\frac{C_t}{(1+r)^t}}{P_o}$ | $\frac{\frac{C_t}{(1+r)^t}}{P_o} \times t$ |
|---|---|---|---|---|---|
| 1. | 70 | 0.943 | 66.01 | 0.0638 | 0.0638 |
| 2. | 70 | 0.890 | 62.30 | 0.0602 | 0.1204 |
| 3. | 70 | 0.8396 | 58.77 | 0.0568 | 0.1704 |
| 4. | 1070 | 0.7921 | 847.55 | 0.8191 | 3.2764 |
| | | $P_o$ = Rs. 1034.63 | | | D = 3.6310 |

**Bond 'B' with 8% coupon rate.**

| Year | Cash flow Ct | $\frac{1}{(1+r)^t}$ | PV × CT | $\frac{\frac{C_t}{(1+r)^t}}{P_o}$ | $\frac{\frac{C_t}{(1+r)^t}}{P_o} \times t$ |
|---|---|---|---|---|---|
| 1. | 80 | 0.943 | 75.44 | 0.0706 | 0.0706 |
| 2. | 80 | 0.890 | 71.200 | 0.0666 | 0.1332 |
| 3. | 80 | 0.8396 | 67.168 | 0.0628 | 0.1884 |
| 4. | 1080 | 0.7921 | 855.468 | 0.8000 | 3.2000 |
| | | $P_o$ = Rs. 1069.276 | | D = 3.5922 | |

| Example | 'A' Bond | 'B' Bond |
|---|---|---|
| Face value | Rs. 1000.00 | Rs. 1000.00 |
| Coupon rate | 7% | 8% |
| Years to maturity | 4.0 | 4.0 |
| Macaulay's duration | 3.631 Years | 3.592 Years |

From the example it is clear that the bond with larger coupon payments has a shorter duration compared to the bond with low coupon rate.

*General rule*

- Larger the coupon rate, lower the duration and less volatile the bond price.
- Longer the term to maturity, the longer the duration and more volatile the bone.
- Higher the yield to maturity, lower the bond duration and bond volatility, and vice versa.
- In a zero coupon bond, the bond's term to maturity and duration are the same. The zero coupon bond makes only one balloon payment to repay the principal and interest on the maturity date.

Importance of duration- The concept of duration is important because it provides more meaningful measure of the length of a bond, helpful in evolving immunisation strategies for portfolio management and measures the sensitivity of the bond price to changes in the interest rate.

Duration and price changes- The price of the bond changes according to the interest rate. Bond's price changes are commonly called bond volatility. Duration analysis helps to find out the bond price changes as the yield to maturity changes. The relationship between the duration of a bond and its price volatility for a change in the market interest rate is given by the following formula.

$$\text{Percentage change in price} = \frac{-MD\,[\Delta BP]}{100}$$

MD = Modified duration

BP = Basis point is 0.01 of 1% (1% = 100).

$$\text{Modified duration MD} = \frac{D}{1+\frac{R}{P}}$$

Where

D = Duration

R = Market Yield

P = Interest payment per year (usually two)

*Immunisation:* Immunisation is a technique that makes the

bond portfolio holder to be relatively certain about the promised stream of cash flows. The bond interest rate risk arises from the changes in the market interest rate. The market rate affects the coupon rate and the price of the bond. In the immunisation process, the coupon rate risk and the price risk can be made to offset each other. Whenever there is an increase in the market interest rate, the prices of the bonds fall. At the same time the newly issued bonds offer higher interest rate. The coupon can be reinvested in the bonds offering higher interest rate and losses that occur due to the fall in the price of bond can be offset and the portfolio is said to be immunized.

The process- The bond portfolio manager or investor has to calculate the duration of the promised outflow of the funds and invest in a portfolio of bonds which has an identical duration. The bond portfolio duration is the weighted average of the durations of the individual bonds in the portfolio. For example if an investor has invested equal amount of money in three bonds namely A, B and C with a duration of 2, 3 and 4 years respectively, then the bond portfolio duration is

$D = 1/3 \times 2 + 1/3 \times 3 + 4 \times 1/3 = 0.66 + 1 + 1.33.$

$D = 2.99$ (or) 3 years.

By matching the outflow duration with cash inflow duration from bond investment the bond manager can offset the interest rate risk and price risk. The portfolio of money to be invested between the different types of bonds also can be found. The equation is

Investment outflow = X1, ×) Duration of bond 1) + (X2, ×) Duration of bonds 2) X1, X2 proportion of investment on bond 1 and 2.

Illustration Abisekh has Rs. 50,000 to make one time investment. His son has entered the Higher Secondary chool and he needs his money back after two years for his son's educational expenses. As Abisekh's outflow is one time outflow, duration is simply two years. Now he has a choice of two types of bonds.

- Bond'A' has a coupon rate of 7 per cent and maturity period of four years with a current yield of 10 per cent. Current price is Rs. 904.90.

- Bond'B' has the coupon rate of 6 per cent, a maturity period of one year and a current yield of 10 per cent. The current price is Rs. 963.64.

Risk- The two bonds pose two types of risk to him. He can invest all his money in bond'B' with the aim of reinvesting the proceeds from the maturing bonds into another issue of one year period. If the interest rate declines in the market during the next year, he has to reinvest his money in low yielding bonds and may incur a loss. Now, he has to face the reinvestment risk. On the other hand, if he invests his money in'A' bond, that also involves certain amount of risk. He cannot hold it till it matures, because he needs the money after two years and has to sell it in the middle. If there is a rise in the market interest rate then the price of the bond will fall down and vice versa. If a rise in interest rate is assumed, the investor has to incur loss.

*Solution.* Abisekh can solve the problem by investing part of the money in one year bonds and a part in four year bonds. But, he should know how much to be invested in each of these bonds. This can be got by solving the following equation.

$(X_1 \times D_1) + (X_2 \times D_2) = 2$

That is $X_1$ = the proportion of investment in bond'A'

$X_2$ = the proportion of investment in bond'B'

$D_1$ = Duration of bond'A'

$D_2$ = Duration of bond'B'

one time payment.

Duration of bond 2,

$$D = \left[\sum_{t=1}^{T} \frac{P_V(C_t)}{P_O} \times t\right]$$

| Year | Cash flow $C_t$ | Present value factor 10% | $P_v(C_t)$ | $\frac{P_V(C_t)}{P_O}$ | $\frac{P_V(C_t)}{P_O} \times t$ |
|---|---|---|---|---|---|
| 1 | 70 | 0.9091 | 63.64 | 0.0703 | 0.0703 |
| 2 | 70 | 0.8264 | 57.85 | 0.0639 | 0.1278 |
| 3 | 70 | 0.7513 | 52.59 | 0.0581 | 0.1743 |
| 4 | 1070 | 0.6830 | 730.81 | 0.8076 | 3.2305 |
| | | | $P_0$=904.89 | | D=3.6029 |

Applying the formula,

$(X \times 1) + (X_2 \times 3.6030) = 2$

$X_1$ can be written as $(1 - X_2)$, then

$[(1 - X_2)1] + [X_2 . 3.603] = 2$

$1 - X_2 + 3.6030\ X_2 = 2$

$X_2 = 0.3842$

$X_1 = 0.6158.$

Abisekh should put 61.58% of his investible funds in one year bond and 38.42 per cent in the four year bond.

For investing in both the bonds he needs Rs. 41322.31 = Rs. 50,000% (1.10)2] to have fully immunised bond portfolio. The money to be invested is,

One year bond = Rs. 41322.31 × X1 = Rs. 41322.31 × 0.6158
= Rs. 25446.28.

Four year bond = 41322.31 × 0.3842 = 15876.03.

From here we can find out how many bonds he can buy,

One year bond price Rs. 963.64,

$$=\text{Rs.}\frac{25446.28}{963.64} = 26.4$$

Approximately 26 bonds,

Four year bond price = 904.89

$$=\text{Rs.}\frac{15876.03}{904.89}$$

$$= 17.54$$

Approximately = 18 bonds.

The theory the rise in the market interest is offset by the reinvestment of matured bonds at a higher rate of interest.

Theoretically it seemed to be very simple, but in practice it is not so simple because of the following reasons:

- Immunisation and duration are based on the assumption that the change in the interest rate would occur before payments are received from both the bonds. This may not be true always. The shift may occur after receiving the cash flow.
- Another assumption is that the bonds have same yield. This also may not be applicable. The yield may vary according to the period of maturity.

- It is assumed that the shift in the interest rate affects all the bonds equally. Many a time, the shift in interest rates affects different bonds differently.
- The whole analysis is based on the belief that there will not be any call risk or default risk. But evidence has proved that bond investment is not free from call risk or default risk.

# 5

# Risk Management

## INTRODUCTION

Is there something special, with respect to risk and capital, about a financial conglomerate that combines banking, insurance and potentially other financial and non-financial activities? To what degree is the risk of the whole less than the sum of its parts? This seeks to address these questions by evaluating the risk profile of a typical banking-insurance conglomerate and highlighting some of the key analytical issues relating to risk aggregation. We provide a framework of analysis which builds up this risk profile and allows for coherent dissection of a financial conglomerate's diverse set of risks. We then use the analytical results to frame a policy debate for regulating the solvency of a multi-line financial conglomerate.

Increasing industry consolidation, financial deregulation, and globalization are fuelling rapid growth in the scope of large, multi-line financial conglomerates. The Joint Forum defines a financial conglomerate as "any group of companies under common control whose exclusive or predominant activities consists of providing significant services in at least two different financial sectors (banking, securities, insurance)." In fact, it is fair to say that virtually all of the large, multinational financial institutions operating around the world today are, to some degree, financialconglomerates by either the strict

The merits and sins of specialization vs. conglomeration, small vs. big, have been debated at length, and most of that debate has been conducted using data and experience from the U.S. banking industry.4 There is some evidence suggesting that economies of scale exist in banking (Berger, Hancock and Humphrey, and Hughes and Mester. However, to achieve those gains from strict cost efficiency has proven to be difficult, Are bigger banks less risky? Demsetz and Strahan show that while large U.S. bank holding companies are better diversified than small ones, this diversification does not translate into lower risk. Effectively they 'spend' their diversification benefits through larger C&I portfolios.

Economies of scope have also been used to explain the existence (or creation) of financial conglomerates. These economies of scope can take different forms: lower joint production costs, consumers desiring (and being willing to pay for) one-stopshopping, and more efficient internal capital markets. Putting these together firms might achieve economies of scale and scope to lower monitoring costs, or perhaps by using very large customer databases to cross sell retail financial products and services (reference). Using the U.S. insurance industry as their labouratory, Berger, Cummins, Weiss and Zi (2000), try to explain the coexistence of, in their terminology, the "conglomeration hypothesis" — diversified insurers — with the "strategic focus hypothesis" – pure life or P&C insurers. They do so using a concept of "profit scope economies, which measures the relative efficiency of joint vs. specialized production, taking both costs and revenues into account.". They find that "the conglomeration hypothesis tends to apply more to insurers that are large, emphasize personal lines of business, [and] use vertically integrated distribution systems while the strategic focus hypothesis tends to apply more to insurers that are small, emphasize commercial lines, [and] use non-integrated distribution systems" But are conglomerates more or less risky? A stylized story promises reduction in earnings volatility as the business activities generating those earnings become more diverse. Stiroh (2002) debunks this story for the case of banking by showing that the U.S. banking industry did not achieve any obvious diversification benefits, in the form of stable profits or revenue, through an ongoing shift away from traditional interest income during the last twenty years. all argue that correlation will likely go up once business and product silos are placed under one roof. Moreover, risk may actually increase because monitoring goes down, either report that consolidation appears to have increased profit efficiency in banking.

The idea of risk mitigation as a merger motivation is not new. There is a rich literature on co-insurance following the seminal paper, which discusses the impact of mergers on debt holders (and, indirectly, shareholders).through the bank monitoring its counterparties or the bank being monitored by others such as rating agencies argue that the risk of the whole may be greater than the sum of its parts, largely due to spillover effects from reputation risk. Moreover they point out that the practicalities of achieving integrated risk management are daunting and"appear to have discouraged firms from adopting consolidated risk management". Once those systems are in place, however, firms should expect to reap economies of scale in risk management

As suggested, examine the risk reduction, in terms of economic capital, that might be experienced by possible conglomerate profiles. Others have also considered different inter-sector marriages. Lown e, using pro-forma analysis of potential combinations of banks with either of securities firms, life or P&C insurers, find that the merger of bank with a life insurer resulted in the best risk-return benefit, largely because of enhanced revenue opportunities (economies of scope) and anticipated risk reduction, rather than anticipated cost savings or manufacturing scale (economies of scale). Estrella (2001), using a different approach based on options pricing and the arbitrage pricing theory (APT), finds potential diversification gains from virtually all combinations of banking and insurance (both life and P&C) arising from revenue gains and the already well diversified nature of an insurance portfolio. While these results are in harmony with ours, and as suggested, use some of Estrella's correlation estimates as a robustness check on our analysis later, we are less bullish about the degree of diversification that is actually realizable.

Finally, systemic risk concerns have been raised by several authors, either because the conglomerates are larger and might be considered too-big-to-fail —TBTF –, or that even if they are not "too big" they may become too-complex-to-fail – TCTF –. Moreover, one might be concerned that bank supervisors, in order to help prevent failure of a non-bank affiliate, might be tempted to extend the.

In his literature review, Stiroh points to eighteen studies collected in Saunders and Walter that examine safety net beyond just the bank. This would inhibit market discipline by reducing the incentive to monitor the financial institution and increase the risk of contagion across the pieces of the holding company.

Against this backdrop, we turn to a question that has not been examined in the literature: What does the risk structure of financial conglomerate imply for capital adequacy, particularly at the holding company level? In fact, where are the major sources of risk, and of equal importance, where are the diversification benefits within a financial conglomerate? As suggested, not speculate on possible revenue synergies or management span-of-control issues, but rather focus on the size and composition of the risk pie (e.g. how big is market risk in banking vs. insurance) and what that implies for different financial conglomerates (e.g. large universal bank merging with a small P&C insurer) from the perspective of capital adequacy.

Despite the increasing importance of financial conglomerates, the regulatory structure in most jurisdictions is still largely based around single business lines, on the notion that financial institutions, or their business lines, can be classified as banks or insurance companies or securities firms.9 This is particularly true of the regulatory approach to capital adequacy, which historically has treated different regulated businesses as independent 'silos' in setting capital requirements.

Analytically, the special problem of capital management in a conglomerate stems from the need to aggregate risks across diverse business lines, such as banking and insurance. Our suggested approach for constructing a composite risk picture is to follow a 'building block' approach that aggregates risk at three successive levels in an organization (corresponding to the levels at which risk is typically managed):

Whether non-bank activities broadly are risk reducing; nine conclude yes, six no, and three have mixed results.Securities and asset management activities for third parties are deemed part of the bank or insurance group. These activities are, therefore, not explicitly and separately. Level I: The first level aggregates the standalone risks within a single risk factor (e.g. credit risk in a commercial loan portfolio)

*Level II:* The second level aggregates risk across different risk factors within a single businessline (e.g. combining the asset, liability, and operating risks in P&C or life insurance)

*Level III:* The third level aggregates risk across different business lines (e.g., banking and insurance).

Our analysis adopts this building block approach because it isolates the incremental effects of crossbusiness diversification that are unique to a conglomerate.

Empirically, diversification effects are greatest within a single risk factor (Level I), decrease at the business line level (Level II), and are smallest across business lines (Level III). Our estimates suggest that the *incremental* diversification benefits achievable at Level III by combining a bank with an insurance company are on the order of a 5-10% reduction in capital requirements, depending on business mix. In such a building block approach, the result of adding risks at the holding company level can be no more accurate than the standalone capital measures for individual risk factors (Level I) and business lines (Level II).

The existing regulatory capital measures at these levels are inherently limited, and in particular, fail to reflect important diversification effects at Levels I and II. In our view, a well-constructed economic risk and capital management framework offers the best chance of overcoming the limitations of the silo approach to capital regulation.

Specifically, such a framework can have the potential to address – in a flexible way that is sensitive to business mix– both the standalone distributions and correlation structures of different risk factors, leading to a composite 'aggregate' risk picture of the organization. Finally, by defining economic capital as a 'common currency' for risk, the framework has the potential to overcome inconsistent measurement of risks based on where a transaction is booked.

We suggest that supervisors respond to industry developments in risk measurement and management by supplementing existing supervision of regulated subsidiaries with oversight at the holding company level of a conglomerate's internal risk and capital management framework. This oversight should seek both to validate – and to leverage – internal capital models, harnessing their power to frame the right questions for each institution. Ultimately, rather than focusing just on the numbers, supervision of the holding company should focus on the effectiveness of the capital decision making process.

We discuss the limitations of a 'silo'-based approach to regulation and describe how these limitations give rise to the questions posed by the Project Sponsors. An analytical framework for assessing the risk profile of a typical banking-insurance conglomerate and examines the scale and scope of aggregation effects. Industry practices for measuring and managing risk and capital in a financial conglomerate.

## CURRENT 'SILO'-BASED APPROACH TO REGULATION

Despite the increasing significance of financial conglomerates, the regulatory structure in most jurisdictions is still largely based around single business lines, on the notion that financial institutions, or their business lines, can be classified as banks or insurance companies or securities firms.

The current Basel Committee (BIS I) rules for the banking industry, for example, limit capital requirements to the credit and trading activities of licensed banks.

Life insurance capital regulation similarly focuses on reserve requirements for authorized underwriting activities. Capital requirements for securities firms, meanwhile, vary by jurisdiction. In countries with a universal banking heritage, such as the Netherlands and Germany, the requirements for securities firms fall under bank capital guidelines. In other countries, such as the U.S., the requirements for securities firms fall under different 10 Estrella was one of the first to highlight the importance of this issue.

The rules set by a separate authority The UK and Japan, through their respective Financial Services Authorities, have placed regulation of all three sectors underone roof.

## LIMITATIONS OF THIS 'SILO' APPROACH

The approaches to capital regulation for banks, insurance companies, and securities firms have evolved from very different starting points, under different statutory regimes, accounting conventions, time horizons, intervention triggers, and policy objectives.

This 'silo' approach to capital adequacy raises a number of issues: First, the silo approach is inconsistent: it may lead to different treatment of similar risk types depending on where the risk is booked.

As an example, consider a credit exposure to an 'A' rated counterparty. If the exposure were booked in a bank as a loan, it would, under current (BIS I) capital rules, require Tier I capital of 4% of outstandings.

If it were booked as a credit insurance transaction in a P&C insurance company, the same economic exposure would, under EU regulation, require capital of only 0.16% of outstandings – or twenty-five times less capital than a bank loan. By comparison, if the credit exposure were held as a bond in a life insurance company investment portfolio, it would, under EU regulation, require an (implicit) asset risk charge of 3% of outstandings.

Inconsis-tent treatment creates the potential for regulatory arbitrage: It may encourage institutions to book business in those subsidiaries or shell companies that face the lightest regula-tion, irrespective of their ability to manage or sustain the level of risk. Gramm-Leach-Bliley, with the Financial Holding Company (FHC), makes this now possible in the U.S. as well. An interesting recent proposal from the UK's FSA is in the form of CP136 which seeks to draft a framework for capital adequacy standards for each financial sector.

Banking Regulation/(BIS I)

EU Credit Insurance Regulations EU Life Insurance/ Regulations

- Treat as commercial loan
- Tier 1 capital = 4% ofoutstandings
- Treat as credit insurance payingcredit insurance premium of 1%per annum
- Solvency capital = 16% of premiums Ò! 0.16% ofoutstandings
- Treat as an investment
- Implicit asset risk charge = 3% of outstandings

Second, the silo approach ignores aggregation because it fails to take account of risk concentrations or diversification across different operating subsidiaries. It is possible that an acceptable level of credit risk to a given counterparty in a firm's banking book may become a possibly unintended concentration if added to exposures to the same counterparty in the firm's trading book or insurance investment portfolios.16 For example, if a bank has extended a credit facility to the same business to which the insurance company has issued a catastrophic (CAT) risk insurance policy, the concentration of risks will be lost in the silo approach. More fundamentally, many of the major risk factors within an operating subsidiary will tend to be mitigated by offsetting and diversifying exposures in other businesses.

Third, the silo approach is incomplete because it ignores the capital requirements of unlicensed subsidiaries, including a top holding company. Unlicensed subsidiaries that are engaged in commercial activities impose incremental risk, even if limited to non-financial factors (such as business and operational risk), which suggests a need for additional capital. At the same time, it is at the holding company level that the benefits of diversification across business lines are ultimately realised. These diversification benefits, however, need to be evaluated in the context of a holding company's funding 16 In the EU, banking and trading book exposures within one firm (and group) are together subject to the large exposure rule practices and capital structure, taking into account such factors as the potential for double leverage. We summarize the problems of inconsistency, aggregation, and incompleteness

**Inconsistent Treatment**
**Aggregation Incompleteness**

- Capital requirements dependent on where risk is booked
- Boundaries breaking down due to product innovation
- Increased demand/potential for regulatory arbitrage
- Concentration of risks across legal boundaries
- Diversification across risk classes within a legal entity
- Diversification of risks across business activities and operating companies
- Capital requirements of unlicensed operating companies
- Capital requirements/funding structure of holding company
- 'Strategic' investments in non-financial companies

The limitations of the current silo approach will continue to be exacerbated by industry consolidation and product innovation, which will further blur the boundaries between traditional business lines and risk classifications. If the regulatory structure fails to keep pace with these developments, the whole purpose of rule-based capital requirements may prove to be self-defeating.

There is a danger that institutions will increasingly view risk and capital reporting as a game to be arbitraged, rather than as an opportunity to communicate their financial strength to the outside world.

While there are no simple answers to these challenges, the development of integrated risk and capital frameworks for evaluating capital adequacy in a conglomerate context is progressing. These developments are being driven by a number of factors, including:

- The introduction of risk measurement methodologies

and analytical tools for risk and capital management as well as performance measurement

- The evolution of enterprise risk management as a key corporate centre function
- The blurring of product boundaries through financial innovation, and the potential for regulatory capital arbitrage
- The increased reliance by rating agencies on enterprise-wide capital models for evaluating the ratings of financial conglomerates
- The pressure from some regulators for a consolidated view of risk and capital at the holding company level

Advances in internal risk and capital management practices offer the potential for innovative and more powerful regulatory approaches.

**Recent Regulatory Debate**

The debate in the regulatory arena around these issues has intensified in the last three to four

years. Notably, the New Basel Accord, sometimes called BIS (or Basel) II, proposes to "include, on a fully consolidated basis, holding companies that are parents of banking groups to ensure that it captures risks within the whole banking group" (Basel Committee on Banking Supervision. This includes especially securities and even insurance subsidiaries.18 More recently, in September 2002, the EU Council of Ministers approved an EU directive on the supervision of financial conglomerates.

This directive had four main objectives: 1) to ensure that the conglomerate be adequately capitalized, with particular attention focused on preventing 'multiple gearing;' 2) to introduce methods for calculating a financial conglomerate's overall solvency position; 3) to deal with issues of intra-group transactions, group-level risk exposure and internal risk management and control processes; and 4) to adopt a provision for lead supervisor by the member states for each financial conglomerate.

The Joint Forum at the BIS has also tackled the issue of

risk measurement and management in a financial conglomerate head-on.20 This Joint Forum grew out of a "Tripartite Group" formed in 1993. The purpose of the Group was to identify and provide solutions for problems that financial conglomerates pose for supervisors. It was the first time three sets of supervisors worked.

A bank that owns an insurance subsidiary bears full entrepreneurial risks ofthe subsidiary and should recognise on a group-wide basis the risks included in the whole group."

Together. In 1995, the Group submitted the Tripartite Report, which, while not officially endorsed by the Basel Commission, the International Organization of Securities Commissions (IOSCO), and the International Association of Insurance Supervisors (IAIS), served as the launching point for the Joint Forum consisting of these three regulatory bodies. Fundamentally, the Tripartite Group agreed that supervision of financial conglomerates cannot be effective if individual components of a group are supervised on a purely solo basis. The solo supervision of individual subsidiaries continues to be of primary importance, but it needs to be complemented by an assessment from a groupwide perspective.

The paper laid out simple policy alternatives and proposed some accounting and managerial guidelines but did not provide any answers to the questions of diversification or concentration.The 1999 Joint Forum Report, under the aegis of the Basel Committee on Banking Supervision(Basel Committee), IOSCO and IAIS, was meant to take forward the work completed by the 1995 report.

The report is a set of five papers around capital adequacy, supervisory principles and information sharing and co-ordination. While the first paper on Capital Adequacy made significant progress on the 1995 effort, it focused less on diversification and concentration effects and more on issues such as double (or multiple) leverage, regulatory arbitrage (across distinct bodies), and provided a very simple, banking focused approach to risk aggregation.

The most recent report explicitly compares approaches to risk management and capital regulation across the three sectors of banking, securities and insurance. It not only gives the comparative regulatory view but also summarizes many of the different approaches employed by financial firms across the three sectors, including, of course, practices by financial conglomerates.

EU Directive on Supervision of Financial Conglomerates, Commission to the European Communities,SEC(2002) 995 Final. This report in turn builds on their earlier work.

## Risk Profile of a Financial Conglomerate: Measurement and Management

The special problem of capital management in a conglomerate stems from the need to aggregate risks across a diverse set of businesses. This size the magnitude of aggregation effects by examining the risk profile of a banking-insurance conglomerate.

In effect, it asks just how big a problem risk aggregation actually is: are aggregation effects so severe that a typical conglomerate is over-capitalized to the point of inefficiency (in particular to shareholders), or under-capitalized to the point where it causes undue risk of insolvency to debtholders and policyholders? Very High Very Low/ None

## Illustrative Financial Conglomerate Risk Profile

A financial conglomerate is, by definition, a combination of diverse businesses operating under a common ownership structure. The organization can be broken down into major 21 The 2002 EU directive on the supervision of financial conglomerates adopted the 1999 Joint Forum recommendations.

Business lines, each of which has a distinct risk profile. For example, the universal banking activities – consisting of retail, corporate, and investment banking — are dominated by credit risk. Life insurance activities are dominated by market (investment) risk, and P&C activities by insurance (CAT) risk. In addition, non-licensed subsidiaries may be part of the conglomerate structure. While the common ownership structure is typically in the form of a holding company, it need not be. The analysis and results in this part are independent of the specific legal structure of the conglomerate.

The capital management problem for a conglomerate is to determine – both within and across businesses – how much capital is required to support the level of risk taking. The problem is of concern to different constituencies. On the one hand, debtholders, policyholders, regulators and rating agencies are primarily concerned with the *solvency* of the institution. For them, the key issue is whether the institution holds sufficient capital to absorb risk – or the potential for loss – under all but the most extreme loss scenarios. Put another way, they are seeking capital to backstop the organization's risk taking at a high degree of confidence.

On the other hand, shareholders, participating policyholders, and investment analysts are primarily concerned with the *profitability* of the institution. For them, the key issue is whether the institution is earning a sufficient return on the capital invested to support risk taking. While capital is the common denominator that links the debtholders and shareholders, their interests pull in different directions. Lower capital for a given degree of risk taking will make an institution less solvent, but more profitable, and vice versa.

A conglomerate poses special challenges for capital management: internally, for managers charged with balancing the risk, capital, and return equation, and externally, for regulators concerned with the safety and soundness of the institution. The first challenge is to determine the standalone risk of an activity within a business line – such as the credit risk in a commercial loan portfolio or the 22 Given the myriad ways in which a financial conglomerate can be structured, the only valid method for aggregating risks is one that is based on underlying risk fundamentals and is independent of legal structure. catastrophe risk in a P&C insurer's homeowners portfolio. A number of techniques have been developed within banks and insurance companies to assess risk at this level.

The next challenge is to combine the different risk factors within a business line or licensed subsidiary. Because risks are less than perfectly correlated, they cannot be strictly added together. The licensed subsidiaries include banks, insurance companies, and securities firms that are subject to specific capital requirements. The potential for diversification suggests that the whole will be less than the sum of the parts.

A further challenge for a conglomerate results from the presence of unlicensed subsidiaries. They generally fall into two categories: financial subsidiaries that engage in financial businesses such as financing, insurance, and brokering outside of a licensed banking group, insurance company or securities firm; and commercial subsidiaries that are principally engaged in non-financial activities.

In both cases, unlicensed subsidiaries impose an incremental need for capital, at a minimum to cover the incremental operating risks (including both business and event risk) inherent in the business. For a nonlicensed financial subsidiary – such as a consumer finance or leasing company – the need for capital will be similar to that for other regulated activities. For an unlicensed commercial subsidiary, the incremental capital will be analogous to that held by a non-financial firm, and will be needed to cover operating risks, including business and event risk.

At the same time, the top holding company within a conglomerate structure may also be an unlicensed entity. Because of the scope of activity, the holding company raises unique issues of aggregation.

## Economic Capital as a Common Currency for Risk

In order to assess capital requirements in a diverse conglomerate, there needs to be a 'common currency' for risk that can equate risk taking in one activity or business line with another. Economic capital is often used as that common currency for risk measurement, irrespective of where the risk is incurred. Under the economic capital approach, the risks of a conglomerate – or of the individual businesses within it – can be classified into primary components of asset risk, liability risk, and operating risk. These risks can be further decomposed. Asset risk is typically broken down into credit risk and market/ALM (asset/liability mis-match or management) risk. Insurance liability risks can be separated into P&C catastrophe risk; P&C experience-based risks; and life risks. Operating risks can be split into business risk and event risks.

This framework does not explicitly address what is sometimes referred to as "reputation risk." Reputation risk has two separate connotations: the first is the spillover risk to one business resulting from the insolvency of an affiliated entity. This effect is not incorporated in an economic capital framework because it is not a result of risktaking per se. Rather, it is a result of the failure to hold sufficient capital to prevent the insolvency of the affiliate, and of the legal or market conventions that transfer some or all of the resulting loss to the surviving business. This "risk" can be mitigated by setting high solvency standards for all entities within a conglomerate. Equally, if risks are correctly aggregated, then the total amount of economic capital at the top of the organization will determine the amount of financial resources (capital) necessary to support all of the organization's risk taking at the desired confidence level, inclusive of any spillover effects.

Another meaning of "reputation risk" refers to franchise risk associated with a major fiasco – such as the damage to a financial institution that could result from a large internal fraud or involvement in illegal money laundering. In principle, any direct losses stemming from such occurrences should be captured as an "event" risk within an economic capital framework. The more diffuse harm to franchise value is not something which capital resources are effective at alleviating.

Although each of these risks has distinct statistical properties – as reflected in the stylized risk distributions shown for them – economic capital sets a common standard for measuring the degree of risk taking. The standard is defined in terms of a confidence interval in the cumulative loss distribution, assessed over a common time horizon.25 By setting capital for different risks at the same confidence interval, the economic capital requirements for different risk factors and types of activities can be directly compared. Only by having such a common standard can one meaningfully assess the risk for a complex conglomerate with a diversity of business activities across the financial spectrum.

A typical approach is to tie the degree of capital protection to the target debt rating of the institution. One convention is to adopt a one-year time horizon.26 The economic capital requirement is set to protect against losses over one year at the 99.9% level – roughly equivalent to the default risk of an 'A' rated corporate bond. Put another way, a business that holds capital to protect against one-year losses at the 99.9% confidence interval would have a default risk consistent with a 'A' debt rating. Setting capital for the individual risks within a conglomerate at this confidence interval assures that each of them, on a standalone basis, is protected to a level consistent with the target rating.

Economic capital models are typically built up from the specific analytical approaches for individual risk factors. While the specific tools for risk factors such as credit, CAT, P&C experience and market risks differ, the common denominator in an economic capital framework is the attempt to describe the risk distribution in probabilistic terms, and set capital at a common confidence interval.

The different risks have traditionally been measured at often rather different time horizons. The one-year horizon is indeed typical for banking. In insurance, longer time horizons are considered. Just as risks can be decomposed into individual factors, they can also be re-aggregated. The distribution drawn at the bottom of shows conceptually how the various risk distributions of a financial conglomerate can be combined to yield a single, cumulative loss distribution – and economic capital requirement — for the institution.

In practice, aggregating the various risk distributions in a complex financial organization is a challenging task and somewhat arbitrary. Ultimately, the total amount of economic risk at the top of an organization is independent of how risks are aggregated within it. One proposed method for constructing a composite risk picture is to follow a 'building block' approach that aggregates risk at successive levels in an organization. There are three key levels, corresponding to the levels at which risks are typically managed:

- *Level I:* The first level aggregates the standalone risks within a single risk factor in an individual business line. Examples include aggregating the credit risk in a commercial loan portfolio; the equity risks in a life insurance investment portfolio; and the catastrophe risks in a P&C underwriting business.
- *Level II:* The second level aggregates risk across different risk factors within a single business line. Examples include aggregating the credit, market/ALM, and operating risks in a bank; or combining the asset, liability, and operating risks in P&C or life insurance.
- *Level III:* The third level aggregates risk across different business lines, such as banking and insurance subsidiaries. This leads to the composite picture – or cumulative loss distribution – at the top (holding company) level.

Our analysis adopts the building block approach because it allows the risk profiles of each of the businesses within a conglomerate to be considered separately, *before introducing the cross-business aggregation effects that are unique to a conglomerate.* Put another way, Level I and Level II aggregation effects are already present within regulated banks and insurance companies. The unique problems of a conglomerate are associated with Level III.

Differences in corporate structure, business line definitions, legal requirements, or risk management philosophy may lead some organizations to follow other hierarchies in aggregating risks than the three-level building block approach of overall risk at the top of the organization, alternative approaches to risk aggregation will yield different results at lower levels.

## Estimating Aggregation Effects: General Principles

The starting point for risk aggregation is to begin with

standalone estimates of the economic capital required for individual risk factors. While the general concept of economic capital is explained, the specific techniques for calculating risk at this level are beyond the scope of this paper. Given estimates of standalone economic capital, one can aggregate risks – to a first-order approximation — based on the relative amounts of economic capital, and then consider correlations between risk factors. The diversification benefits that accrue from aggregation are driven by three main factors:

- The number of risk positions (*N*)
- The concentration of those risk positions, or their relative weights in a portfolio
- The correlation between the positions

In general, the diversification benefit increases with the number of positions, decreases with greater concentration, and decreases with greater correlation. The diversification benefits for a portfolio of equally weighted assets or liabilities for two different levels of correlation.

## Diversification within a Risk Factor

As the number of positions28 increases for a given level of correlation, the diversification ratio decreases – i.e., there is an increase in the diversification benefit. For a given number of positions, as the correlation decreases the diversification benefit increases. For a correlation level typically experienced in market risk – around 40% – the full diversification benefit amounts to about one-third; this is achieved fairly rapidly, after about 30 positions. For the much lower correlations typical of a credit portfolio – around 2% – the diversification benefit is significantly greater – around 75%. However, it takes longer to get there; this limit is achieved after around 100 positions.

Though the deals with equally weighted positions, as concentration increases thediversification benefit decreases. This is most easily seen at the extreme. The diversification benefit obtained by one risk factor that is nine times the size of another will be very small, even if the two risks The term 'positions' is used to highlight the fact that this holds universally for assets, liabilities, number of risk factors, etc.

It is important to note that some credit portfolios with considerably more than 100 loans do not converge on the systematic risk limit, because the loans are not equally weighted. Often, a few individual loans can each account for as much as 2-3% of the portfolio, which limits diversification because of concentration effects. are completely uncorrelated (independent). At zero correlation, the largest diversification benefit possible cannot exceed 10%.30.

The Capital Asset Pricing Model (CAPM) breaks total risk into specific (or idiosyncratic) and systematic risk. While the two curves represented in the graph show the systematic risk associated with average correlations of 40% and 2%, respectively, it is possible to conceive of different systematic risk curves for a given risk factor, reflecting different average levels of correlation. For example, a systematic risk curve for a domestic equities portfolio will have a higher level of average correlation – and lower diversification benefit – than a systematic risk curve for a globally diversified equities portfolio. Similarly, the systematic risk curve for a regionally concentrated credit portfolio will have a higher level of average correlation than a systematic risk curve for a globally diversified credit portfolio. Thus, the diversification benefit obtainable within a given risk factor will vary with the scope of activity.

With these principles in mind, the general characteristics of the three levels of aggregation can be stated as follows:

- Level I has many risk factors (individual assets or liabilities) that are neither strongly concentrated nor highly correlated. As a result, there should be a high diversification benefit at Level I. The achievable diversification benefit will be driven by the scope of activity.
- Level II has fewer risk factors, and they are likely to be more concentrated and more correlated. Consequently, there should be a lower diversification benefit at Level II than at Level I.
- At Level III, there are only a few risk factors; some are likely to be much more highly concentrated than

others, and correlations will tend to be high. Level III should therefore If *EC*1 = 9 and *EC*2 = 1, and ñ = 0, then *ECT*= 92+12>9 and the diversification benefit *DB* < 10%. yield the smallest diversification effects of the three levels.

**Level I Diversification**

Level I diversification benefits reflect the degree of diversification achievable for a single risk factor within a given business line. At this level, the number of positions in a portfolio is quite large – typically well over 1,000 policies or loans in an insurance or loan portfolio, and over a hundred positions in an investment portfolio. As a result, diversification benefits will converge fairly rapidly to the systematic risk limit. An equity portfolio, a one-third reduction is achievable due to diversification of idiosyncratic risk alone, while for credit risk the lower correlations allow for a fourfifths reduction.

Beyond the number of positions, differences in the scope of activity can have a dramatic impact on the level of systematic risk, and hence the achievable diversification benefits. As an example, the increasing benefit from diversifying the credit risk of an equally weighted commercial loan portfolio internationally across geographies, essentially diversifying the portfolio with respect to the most fundamental of systematic risks, the (national) business cycle.31 We present results using correlation based on GDP changes from 1991 to 2000.32 31 The economic capital requirement for a U.S. only portfolio is indexed to 1.0 If that portfolio were combined with an equivalent sized portfolio of U.K. commercial loans of similar ratings, the capital requirement (as a percentage of exposure) would be reduced by about one-fifth. Adding a German portfolio of equal size would increase the diversification benefit to 30%, while a fully diversified global credit portfolio would require slightly less than half as much capital, per unit of exposure, as the regionally concentrated U.S. portfolio. Not surprisingly, diversification is a major rationale for financial institutions to internationalize portfolios. For a given amount of expected loss, the same notional exposure leads to less loss volatility and lower capital requirements. Note that this result is not unique to credit risk, rather it can be generalized beyond just banking to insurance as well as non-financial activities.

The same principles apply to equity portfolios – where international diversification is the only means of lowering the systematic risk in any one market. And equally, in P&C insurance, diversifying CAT risk across product lines and geographies produces a similar effect. Since CAT risk for hurricanes and earthquakes is uncorrelated, a U.S. insurer exposed to Florida hurricanes can lower systematic CAT risk by underwriting Tokyo earthquake policies. This explains one of the key benefits of internationalization for insurance companies, particularly P&C and reinsurance. As in the credit example, single risk factor diversification benefits can be on the order of 50% or more.

Significantly, existing capital requirements typically ignore differences in Level I diversification by assuming some 'average' level of correlation and hence systematic risk. As an example, current (BIS I) rules for bank credit risk set a 4% Tier I capital requirement for all commercial lending – irrespective of the degree of diversification in the portfolio. This would continue to be true under the internal ratings based capital reforms proposed in BIS II.33.

*Level II Diversification:* Level II diversification depends on the correlation of risks within a business line. The magnitude of Level II effects will differ systematically for banks, life insurers, and P&C insurers. For banks, the dominant risk, as reflected in BIS capital rules, is credit risk. This is corroborated by two benchmarking studies conducted in 2000. One was conducted by Oliver, Wyman & Company, which surveyed the internal economic capital allocations of ten large international banks in Europe and North America. Capital Market Risk Advisors conducted its own survey of 38 banks, six of which were classified as "large, global". The standalone economic capital requirements for the banks – as determined by their internal models – was broken down into three major risk factors: credit risk, market/ALM risk, and operating and other risks. On average, credit risk accounted for about half of the total economic capital requirement, market/ALM risk accounted for one fifth and operating and other risks accounted for one quarter to one third of the total economic capital. 33 The same applies to insurance, both under EU and NAIC guidelines.

*Economic Risk Capital Breakdowns:* Given the relative weights of the standalone economic capital for the risk factors, the Level II diversification benefits can be estimated from the risk factor correlations. In practice, there are a number of approaches for calculating correlations and diversification benefits. Taking the OWC economic capital breakdown as an example. The first set is taken from Dimakos and Aas who estimate correlations for a Norwegian bank which also owns a life insurance subsidiary. The second set comes from Ward and Lee who present risk aggregation results for a diversified insurer with the risk types broken out. Ward and Lee have separate correlations for market and ALM risk. 34 As we aggregate those risks here, we took the higher of the two correlations. Finally we present results based on the correlations used in Kuritzkes, Schuermann and Weiner,35 which are based on interview findings and reflect the values used by Dutch and other financial conglomerates in their internal capital models. 34 We group market and ALM risk together as the interest rate risk associated with ALM is typically the dominant risk factor in market risk.

Supports the proposition that as the level increases, the magnitude of the diversification benefit decreases. The explanation is straightforward: at the bank level, there are only three risk factors; they are concentrated (credit risk alone accounts for over half of total capital); and have relatively high correlations (for the more conservative KSW case, 40% or greater).36 This provides a possible justification for why existing bank capital regulations ignore Level II benefits: both the present and proposed BIS guidelines treat credit and market risks on a standalone basis, and simply add together the combined requirement without any deduction for cross-risk factor diversification. Many banks do the same in their internal economic capital frameworks. This underscores the importance of Level I diversification relative to Level II for the banks.

The same analysis can be repeated for insurance companies. We show three risk profiles: a life insurer, a P&C insurer and a diversified insurer. Note that the risk profile of the insurers differs significantly from that of a bank and also from each other. Credit risk, for example, accounts for only about 5% and 10% of the total economic capital of a typical P&C and life insurer respectively, although the Ward and Lee estimate is closer to 20% for the diversified insurer, compared to 50% for a bank. At the same time, market/ALM risk accounts for 50% of the capital requirement of a life insurer, 44% of the diversified insurer, 37% of the P&C insurer while only 21% of the total risk of a bank. They may, in fact, not be all that conservative. It is well known that in times of stress, correlations oftenincrease

While grouping ALM and Market Risk is generically useful, life insurance has potentially distinctive ALM features stemming from the unique obligations to its policy holders. Specifically, the policyholders (i.e. liabilitiesto the insurer) often bear some of the market risk from the asset side of the balance sheet.

Studies reporting inter-risk correlations for insurers are harder to come by than for banks. We are aware of only one,, who do so for a diversified insurer. Thus we present diversification benefit results for a life, P&C and diversified insurer using their correlations as well as the correlations used in KSW. With only one exception (the correlation between operating and life risk), our correlations are higher (often much higher) than those of Ward and Lee. Level II diversification benefits for a life and P&C insurer using two different correlation assumptions. The lower correlations of Ward and Lee result in larger diversification benefits than do our more conservative estimates. This benefit is 46% for a P&C and 38% for a life insurer, while the higher correlation version results in 27% and 19% respectively.

*Diversification at Level II (Insurance):* In both cases, the larger diversification benefit for the P&C insurer result from P&C risk being relatively uncorrelated with other risk types. This lower level of correlation overcomes the high concentration that P&C risk represents in the risk profile of a P&C insurer.

Despite the larger diversification benefits at Level II for the insurers relative to a bank, the main hypothesis holds, namely, in moving from Level I to Level II, the diversification benefit decreases.

The results for the diversified insurer are very similar to those of the P&C insurer. While the incremental diversification benefits encountered at Level II are less than at Level I, they can nevertheless be economically important and often are not accounted for by regulatory capital rules. For example, the bank capital regulation (under both BIS I and BIS II) simply adds together the standalone requirements for credit, market, and prospectively, operational risk without any offset for diversification. Similarly, existing European insurance capital requirements assume some "average" level of correlation within one licensed insurance entity. If several such entities form part of an insurance group, as is typically the case, any diversification effects (e.g., geographic diversification) are ignored.

Considering an example from insurance, in the U.S. the P&C risk based capital (RBC) formula for underwriting risk capital has two components: reserve risk and premium risk. The reserve risk charge is calculated by multiplying net premiums written with a set of RBC factors. The factors are different for each line, thereby introducing some diversification benefit.

This is called the Loss Concentration Factor (LCF), which is linearly related to the ratio of the volume of the reserves for the largest line to the total reserves. Suppose that for two companies A and B, the largest line comprises one-fourth of total reserves – but the two lines are different. Then each line will have a different standalone risk and different correlations with the rest of their respective business lines. Nevertheless the capital requirements will be the same.

*Level III Diversification:* Having addressed the diversification benefits at Level II, the incremental diversification benefits at Level III can be estimated by combining banking and insurance activities in varying proportions. As discussed earlier, the three key factors in quantifying diversification benefits are the number of assets or liabilities, the concentration of risk factors, and the cross-risk factor correlations.

Note, however, that in Existing European insurance capital requirements assume some 'average' level of correlation within one licensed entity. In case several of such entities form part of an insurance group, any additional diversification effects (e.g., geographic diversification) are ignored, combining an insurance company with a bank, there are only two business lines, and they share many of the same risk factors (e.g. exposure to a common business cycle). In addition, one of the subsidiaries may well be larger than the other one. These factors will tend to limit the possible diversification benefits.

To aid in understanding the potential diversification benefits at Level III, we consider five different conglomerate profiles reflecting possible different mixes of a universal bank (bank plus securities firm), life and P&C insurers, plus in one scenario, the addition of a small non-financial, commercial subsidiary.

The proportions represent the unit's level of standalone economic capital. These risk profiles are meant to capture a wide range of possible structures, from banking-dominated conglomerates to insurance-dominated conglomerates. For each profile, the diversification benefits were calculated by breaking down the bank, life, and P&C businesses into their Level II risk factors. The Level II risks were then re-aggregated based on the cross-risk factor correlations.

*Sub Units*
*Universal*
*Bank*
*P&C Life Non-financial*
Profile 1 "Bank/P&C-lite" 70% 30% 0% 0%
Profile 2 "Bank/Life-lite" 70% 0% 30% 0%

Profile 3 "Bank/P&C" 50% 50% 0% 0%
Profile 4 "Life/Bank-lite" 25% 0% 75% 0%
Profile 5 "Mixed" 35% 30% 30% 5%
*Conglomerate Profiles*

The LCF formula is LCF=0.7+0.3*ratio. This adjustment reduces the capital required for reserve risk.

Obviously, LCF is a rough approximation for the true diversification benefit.

We then estimate diversification benefits for these profiles given the standalone levels of economic capital by risk type and their correlations as described We do so using several different sets of inter-risk correlations taken from different studies, including the correlations used in our original study. These correlations are presented as well as a brief synopsis of each study. we present the results, including an average across all four correlation specifications.

## Conglomerate Diversification Benefits

Several observations come to light. First, the overall results confirm our initial hypothesis: the benefits at Level III are smaller than at Level I and Level II.

For three of the four correlation specifications, the benefits only range from 0% to 12%.44 For the specification which combines correlation estimates from Dimakos and Aas for banking and from Ward and Lee for insurance, the implied diversification is larger: 5% to 16%. Indeed, under any of the correlation assumptions from this broad range, diversification benefits are modest. Expected benefits likely fall in the 5% to 10% range Second, across the range of estimates, the largest diversification benefits stem from combining a bank with a P&C insurer. This follows because credit risk (the dominant risk in banking) is uncorrelated with catastrophe risk (the dominant risk in P&C). Third, relative size matters. The biggest bang for the diversification buck comes from combining risks of equal size. Moving from an equally weighted Bank-P&C group, for example, to a 70% bank – 30% P&C combination reduces the diversification effects by about five percentage points on average.

## The Fallacy of Composition

The diversification effects estimated through the building block approach reflect an *economic* view of risk aggregation, in which risks are first aggregated within a single risk factor; then within a business line; and then across business lines at the level of the conglomerate. This approach to risk aggregation isolates the *incremental* effect of diversification across business lines. It also corresponds to the way risk and capital is managed at the group level in leading banking-insurance groups.Ultimately, the total amount of economic risk at the top of an organization is independent of how risks are aggregated within it. However, to the extent that risks are added differently at each of the three levels above, then the magnitude of the diversification effects at those levels will also differ.. Insurance companies tend to be broken down If a bar is missing, the diversification benefits are near zero. The results differ somewhat from KSW due to slight differences in standalone risk specification.

There is an effect that may tend to reduce capital requirements at Level III beyond the potential for diversification. Certain risks could actually be offsetting in different subsidiaries, e.g., if one subsidiary is "long"the risk and the other subsidiary is "short" the risk. This could lead to a net reduction in the particular risk factor.

Although theoretically possible, the only major risk for which an offset is likely to occur is interest rate risk between banks and insurance companies. The magnitude of this effect will depend on a number of factors, including the size of the bank asset/liability mismatch gap and the insurance investment portfolio mix. For other major risk factors, banks and insurance subsidiaries are each likely to be long the risk. by geography and product line into a number of operating subsidiaries, each of which is separately capitalized under local law. In many cases, the operating subsidiaries carry their own ratings in terms of default and policyholder protection. Historically, this has made centralized risk and capital management less of a pressing issue for insurance companies than for banks. However, the trend currently is increasingly towards centralization, especially for large, globally active insurers and more particularly for financial conglomerates, which require this centralized view of risk and capital.

**Fallacy of Composition**

The two possible structures for a conglomerate. They differ in the way the insurance subsidiaries are aggregated at Level II. If the insurance subsidiaries are *not* aggregated into one business line at Level II, then the *perceived* aggregation benefits from Level II to III could be greater than the 0-12% range, simply because there are a greater number of small businesses at Level II. 46 But this is an artifact of organizational structure; the amount of risk and the cross-business line diversification effects do not differ, where the insurance subsidiaries are first aggregated into one insurance line. To be sure, there is nothing to prevent management from also splitting up the banking line into many individual subsidiaries at Level II.47 Obviously this would not change the amount of risk or cross-business diversification effects either. It is not uncommon for large insurers to have well over 50 separate subsidiaries. An extreme case would be if each bank branch were a distinct subsidiary and separately capitalized.

In practice, the diversification potential for insurance subsidiaries located in different geographies and hence capitalized (and regulated) separately is often not exhausted prior to Level III aggregation. But the problem here is that the standalone insurance capital requirements fail to take account of the level of diversification already present within the insurance "silo." It is not a feature of cross-business line diversification associated with a conglomerate.

The "fallacy of composition " – or the sensitivity of perceived diversification benefits to how risk units are added within an organization – drives home a central point: Given the myriad ways in which a financial conglomerate can be structured, the only valid method for aggregating risks is one that is based on underlying risk fundamentals, such as the economic capital approach, and is independent of legal structure.

## Compounding Risk and Model Mis-Specification

The diversification effects also underscore a basic tenet of portfolio theory: the risk of the whole cannot be greater than the sum of the parts. *Provided standalone risks are correctly measured,* this means that the economic capital for a conglomerate cannot exceed the total standalone economic capital of the individual business units. Concern that combining businesses within a single entity can somehow increase, rather than reduce, total capital is really a concern about mis-specification of risks at lower levels.

For example, in the case of Long Term Capital Management, there was a compounding exposure to credit spread risk, as positions in different trading books were aggregated, Lowenstein (2000)). But the fundamental problem was that the underlying risk estimates for individual positions were mis-specified since they failed to account of the potential for extreme credit spread movement.

Ultimately, no method of risk aggregation can overcome mis- Legal requirements will, however, imply restrictions on the use of capital and assets within a conglomerate. Cumming and Hirtle argue that the spillover effects resulting from reputational risks may result in this inequality not necessarily holding.

50 Some have argued that the whole may actually be riskier than the sum of the parts (Santomero and Eckles due to reputation and spillover effects. for sound arguments why it is very difficult to cleanly separate market and credit risk. specification of underlying risks. The best antidote to mis-specification is to stress the model parametres and supplement traditional analysis with scenario testing across a wide range of market movements.

Indeed the industry is placing greater importance on stress testing and scenario analysis to explore the edges of the risk space for the very reason that the models are almost always estimated with data dominated by "normal" times. Yet risk managers care disproportionately about the "non-normal" times, i.e., the tails and not the middle of the distributions.

This is the risk manager's dilemma: she understands the unimportant part of the loss (or value change) distribution quite well but not the part which really matters to her, namely the tails. With the current state of the art this can only be characterized through stress testing and scenario analysis.

**Time Horizon**

Another challenge of evaluating risk within a conglomerate is specifying a uniform time horizon. At one end of the spectrum, market risk is typicallymeasured on a daily basis and scaled up to ten days for capital requirements under Basel. Credit risk istypically calibrated to a one year horizon, as is operational risk. In banks, the convention for modelingrisks and assessing capital is to adopt a one-year horizon. The logic to a one-year horizon is that it typically ties to reported business line P&Ls, corresponds to the internal capital allocation and budgeting cycle, and is a period in which an institution can access the markets for additional capital. It is also the horizon used in the New Basel Accord (BCBS. Alternatively, insurance companiesare often capitalized for longer decision horizons. This is particularly true for life insurers, where the obligation to policyholders is unique and often extends to 30+ years. In our approach, in order for economic capital to serve as a 'common currency' for risk, a common time horizon needs to be specified. We adopt a one-year perspective rather than a longer-term Industry

**Practices**

Provided a foundation for evaluating the risk profile and aggregation effects of a financial conglomerate, this part highlights industry practices for risk modeling and capital management within conglomerates. These trends are important for defining the "world of the possible" for policy reform.

Perhaps the most important trend, as noted by the Joint Forum, is that internationally active financial institutions are adopting economic capital as the fundamental measure of risk. This is true of major banking-insurance groups, which have either implemented, or are in the process of implementing, economic capital frameworks across both banking and insurance business lines.

Our earlier study (KSW) confirmed that all of the major banking-insurance groups in the Netherlands are adopting economic capital as the cornerstone of an integrated risk and capital management framework.

The economic capital framework allows for consistent measurement of risk factors across both banking and insurance lines. It also addresses risk aggregation at successive levels in an organization, through internal models that are sensitive to differences in risk profile and business mix. Yet risk modeling and measurement is only relevant to the extent that it drives management decision making. The corollary is that the structure of risk modeling and measurement needs to reflect both management processes and organization structure.

Financial conglomerates are building up group risk and capital management functions to oversee capital planning and decision making at the holding company level. This trend overcomes significant differences in the evolution of capital management for banks and insurance companies.

Banks historically expanded through branching. Branching, in turn, depends on a single balance sheet with centralized capital resources. When a bank entered a new market it typically did so on the strength of the capital resources at the head office. This created a natural need for centralized risk and capital management in banking organizations.Insurance companies, by contrast, typically expanded either by starting up or acquiring new subsidiaries – whether in adjacent product lines, or in new geographic markets.

Each of the subsidiaries, in turn, was subject to separate, standalone capital or reserving requirements, independent of the parent. As a result, insurance companies tended to be locally capitalized – in many cases, with operating subsidiaries rated separately in terms of debt and policyholder protection. Historically, this made centralized risk and capital management less of a pressing issue for insurance companies than for banks. Notwithstanding these differences, internationally active financial conglomerates – including banking-insurance groups – are putting in place centralized risk and capital management units. The dominant approach is to adopt a 'hub and spoke' organizational model that corresponds to the three levels of risk modeling and measurement identified previously. At Levels I and II are the spokes, which are responsible for risk management within business lines.

Examples of activities at the spoke include the credit function within a bank, or the actuarial function within an insurance subsidiary or group, each of which serves as the front-line managers for most transaction decision making. Level II risk management – across risk factors within a business line – also typically takes place in the spokes, often in a finance unit that is responsible for funding and business reporting for the subsidiary.

At Level III is the hub, which provides centralized oversight of risk and capital at the Group level. While the hub is dependent on risk reporting from Levels I and II, in many cases it is also responsible for overseeing the methodology development of an integrated economic capital framework that is then implemented within the spokes.

The specific roles of the hub vary, but tend to include assuming responsibility for Group-level risk reporting; participating in decisions about Group capital structure, funding practices, and target debt rating; liaising with regulators and rating agencies; advising on major risk transfer transactions, such as CLOs (collateralized loan obligations) and securitizations; and, in some institutions, actively managing the balance sheet.

The 'hub and spoke' system is both a reflection of – and a reinforcement of – the importance of economic capital modeling. Risk measures, as manifested by internal economic capital models, increasingly drive management decisions, not just for loss prevention but for business optimization through efficient capital management. The group capital structure considers disparities in the different kinds of capital:

Accounting capital vs. economic capital vs. regulatory capital vs. rating agency capital. As there is no single view on the relevant measure of capital, the group's task is to balance the requirements of different constituencies (regulators, shareholders, debtholders, rating agencies) with efficient yet prudent capital management.

The net effect is increasingly proactive management of risk, capital and value in conglomerate companies, both within business lines and at the group level. It strongly suggests a need for regulation to keep pace with internal developments and market structure.

## Policy Discussion

So how should one interpret our analytical results? A naive interpretation would be that since Level III diversification effects are small, silo regulation is adequate and capital at the holding company level should simply be the sum of the parts.

This would suggest that the de-consolidation approach taken in the New Basel Capital Accord (BIS II) is essentially correct – that insurance company capital should be subtracted, dollar for dollar, from holding company capital for a predominantly banking group. This is the equivalent of saying that holding company capital must equal banking capital plus insurance company capital.

A more nuanced interpretation of our results, however, would be that the naive interpretation is only correct if diversification effects are already fully captured at Levels I and II. But we know that is not the case with existing regulatory measures: Rules-based capital measures at both levels are based on a "lowest common denominator" approach that assumes an average level of correlation within a single risk factor and ignore cross-risk factor diversification at the business line level.

As an example, consider the proposed credit risk capital rules under BIS II. The Level I capital requirements for credit risk under the internal ratings-based approaches assume just a single correlation factor for all commercial and industrial loan portfolios. Similarly, for the bank, the Level II requirements for credit, market, and operational risk will simply be added together, with no offset for cross-risk factor diversification. A key point is that capital regulation at Level III can be no more accurate than the standalone measures on which it is based.

Given the inherent limitations of existing regulatory measures at Levels I and II, a better approach to capital regulation for conglomerates would be to adopt a more supervision-intensive approach such as that contemplated by BIS II's second pillar. Such an approach would require conglomerates to put in place their own economic capital models for assessing risk and capital at successive levels. These customised models are the only real hope of being able to capture the complexity of diversification at all levels within a conglomerate.

In advocating new policy, we are not starting with a clean slate. Any new policy proposal focused on addressing some of the unique problems of a multi-line financial conglomerate will have to reflect the very different starting points and traditions of banking, insurance, and securities capital regulation. In short, the silo approach is here to stay, at least for the foreseeable future.

Estrella (2000) provides a thoughtful discussion of the difficulties and trade-offs encountered in design of regulation for financial institutions. They include the different goals and objective functions of the different constituencies ( for instance); the desire for simplicity (emphasis on rules) and flexibility (emphasis on supervision); at the same time we want to allow for market forces to provide a powerful monitoring and correction mechanism.

The framework of the New Basel Accord is partly motivated to strike a balance among these apparently competing forces. We think the main issues surrounding risk measurement and management in a financial conglomerate can fit within that framework of the New Basel Accord, perhaps with renewed emphasis on legal firewalls as a possible structural response to contagion of risks across distinct entities.

*I: Rules* *II: Supervision*
*III: Market Mechanisms* *IV: Legal Firewalls*

- Specific minimum capital requirements
- Lowest common denominator
- Imposed by regulator
- Non-discretionary, non-judgmental
- Review of internal capital approach
- Institutionspecific
- Internally driven
- Flexible
- Market evaluation of capital adequacy
- Aggregate judgment of multiple views
- Externally driven
- Limited to publicly disclosed information
- Legal mechanism for separating risks
- Jurisdiction & institution specific
- Recognized under law
- Both statutory and contractual
- *Proposed '3+1' Pillar Framework*

The pillars would combine rules-based, supervisory-based and market-based approaches to capital regulation with legal mechanisms. Importantly, the pillars are designed to be mutually reinforcing; no one pillar by itself is sufficient.

The first pillar would incorporate specific, rules-based minimum capital requirements for a conglomerate at the holding company level. Given the findings on the magnitude of Level III aggregation effects, a simple rule-based approach to capital adequacy would be to add up the individual capital requirements for regulated subsidiaries at the parent holding company level, without any offset Estrella and Santos stress that risk and capital are hard to determine in the presence of safety net such as deposit insurance, and that the two design problems (capital adequacy, deposit insurance) should be addressed simultaneously for diversification. While this would tend to overcapitalize the conglomerate to some extent, the degree of overcapitalization attributable to cross-business line diversification is likely to be small – on the order of 5-10%.56 The incremental capital might be justified as compensating for the increased complexity of a multi-line financial conglomerate, for measurement and modeling error at Levels I and II, or alternatively, as imposing a somewhat higher solvency standard for a conglomerate.

The second pillar, however, should be the main load-bearing column of the regulatory framework. In the words of Estrella, this pillar would allow regulators to reap "the benefits of informed supervision. Mechanical formulas may play a role in regulation, but they are in general incapable of providing a solution to the question of how much capital a bank should have. At the margin, scarce public resources are better employed to enhance supervision than to develop new formulas whose payoff may be largely illusory."

Especially for a large, complex conglomerate, the supervisory review is likely to be far more important than the rule-based approach. It would enable the supervisor to evaluate the adequacy of an institution's internal risk management and capital decision processes along a number of dimensions. Importantly, this pillar should be a flexible approach that allows for differences across institutions. Such differentiation is necessary to accommodate variations in business mix, risk profile, legal structure, and level of sophistication.

The third pillar would leverage market judgements on capital adequacy. In the end, the market's judgement of capital for the holding company (and potentially individual subsidiaries) will be decisive, through its influence on pricing and access to funding. While it is attractive from a theoretical standpoint to place great weight on the market's consensus, in practical terms there are too many limitations in current accounting conventions and disclosure standards for this pillar to be sufficient on its own. Similar to the sentiment expressed by the Basel Committee in BIS II, our recommendation is A 5-10% difference in capital is likely within the tolerance range for capital planning, and is unlikely to prompt specific management action. This is especially true since regulatory capital for major financial conglomerates is a floor – and often non-binding. The capital ratios for banks in G10 countries, for example, currently average11.2%, or 40% above the 8% (Tier I plus Tier II) regulatory requirements. that regulators encourage improved accounting rules and better disclosure of the risk and financial structure of a conglomerate, to enable the market to do its job better.

The fourth pillar – legal firewalls – is a possible structural response to contagion of risks. Legal firewalls might be appropriate for a 'mixed conglomerate' that combines both financial and unlicensed commercial subsidiaries.

In practice, there is a very broad range of non-financial subsidiaries that are owned by or affiliated with financial conglomerates.

Given the difficulty of evaluating the capital requirements for such a broad array of businesses, an alternative might be to segregate the risks of these activities from the financial activities in a conglomerate. They could be erected by requiring that nonfinancial subsidiaries be separately capitalized, and by preventing inter-company funding of the subsidiary and cross-company guarantees. Such barriers might not fully mitigate against reputation risk, but they should go a long way towards limiting financial contagion.

The specifics around legal firewalls – what exactly are they? how will they be enforced? – are very important and complex. We simply want to propose for discussion a possible solution to an obviously complex problem, namely that of assessing capital for unlicensed commercial (i.e. non-financial) subsidiaries.

Our proposed '3+1' framework will inevitably require more detailing – and debate – both within the regulatory community and among other constituencies. We look forward to the exchange. firms from 1.2 to 1.3 times the warning level and insurance companies more than 5 times required capital. 57 To be sure, financial institutions are particularly opaque, making assessments by delegated monitors such as rating agencies and equity analysts more difficult. Indeed Morgan (2002) measures this opacity by showing that bond raters disagree more about banks and insurance companies than about any other kind of firm.

## Global Management and Asset Allocation

For the past 20 years, students of stock-market investing have worshipped at the twin altars of modern-portfolio theory and efficient-market theory. The first holds that the more diversified a portfolio, the less the risk from each of its components. The latter posits that active money managers have no more stockpicking prowess than a bunch of randomly tossed darts. Marry these theories, and what do you get? An index such as the S&P 500, which has vanquished all but a few extremely gifted — or is it merely lucky? — active managers, especially in recent years.

No surprise, you won't find too many portfolio jockeys at the wedding, throwing rice. Instead, the S&P's compelling example to the contrary, a small but growing cadre of investment pros is turning its back on both revered theories. These particular managers seek to beat the mighty index — and some have done so resoundingly — by concentrating their bets on no more than 25 stocks. And they're in arguably excellent company: Warren Buffett, the king of concentrators, confines his stock holdings to fewer than 10 anointed names.

Though it flies in the face of business-school doctrine, portfolio concentration has intuitive appeal. "If one manager holds 40 stocks, you might get his 10 best ideas, while the other 30 are filler," Greg Horne, president of Ashbridge Investment Management, a Philadelphia-based investment adviser. "I would just as soon get the filet."

Others see no hope for glory without commensurate guts. "No hospital wings or college dormitories have ever been named by an indexer," declares James Oelschlager, founder of Akron, Ohio-based Oak Associates, which manages almost $5 billion in mutual funds and institutional accounts. "They've been named by people who invested in one or two stocks and rode them for a period of time."

By fund-manager standards, Oelschlager too might qualify for his own wing or dorm. Screening Morningstar's Principia Plus database turned up only three mutual funds with 25 or fewer stocks that beat the S&P 500 over three- and five-year periods: Oelschlager's White Oak Growth Stock, Oak

Value and Sequoia, a 15-stock fund run by Buffett confreres William Ruane and Richard Cunniff, that long has been closed to new investors. A few other relatively concentrated funds, including Clipper, Longleaf Partners and Ken Heebner's CGM Capital Development, also have amassed outstanding long-term records, but the slim ranks of tenured superstars hasn't deterred a batch of newcomers in the past year or two.

"Although some concentrated funds have been around for quite a while, it's just in the last 18 months that we've seen funds launched specifically to play on a concentrated theme," Ken Gregory, a San Francisco investment adviser and newsletter writer. Some upstarts, such as Yacktman Focused, CGM Focus and PBHG Large Cap 20, were spawned by successful, more diversified parents. The infant Marsico Focus (along with a more diversified offering) is manager Tom Marsico's new act; the popular fund manager departed Janus Funds last fall. Lately, $1.2 billion Oakmark Select has had industry jaws dropping: the 19-stock fund, managed by William Nygren, returned 55% in '97, its first full year, and another 13.4% in the quarter ended March 31. Nygren's top holdings include U.S. Industries, USG, Tele-Communications Liberty Media Class A and PartnerRe.

Concentration seemingly is more popular, or at least has met with more widespread success, among institutional money managers. Screening Invest-Works Pro, a database maintained by Barra RogersCasey, for similar composition and performance characteristics yielded 14 products, ranging from $25 million in institutional tax-exempt accounts run by Sorema Asset Management to $4.3 billion in accounts managed by the aforementioned Oak Associates. And that list doesn't include firms that lack five-year track records or have trailed the S&P by so much as a whisker.

Wilson/Bennett Capital Management, of McLean, Virginia, is in the latter camp. In the last 10 years value investor John W. Fisher, the firm's founder and CEO, has managed to keep pace with and frequently beat the market by holding just 12-15 stocks. "I didn't make a conscious decision in 1987 to run concentrated portfolios," "The analytical process —

valuing businesses and pieces of businesses — lends itself to a concentrated approach. We get to know the companies well, and if you're following 12 or 13 stocks, it's much easier to know what's going on in the underlying businesses."

Fisher is on intimate financial terms with, among others, Bankers Trust, Texaco, Mobil and Philip Morris. In Big Mo's case, he charges, the market currently is placing "almost $2 negative value" on the tobacco business.

In the past year, Fisher claims, he's received as many phone calls inquiring about concentration as he did in the previous nine. "The Buffett effect has had a lot to do with it," he surmises. "Also, some people finally have come to the cease that there is no way to follow 100 different companies, particularly large-cap multinationals. The guys buying 90-100 stocks really are closet indexers. They're simply trying to keep up with a benchmark."

Brett Robertson, president of Dallas-based Richmont Investment Management, seconds that rather inflammatory notion. Academic and industry studies, he notes, have shown that the inclusion of as few as 16 stocks in a portfolio eliminates as much as 93% of stock-specific risk, provided, that is, the stocks aren't closely correlated. "Yet in spite of the statistical facts, many managers hold more than 100 stocks," he marvels. "A lot of traditional shops don't concentrate because it means taking a lot of risk to the mother ship, and major blowups can mean the end of marketing. If they don't do anything wrong, money is going to pile into their funds, even if they're just mediocre. We think diversification is a recipe for mediocrity, especially if you measure the fees of a diversified portfolio against an S&P index fund."

Those are fighting words to proponents of diversification — namely, the vast majority of active managers, some of whom have racked up sterling returns with 100 stocks, and more. But they get to the heart of the increasingly raucous debate about whether less is more. And they lend credence to Bill Nygren's assertion that the current interest in concentration "stems directly" from the success of indexing.

How so? Investors who allocate their assets to a variety

of managers or funds, each with a diversified portfolio, in short order find that they have replicated the S&P or another index, albeit at greater cost. Yet, the two investment approaches need not be opposed. "We believe concentration works hand in hand with indexing," he adds, suggesting that concentrated and diversified funds together can make better music than a collection of diversified funds alone.

It's easy to see the drawbacks to pure concentration, which Morningstar highlighted in several studies in the past two years. Sharply limiting the number of holdings in a portfolio does not, in itself, provide any performance edge. It's the manager who makes all the difference. In the hands of a great stockpicker, a tightly focused portfolio has an excellent chance of outperforming the market, as each winning issue packs much more of a wallop. But the exaggerated impact of a rotten egg or two, conversely, can spell disaster.

Some concentrated funds also are more volatile than their diversified brethren, although not necessarily more risky. Investors who take their financial temperature daily should steer clear, as White Oak Growth Stock's recent adventures emphasise. The fund "got slaughtered," in manager Oelschlager's words, in last year's tumultuous fourth quarter, only to snap back with a handsome first-quarter gain of 17%.

If concentration isn't for cardiac patients, neither is it for most short-term investors. In fact, Dennis Bertrum, founder and president of New York's Bank Street Advisors, believes that concentrated-fund holders must be willing to hang on for five years, at least, in order to reap maximum reward.

Nor should these investors confuse volatility with risk. "As soon as some people see higher volatility numbers in their portfolios, their minds shut down and they see risk," Richmont's Robertson. "To me, if 20 years from now you haven't met your investment goal, that is the real risk."

Proponents of concentration, on the other hand, see ponderous problems with diversification. Chiefly, they cite diminished opportunities to beat the market as one's holdings collectively grow to resemble it.

To Ronald Surz, a managing director of Roxbury Capital

Management, in Santa Monica, California, the effort to diversify is a "distraction." Risk increases as "a manager populates a portfolio with the unfamiliar for the sake of matching index characteristics. Once committed, the manager becomes dependent on others for both buy and sell signals, thus following the herd and incurring unnecessary turnover." That's particular problematic in today's market, with the leaders of the S&P 500 achieving the status of momentum stocks.

Indeed, minimal turnover sometimes is a happy byproduct of a more focused approach, as a manager who falls deeply in love with a few good, exhaustively researched ideas presumably will be less likely to fall out of love on a regular basis. Charlotte Beyer, director of the Manhattan-based Institute for Private Investors, concentration is particularly appealing to tax-sensitive investors, including the heirs to numerous family fortunes — especially considering that most of those fortunes were built on one or two great ideas.

How can individuals best utilize concentration? The answer lies less in the concept than the recipe. Oakmark's Nygren puts most of his own eggs in the basket he manages, although the idea probably won't appeal to more timid souls. For these nail-biters, a touch of Tabasco, achieved by blending concentrated with indexed assets, might be just enough.

Yet, such an admixture would seem to subvert the whole point of concentration — namely, the possibility of scoring a grand slam with a crackerjack stockpicker's very best ideas. Greg Horne, of Ashbridge, suggests a better way. "When you combine several concentrated portfolios using noncorrelated strategies, you have the best chance of beating a benchmark,".

Ken Gregory certainly hopes so; he and partner Craig Litman have designed the 15-month-old Masters Select Equity fund around the concept of an all-star team of concentrators. They've parceled out assets to six distinguished managers with distinct investment styles, and have charged each — Shelby Davis, Spiros Segalas, O. Mason Hawkins, Richard Weiss, Foster Friess and Jean-Marie Eveillard — with buying no fewer than five, and no more than 15, favourite stocks.

Last year, the fund returned a total 29.1% — easily beating the Dow Industrials and the average equity fund, though not the turbocharged S&P 500.

Still, proponents of few-stock portfolios think they can best the S&P, and some boast dazzling returns to prove it. Never mind fancy theories; all it takes are a few great ideas, a bit of time — and a lot of concentration.

# 6

# Analysis of Equity Investments

Different procedure for valuing stocks are presented. The basic framework for valuing a stock is stated to consist of computing the present value of all future expected dividends from the stock. The most sophisticated model estimates future dividends using projected financial statements. However, using a simple model of constant dividend growth, a more subjective valuation procedure is explained in the form of P/e ratio analysis is described in terms of both comparative and absolute valuation.

## THE DIVIDEND DISCOUNT MODEL

Payments from equity investments in productive enterprises are made in the form of dividends.

To value stocks based only on the present value of all dividends is analogous to valuing bonds using only the present value of all expected interest and principal payments on a bond. Even if one were planning to hold a long-term bond for just one year, the bond would still have to be valued using the present value of all interest and principal payments expected on the bond (even those expected after one year), since the sales price of the bond in one year would be a function of these payments (just as the sales price of a stock to be sold in one year would be a function of all dividends subsequent to that date). It shows that stock values have investor expectations incorporated into them. As a result, stock values will be high for equities with expectations of high future dividends and low for stocks with low expectations, regardless of current dividend levels. Because dividends are paid from earnings, and because earnings and the future potential dividends from them can be increased by retaining more earnings in the business as opposed to paying them out to shareholders, values.it can be extremely high, even for companies that pay low or no dividends currently, or for companies that aren't even earning a profit, if earnings and dividends at some point in the future are expected to be high.

Because stock values are based on expectations, stock values tend to rise and fall with changes in expectations. In particular, if expectations of future earnings and dividends are lowered, stock values will fall, while stock values will rise when forecasts of earnings and dividends are raised. A number of different events can cause investors to change their expectations on future earnings and dividends, including changes in forecasted economic growth, changes in the industry environment, and changes in the company's own operating situation. Changes in a company's operating environment are often revealed in public company announcements (or press releases, as they are commonly called) that often provide information on a company's new products and cost-cutting measures.

Company earnings reports also affect investors' expectations of future earnings, as they provide an indication of the current profit situation of the company. In particular, when reported earnings are less than expected, investors may determine that the company's situation and future earnings potential are not as good as previously thought, and the stock's value may fall as a result (and vice-versa for reported earnings greater than expectations). A stock price decline is possible even if earnings are reported to increase substantially from the earnings of the prior period if the increase is less than expected. For instance, it is not uncommon for a stock price to decline after a 20% increase in reported profits if investors were expecting a larger 30% increase in earnings Dividend announcements can also affect investor expectations. In particular, companies tend to pay out dividends only if they believe that their earning power is maintainable, so that there is no perceived need to lower the dividend in the future. As a result, an increase in the dividend payment is often taken to be a positive statement about the company's ability to earn profits in the future.

However, as with earnings announcements, the effect that dividend announcements may have on stock values depends on whether the dividend is higher or lower than expected. For instance, if the dividend is increased 10%, and investors were expecting a 40% increase, the stock price may fall significantly. A detailed analysis of the mechanical effect of each dividend

### *Anatomy of a Dividend Payment*

Each time a dividend payment is scheduled on a stock, a holder-of-record date and a dividend payment date must be announced by the company. The holder-of- record date is the day on which the bookkeepers figure out who is entitled to the dividend payment that occurs on the future dividend payment date.

All those shareholders who owned stock at the end of the day that is 3 business days prior to the holder-of-record date are entitled to the dividend. The date 2 business days before the holder-of-record date is called the ex-dividend date because the stock sells without claim to the scheduled dividend on that date.

As a result, stock values tend to fall by the approximate amount of a distribution on the ex-date (and tend to rise gradually as an ex-date approaches). Because stock values represent the present value of all expected future cash flows, the announcement of a dividend that is already anticipated does not affect stock values.

The only announcements that affect stock values are those that are not fully anticipated and that result in a change in estimated future dividends (or that result in a change in discount rates it, perhaps because of a change in required liquidity premiums, beta, risk premiums on stocks in general, or risk-free rates). In particular, an announced increase in dividends, if less than expected, can result in a decline in a stock price, just as an announced increase can result in a rise in the stock price if it is not anticipated.

For instance, on October 19, 1998, Baltimore Gas and Electric Company announced a $.42 quarterly dividend that would be paid on January 4, 1999 to holders of record on December 10, 1998. This dividend was the same as paid in prior quarter, and investors may have been expecting some chance of a dividend increase. Possibly as a result of such disappointment, the stock price fell 5/16 (or $0.3125) on October 19,1998 to $31.125 per share.

The ex-dividend date would be December 8, 1998 (a Tuesday) for this dividend. As a result, the stock price could be expected to fall by $0.42, or about 7/16 of a dollar, on December 8, 1998. In particular, investors who held the stock at the end of December 7, 1998 (which is the last business day before the ex-dividend date) would be entitled to the dividend payment on January 4, 1999 regardless of whether they sold the stock on December 8, 1998 or thereafter.

As a result, investors would be willing to pay $.42 less for the stock at the open of trading on December 8 than they did at the close of the day on December 7. Naturally, other news and changes in economic conditions (such as changes in interest rates, market risk premiums, and expectations) could cause the stock to rise or fall in value for other reasons before, during, and after this time interval, but stock prices do tend to fall on the ex-dividend date by approximately the amount of the dividend.

Stock splits, stock dividends (which are, like stock splits, dividends paid in the form of more of the same stock), and spinoffs (which are dividends paid in the form of subsidiary stock spun off to shareholders) have mechanics similar to that of a cash dividend. On the announcement date, a holder-of-record-date and a payment date are specified. On the ex-date (which is 2 business days prior to the announced holder-of-record date), the stock will generally sell in two forms: "cum" shares with the right to the payment of the additional shares, and "ex" shares without the right. The "ex" shares should trade at a price equal to the price of the "cum" shares less the value of the new shares to be received on the payment date (e.g., in the case of a 200% stock dividend or an equivalent 3-for-1 stock split, the price of the "ex" shares would be 2/3 lower than the "cum" shares). After the payment date of the additional shares to those investors holding "cum" shares, the "cum" shares disappear.

On the announcement date of a stock split or dividend, there is generally no effect (as breaking up the company into more pieces does not normally create value unless the price per share was previously so high as to have a transaction cost premium due to higher trading costs and less liquidity).

For instance, when there is no change in expected cash flows upon announcement of a stock split or dividend (i.e., when there is no announcement of an unanticipated increase in the effective cash dividend), studies have found no evidence of a positive effect on shareholder wealth resulting from the announcement.

On the other hand, when there is other fundamental news announced (such as rising earnings and dividends), the stock price does tend to react oust as it does when there is a spin-off that creates value if the sum of the individual parts of a company are perceived to be worth more than the whole).

## THE PRO FORMA MODEL

Future dividends can be estimated with pro forma balance sheets and income statements. These projected future financial statements may be estimated by making forecasts on variables such as future sales, profit margins, asset turnover ratios, leverage ratios, and dividend payout ratios.

Because dividends cannot generally be estimated out infinitely in the future, equity valuation models often make simplifying assumptions that, at some future period T, the company will pay out all earnings in dividends, and the dividend stream becomes constant forever thereafter.

The stock can therefore be valued by computing the present value of all dividends until the time period T arrives, and by adding this number to the present value of the value of the stock at period T. Since the constant dividend stream represents a perpetuity, the value of the stock at period T will equal the expected constant dividend at that time divided by the required return.

An example of a pro forma model is the STOCK portion of the SIA software, which values a stock as the present value of all dividends estimated over the next 75 years plus the present value of the expected stock price in 75 years.

Each dividend is estimated using pro forma financial statements that require forecasts on 13 different variables, which include sales, profit margins, dividend payout ratios, asset turnover ratios, and leverage ratios.

The expected value of the 75 future dividends and the stock price in 75 years are all adjusted for the risk of bankruptcy (that is set as a function of the *Value Line* safety rank and leverage) and discounted to a present value). A 100% dividend payout ratio is assumed between 66 and 75 years in the future, with a perpetual dividend thereafter equal to the average dividend paid between 66 and 75 years in the future, so that the stock price in 75 years can be computed as this average dividend far in the future divided by the required return.

A study by Callaghan and Murphy has found evidence that deviations of market prices from pro forma model values (using Value Line or past data to Forecast 75 years into the future) are incorporated into risk-adjusted stock returns over the subsequent 5-10+ years. However, such models were not found to be very powerful in predicting short-term stock prices. Other stock valuation models were discovered to be more effective in predicting short-run stock returns (but were insignificantly related to long-term stock returns).

## THE CONSTANT GROWTH MODEL

If dividends are expected to grow at a constant rate g and the term structure of interest rates.

This model can be used to indicate both direct and indirect relationships between equity prices and various variables. It indicates that equity value is a positive function of dividend growth rates and a negative function of the required return.

However, it indicates an unclear relationship between stock prices an inflation. For instance, during periods of inflation, nominal growth rates in earnings and dividends often increase, as sales tend to grow with inflation as do profits if there isn't a decline in the profit margin.

However, investors also often require higher returns on assets (because of higher risk-free rates) during these times to compensate for losses in purchasing power related to the inflation With an increase in both i and g, the effect on V is unclear. Past history indicates that equity prices often fall when inflation rises, indicating that the increase in i is larger than the increase in g (perhaps because inflation also causes the government to tighten monetary policy to slow down the inflation, thus resulting in interest rates rising faster than inflation, and often resulting in a recession that impedes dividend and earnings growth).

While there are also periods when stock prices rise with increasing inflation (that happen when the effect of inflationary profit growth more than offsets the effect of any increase in interest rates), the overall empirical evidence indicates that stock returns are not positively correlated with inflation over short-term one-month or one-year horizons.

Nevertheless, there is some evidence that stock values do rise with inflation over long periods of time after the short-term effects of interest rate increases are factored out. In particular, once interest rates have risen to a higher level, stock prices can grow with a stable inflation rate.

In addition, if inflation declines to a lower level, interest rates can fall, thereby causing the present value of dividends to rise, so that stock values will reflect the higher value of the earnings that have been increased to an inflated level by past inflation.

While the constant growth model can provide insights on some of the important determinants of stock values, a major problem with direct application of value individual stocks is that the computed stock values are very sensitive to small changes in the estimate of g and sometimes lead to ridiculous valuations. For example, for high values of g relative to i, indicates a negative value for the stock, which is not only counterintuitive but also impossible given the fact that the prices of limited-liability assets like stocks cannot fall below zero. In addition, the formula indicates that a stock which pays no dividend currently is worthless.

Because of these facts and because it is very difficult to estimate g precisely for most companies (except for very stable companies), the constant-growth model is generally not practically applicable (except sometimes as a very rough valuation of very stable companies or the stock market as a whole). However, the constant growth model can be used to derive theoretical relationships between value and important fundamental variables like earnings.

## THE P/E RATIO MODEL

Price/earnings (P/e) ratios measure the price paid per dollar of earnings. These ratios can be computed as the market price per share of stock divided by the company's earnings per share, as well as by the ratio of the aggregate market value of all the shares outstanding to aggregate net income. P/e ratios are often used in both theory and practice to analyse equities.

*General Theory:* Using substitution, can be converted into a model that sets value as a function of the company's earnings e. In particular, the numerator actually equals the dividend expected in the next period, i.e., $d_0(1+g)=d_1$, since g represents the periodic expected growth rate in earnings and dividends. The expected dividend $d_1$, in turn, equals the earnings expected in the next period multiplied by the dividend payout ratio, where the dividend payout ratio is the percentage of earnings paid out in dividends that can be written as d/e.

Thus, the numerator i can be written as $d_1=e_1(d/e)$. This rewriting of equation indicates the amount an investor would be willing to pay for a dollar of the company's earnings in next period. This model of V/e ratios (which equal P/e ratios if V=P, or if the market's valuation or pricing is being analysed) shows that investors are willing to pay more for a dollar of earnings if the earnings and dividends of the company are expected to grow rapidly, and if the discount rate used to compute the present value of the cash flows from the stock is low. The model for V/e ratios can be developed further as a function of operating ratios with an additional assumption. In particular, if a constant return on equity (defined as ROE=earnings/equity) may be forecast for a company, and if future new equity invested into the company may be estimated by a constant earnings retention ratio (1 - d/e), then it is possible to forecast the growth rate in earnings and dividends

***ROE and Dividend Growth Rates***

$$e_1 = (\text{Equity}_{0})r,$$

and

$$e_2 = (\text{Equity}_{1})r,$$

where,

- $\text{Equity}_1 = \text{Equity}_0 + [e_1 (1\text{-}d/e)],$
- which implies from (E-1),
- $\text{Equity}_1 = \text{Equity}_0 + [(\text{Equity}_{0})r\ (1\text{-}d/e)]$
- $= \text{Equity}_0 [1+ \{r(1 - d/e)\}].$
- Inserting (E-4) into (E-2), we have
- $e_2 = \text{Equity}_0 [1 + - d/e)\}]r.$
- Dividing $e_2$ in (E-5) by $e_1$ in (E-1), we get
- $e_2/e_1 = 1 + [r(1 - d/e)]$, thus implying that earnings grow at a rate equal to $g = r(1 - d/e)$.

If d/e remains constant, dividends will also grow at a rate of g per year.

An numeric example of the proof can be provide using the October 24,2007.

Motorola stock, whose $\text{Equity}_0 = \$22.22$, $e_1 = \$2.20$, and $d_1 = \$0.48$ (from the most recent Value Line):

From this data, it can be deduced that,

$$r = \$2.20/\$22.22 = 9.9\%, \text{ and}$$

$$d/e = \$0.48/\$2.20 = 21.8\%.$$

we know that,

$$g = 9.9\% (1 - .218) = 7.7\%,$$

so that earnings are expected to grow to

$$e_2 = e_1 (1 + g) = \$2.20 (1 + .077) = \$2.37$$

in the next year. This same result occurs when the data are input into equation,

$e_2$ = \$22.22[1 =.099x(1 -.218)] x.099 = \$2.37, -

and, assuming price equals value, its P/e ratio would be 8

*The V/e Ratio as a Capitalization Rate*

The foregoing formula for V/e ratios can be used for a variety of purposes. One of the most important uses is to determine the value of a stock's earnings. Determining the value of a stock from its earnings is often called capitalizing its earnings, since the value of a stock essentially represents the present value of the shareholder's claim on the company's earnings (whether the earnings are reinvested or paid out in dividends).

The earnings of a company can be capitalized by multiplying them by an appropriate V/e ratio. The inverse of the appropriate V/e ratio is often called the capitalization rate (e.g., a P/e of 20 represents a capitalization rate of 1/20=5%). Since an equityholder has a claim not only to the current dividend yield but also to reinvested earnings, the capitalization rate measures the current earnings yield on a security.

Equities with similar risk and reinvestment potential should have similar capitalization rates. As a result, assuming P=V (and therefore V/e=P/e), it is possible to use the P/e ratio of stocks with similar risk and reinvestment prospects to capitalize the earnings of equities for which the value is not known. For example, assume a new company with an expected future ROE of 17%, a beta of 1.0, and net income of \$30 million is not traded and has no market price. If other stocks with expected future ROEs of 17% and betas of 1.0 have P/e's of 15 on average, it is possible to estimate the value of the new firm by multiplying its earnings by a P/e of 15 to get a value of \$30,000,000×15=\$450,000,000.

The capitalization rate can also be used for other purposes, such as to determine whether the returns on one class of securities will dominate the returns on another. For instance, if one stock has expected future ROEs of 15%, a beta of 1.1, and a P/e ratio of 9, it is a superior investment to a stock with an expected future ROE of 10%, a beta of 1.5, and a P/e ratio of 11.

Even more broadly, the capitalization rate can be used to make rough comparisons of equity investments with other securities. For instance, it can be shown algebraically that an equity (or group of equities) will earn a return higher than some specified interest rate (such as i or Rf,) only if either the ROE or the capitalization rate exceed that rate. If the ROE and the capitalization rate are both greater than the specified interest rate, the equity (or equities) will definitely be expected to earn a higher return than that specified interest rate. These relationships can be used to evaluate whether equities are likely to earn higher returns than other assets like risk-free Treasury securities.

*P/e Ratio Adjustments for Earnings Quality:* When applying P/e ratio analysis in practice, it is necessary to consider the fact that the earnings portion of the P/e ratio (as well as of the ROE ratio) includes an accounting entry, reported earnings, that may not reflect the true economic or financial earning power of the company.

For instance, accounting earnings can be manipulated by changing accounting procedures for the same cash flow, such as by changing the depreciation method to straight-line from accelerated or by depreciating fixed assets over a longer life as opposed to a shorter life.

Investors are typically willing to pay a higher P/e for companies with more conservative accounting policies, such as ones whose fixed assets are depreciated over a short useful life with accelerated depreciation methods (which result in higher reported depreciation expenses and lower earnings for the same cash flows), and ones that utilize LIFO inventory accounting when prices are rising (which results in higher reported cost of goods sold and lower earnings during such times—when prices are falling, FIFO is more conservative, whereas Average Cost inventory methods are between FIFO and LIFO in all cases).

In addition, investors also tend to be willing to pay more for companies' earnings that are distorted by one-time negative events such as a nonrecurring loss (like from a one-time write-down of fixed asset book values) and pay less for companies' earnings that are distorted by one-time positive events such as a nonrecurring capital gain (like from a one-time gain from the sale of a subsidiary). Any such events that distort reported earnings in comparison to future projected earnings can result in investors valuing the reported earnings differently.

Similarly, investors tend to be willing to pay less for a company's basic earnings per share if the company has issued options on the company's stock (through convertibles, warrants, and employee stock options) that could result in a significant increase in the number of shares outstanding if exercised and thereby dilute earnings per share growth (employee stock options granted by the largest U.S. companies in 1997 alone represented claims on a number of shares equal to about 1.5 of all those outstanding). Note that the *fully diluted earnings per share* reported on financial statements do not fully incorporate the effects of such dilution, as the reported *fully diluted earnings per share* do not take into consideration the effect of dilution resulting from the exercise of options that are currently out of the money but may become in the money in the future if the stock price rises.

P/e ratios, therefore, tend to be a positive function of the quality of earnings, where earnings quality is considered to be higher when more conservative accounting procedures are used, when there are no irregular items that are increasing reported earnings, and when less future dilution is possible. Often, investors attempt to conduct P/e ratio analysis using a normalized earnings figure that adjusts for differences in accounting procedures and irregular items.

For example, an attempt may be made to estimate earnings if companies used the same accounting methods. In addition, analysts often take any nonrecurring items out of reported earnings. However, at least a portion of irregular write-offs or gains may be kept in the normalized net income figure if such items tend to recur periodically. One simple method for determining exactly how much of a nonrecurring item to retain would be to compute the average of such figures over the last 5 or 10 years. For companies with a limited history, a shorter average number of years could be used, and/

or a value of zero for nonrecurring items could be assumed for years when they were not in existence.

For purposes of comparing companies in the same industry, it is possible to make additional adjustments for earnings quality (examples of general intra industry adjustments. For comparisons in some industries, special adjustments must be made (an example for the financial institution industry is provided. In addition, adjustments for different levels of leverage and different amounts of reinvested capital are also sometimes made (an analysis of these factors is provided If earnings are adjusted for difference in earnings quality, it is not necessary to adjust the resulting adjusted P/e ratio.

*P/e Adjustments for Companies in the Same Industry*

- For purposes of comparing companies in the same industry, it is often useful to adjust for depreciation differences by adding depreciation back to earnings. Depreciation plus net income is often labeled cash flow because depreciation is a noncash expense. The ratio price/cash flow can then be used like P/e ratios for purposes of comparison.
- In addition, many analysts add a portion of research and development (R&D) expenses back to earnings or cash flow when analyzing P/e or P/cash flow ratios of companies in the same industry. The reason is that R&D expenses often represent long-term investments that normally do not pay off until far in the future, and so investors may be willing to pay the same amount for a pretax dollar of expensed R&D as for a pretax dollar of earnings. However, because R&D is a tax- deductible item, it is necessary to multiply R&D by (1 - Tax Rate) before adding it back to income in order to compute what earnings would have been if R&D had not been expensed.
- Although such adjustments for R&D and depreciation can be useful, it is important to realise that long-term depreciation and R&D expense requirements differ across industries. As a result, any

adjustment that adds back into income a recurring expense like depreciation and R&D should only be made when comparing companies in the same industry.

*Special P/e Adjustments for Financial Institutions*

- For financial institutions such as banks and savings and loan organizations, a special set of items may be considered to be nonrecurring. The major categories are capital gains from loan and security sales and loan write-offs. To compute normalized earnings, some analysts may leave only the average of capital gains from security and other asset sales over the last 10 years in adjusted net income (i.e., the difference between the year's reported capital gains and the average over the last 10 years would be taken out of reported net income). Also, some average of loan loss and other asset write-offs over the last 10 years should probably be kept in adjusted net income.
- In addition, it is possible to adjust the average write-off figure for inadequate loan loss reserves. In particular, a normal loan loss reserve equal to 0.50% of financial institution loans and a normal ratio of 1% for nonperforming assets to loans can be assumed. Subtracting 0.5% of loans from loan loss reserves and 1% from nonperforming assets therefore computes the extraordinary amount for each.

  Assuming a 50% loss per dollar of extraordinary nonperforming assets (more would be assumed for the case of nonperforming unsecured loans), one can then subtract 50% of extraordinary nonperforming assets from the extraordinary loan loss reserve to determine whether the loan loss reserve is sufficient to cover future losses from the extraordinary nonperforming assets. Any amount by which the losses from the extraordinary nonperforming assets exceed the extraordinary loan loss reserves could then be added to the loan write-offs for the current year (which then would then be included as an input in computing the average loan write-off over the last 10 years).

- Moreover, for financial institutions with mortgage or other callable debt, a portion of interest income represents a premium for call risk. Over time such extra income will be offset by lost interest relating to early repayments. As a result, between 0.25% and 0.5% of the book value of callable debt assets should be considered extraordinary and should therefore be subtracted out of net income to compute adjusted income.
- Finally, income related to financial institutions playing the yield curve should be taken out of net to compute adjusted income. Playing the yield curve refers to having long-term assets financed with short-term liabilities and, as a result, gambling on winning high profits when the yield curve is upward sloping (i.e., when the interest rate on long-term bonds is higher than that on short-term bonds). Since the various theories of interest rates indicate that one can only expect a small profit (if any) from playing the yield curve over the long term, the short-term profits (or losses) that financial institutions gain from playing the yield curve should be taken out of income to compute adjusted net.

  The profits (or losses) from playing the yield curve can be estimated by taking the difference between long-term fixed-rate assets and long-term fixed-rate liabilities for the financial institution (as often computed in an interest-rate sensitivity part of the annual report or financial statements) and multiplying that difference by the average difference between long-term and short-term interest rates over the annual report interval.
- These equations indicate that, for a given ROA, more debt can increase the ROE. In actual fact, the ROA is influenced by the amount of debt taken on (insofar as more debt results in more interest payments and

lower net profit/assets), and higher debt levels may not increase the ROE if the interest rate on new debt exceeds the pretax operating rate of return on assets.

- Increasing ROEs by increasing leverage might be advantageous to stockholders were it not for two potentially offsetting factors. the higher financial leverage increases the stock beta, and so there is some offset to higher ROE-induced growth rates in future earnings and dividends in the form of a higher discount rate on the higher future cash flows, In addition to the effect of a higher beta and discountrate, higher financial leverage can increase the chance of bankruptcy and thereby reduce the expected value of the future reinvestment opportunities of the firm.

  A 1998 empirical study by Walker has indicated that, despite some transitory stockholder gains, there has been little evidence of long-term benefits from leveraged recapitalizations on average. Even in cases where increasing leverage can increase shareholder value long-term, the earnings of companies that have less leverage remain more valuable because they have greater potential to realise such gains from leverage than companies that have already leveraged themselves (one exception to this rule are companies whose stock is heavily controlled by an investor or investors whose concentrated positions in the company result in insufficient diversification and a severe aversion to unsystematic risk that might prohibit even value-enhancing leverage increases). As a result, earnings are generally considered of a higher quality and valued more highly at less leveraged companies (resulting in such companies generally having higher P/e ratios).
- Although the effect of higher leverage on beta and discount rates can be evaluated within the context of a simple quantitative comparison of P/e, beta, and ROE, the effect of higher leverage on the probability

of bankruptcy complicates the analysis. companies with high ROEs have high values based on high future reinvestment rates and futurecash flow growth. To leverage those ROEs with more debt increases the chance of bankruptcy (which would put an end to all operations and reinvestment at any extraordinary ROE) and thereby endangers the vary value created by the high ROES. As a result, many companies with high ROEs and future reinvestment prospects (such as pharmaceutical companies and other high technology firms) tend to have very low levels of debt (in order to maximize the probability of being around to earn those high ROES). Although this bankruptcy effect can be (and is often) incorporated into the expected values of the future cash flow projections for pro forma models, P/e ratio analysis requires the analyst to pay a slightly lower multiple of earnings for a company with more debt, all else (beta and ROE) being equal. Thus, investors are willing to pay more for companies with higher ROES, but they pay more for stocks that generate those high ROEs via greater operating profitability than for stocks that generate high ROEs via greater financial leverage.

- In addition, it should also be the per cent of earnings reinvested at the ROE (as denoted by 1-{d/e}) affects the P/e ratio insofar as reinvesting a large amount of funds at a high ROE is worth more to shareholders than reinvesting a small amount of funds at the same ROE. As a result, companies with high ROEs tend to have higher P/e ratios if they reinvest more funds at that high ROE than if they reinvest less funds at that high ROE.
- It is therefore necessary to consider r, 1-{d/e}, accounting earnings quality, B, and debt when conducting P/e ratio analysis. Higher P/e ratios are justified for companies with higher ROES, higher earnings retention rates (if ROE> i), more

conservatively reported earnings, lower betas, and lower financial leverage.

*Applied P/e Formulas:* For direct applied use, many analysts derive various other formulas for P/e ratios using different assumptions on future dividend growth rates or ROEs. Often, these formulas will be based on dividend growth rates that are assumed to vary over more than one time interval. For instance, a 2-stage dividend growth model assumes that dividends will grow at a constant rate for a number of years, often at a very rapid rate, after which the dividend growth is assumed to stabilize to a more normal constant rate. A 3-stage dividend growth model is also sometimes used that assumes the dividend growth rate moves more gradually from its introductory rapid phase to a normal phase over a time period of up to 50 years.

## P/E RATIO ANALYSIS WITH THE DISCOUNTED CASH FLOW MODEL

Often, forecasts and analysis of a company will produce variable earnings, ROEs, and dividends for a few years (like 5), after which the company will be in a stable growth mode. Once the stable growth mode is reached, it is possible to estimate the V/e ratio for the stock in this time period, and then discount this price and all dividends received until then to compute the present value of the stock.

*The Rel*ationship Between Stock Valuation and Capital Budgeting

- The various models for stock valuation are mathematically and intuitively linked with the formulas and procedures used tomake capital budgeting decisions (such as discounting cash flows). An explanation of the relationship between stock valuation and capital budgeting model.

*Capital Budgeting, Cost of Equity, IRR, and NPV*

- The equations can be useful for understanding the interrelationship between stock valuation and capital budgeting decisions made by the company. For instance, the discount rate used in capital budgeting models is typically computed as the cost of capital, which in turn is a function of the cost of equity capital. In addition, the value of a stock can be computed as the present value of all capital budgeting opportunities. Estimating the Required Return on Equity Estimates of g for individual firms are generally too unreliable for the formula to be applicable, just such growth estimates are too unreliable for meaningful direct application. However, it may be possible to use the average earnings growth estimate of investment analysts for a large group of stocks in order to estimate the required return on the stock market. Several sources exist for such data, such as the Institutional Broker's Estimate System (IBES), which is available on the Internet for a fee (alternatively, one could use *Value Line* estimated earnings growth). Inserting such an estimate for E(Rm) into equation (4-2) can result in the company using a discount rate to estimate the present value of capital budgeting projects that is similar to that used by investment analysts who are computing the present value of the dividends from the company's stock.

- For instance, the Value Line Industrial Composite page forecasts earnings of 3.35 for the index in 2001 compared to earnings of 2.08 in 1997, implying an annual growth of
- It is important to point out, however, that maximization of ROE does not necessarily maximize stock price. The reason is that the value of the abnormal growth opportunities is a function not only of the ROE but also the amount of money reinvested at that ROE. For example, some companies in industries with low or negative growth (such as tobacco) earn fairly high ROEs because of limited competition and heavy brand-name recognition, but the P/e ratios for such companies are often not correspondingly high because there are few

opportunities to reinvest new funds in industries with low or negative growth.

- Another way to look at this phenomenon is to relate Vabnormal growth to NPV and ROE to IRR. A company can invest a small amount of funds at a high IRR and report a very large ROE, but the NPV of the project may be very low because only a small amount is invested. As a result, the Vabnormal growth is very low. For example, the value of a penny invested at a rate of return of 90% for one period is less than a penny, but millions of dollars invested at a rate of 30% typically has a value measured in the millions.
- It is important to point out, however, that maximization of ROE does not necessarily maximize stock price. The reason is that the value of the abnormal growth opportunities is a function not only of the ROE but also the amount of money reinvested at that ROE. For example, some companies in industries with low or negative growth (such as tobacco) earn fairly high ROEs because of limited competition and heavy brand-name recognition, but the P/e ratios for such companies are often not correspondingly high because there are few opportunities to reinvest new funds in industries with low or negative growth.
- It should also be that reported ROEs, or even forecasted future ROEs, only performance as proxies for a company's true IRR and earnings reinvestment rate. Sometimes there are existing operations that appear to earn an extremely high return on existing capital, but the projected return on new projects or investments may be very low, in which case the ROE may not be a very meaningful indicator of the reinvestment rate. A good example might be a company that has had some major writeoffs which have reduced stockholders' equity very close to zero and the stockholders' equity of companies that have repurchased a large amount of stock at prices that

far exceed the book value per share may have their stockholders' equity greatly reduced to a very low level as a result (since the market value of all repurchased shares are subtracted from the balance sheet stockholders' equity account) and may therefore report meaninglessly high (or even negative) ROE figures. In such cases, it may be more useful to back into an ROE estimate based on past (or future projected) earnings growth g using the equation ROE=g/(1-{d/e}).
Or alternatively, in cases of companies that do not seem to have potential to invest at rates that exceed required returns (such as for companies that are not in growth industries), it may be appropriate to assume that ROE=i. In other cases where the computed ROE is clearly a poor indication of the true reinvestment rate of the company, it may be necessary to construct some subjective estimate, perhaps obtained using a pro forma forecasting model stockholders' equity account) and may therefore report meaninglessly high (or even negative) ROE figures. In such cases, it may be more useful to back into an ROE estimate based on past (or future projected) earnings growth g using the equation ROE=g/(1-{d/e}). Or alternatively, in cases of companies that do not seem to have potential to invest at rates that exceed required returns (such as for companies that are not in growth industries), it may be appropriate to assume that ROE=i. In other cases where the computed ROE is clearly a poor indication of the true reinvestment rate of the company, it may be necessary to construct some subjective estimate, perhaps obtained using a pro forma forecasting model.

## FUNDAMENTAL ANALYSIS OF EQUITY INVESTMENTS

First, information sources that are useful in fundamentally

analyzing stocks are described. Next, a top-down forecasting method is evaluated for purposes of estimating the relevant financial variables for stock valuation.

These forecasts are needed to predict the future dividends, whose summed present value equals the stock value. Within this valuation context, the usefulness of scenario forecasting is analysed. Relative P/e ratio analysis within this analytical framework is also discussed. Finally, an actual example of stock valuation is provided.

## INTEGRATING ECONOMIC, INDUSTRY, AND COMPANY FORECASTS

An overall economic forecast is generally necessary before evaluating a stock.

The economic forecast should include predictions of real economic growth as well as inflation in order to provide perspective on the environment within which industries and companies will likely operate. Such forecasts may be obtained from various forecasting services. For instance, *Value Line* provides forecasts of real GDP growth and inflation up to 5 years in the future inside the flap of its weekly company analysis booklet.

In addition, some qualitative economic information should be obtained in order that the analyst may make forecasts for individual industries. The important qualitative information includes analysis of consumer spending, capital spending, exchange rates, government legislation, and other factors that may affect specific industries. Many business periodicals (such as *Fortune, Business Week,* and *Forbes Global Business and Finance*) provide weekly, monthly, or quarterly updates on the economic environment that includes information on various sectors of the economy. For instance, the "Selection & Opinion" part of *Value Line* provides a quarterly report that analyses the economy and qualitatively explains the reasons for its overall economic forecasts.

Information on the economic environment may be used to forecast specific industry factors such as unit sales growth, inflation, and changes in profitability. Some business periodicals regularly provide such information. *Value Line* provides a quarterly analysis of about 100 different industries. *Value Line*'s industry reports include not only a qualitative analysis of each industry but also forecasts of sales, profit margins, and other factors up to 5 years in the future. Forecasts farther in the future are much more difficult to make, although long-term past data—which indicate that real growth in the U.S. has averaged about 3% per year long-term while inflation has averaged about 3% over the last few decades—can be adjusted for the particular situation of each industry (such as by forecasting long-term real unit sales increases in a high-growth industry like electronics above the 3% past average for the economy).

Within the context of economic and industry predictions, it is possible to make predictions for the company whose stock is being investigated. In order to be able to forecast and value future dividends, company market share of industry sales, operating margins, capital structure, taxes, and asset turnover ratios must be predicted. To assist in the analysis, many investment advisory services provide analyses of individual companies and stocks.

Often when making forecasts, analysts categorize companies into groups. Companies whose sales and assets are growing rapidly are often called growth companies, while firms that have been around for a long period of time and whose sales are not growing rapidly are called mature companies. Businesses whose sales fluctuate greatly up and down with the business cycle are referred to as cyclical companies. Firms whose sales are less adversely affected by recessions within a business cycle are called stable companies. The equities of stable companies are often called defensive stocks in recognition of their ability to defend a portfolio against large losses in a recession.

Once the relevant financial variables have been forecast, a pro forma model may be used to value the stock. A general description of such models is provided..

For purposes of individual stock valuation, the "top-down" approach to forecasting for individual companies explained in this part has inherent advantages over alternative methods of analysis, especially for institutional investors operating with many investment analysts. In particular, although a "bottom-up" forecasting method is often used by economists to aggregate the forecasts of individual industries to predict aggregate inflation and economic growth, starting with an aggregate economic forecast (perhaps obtained from a "bottom-up" economic forecast) permits industry and company analysis to be conducted within a unified context. In particular, by assuming the same overall economic and industry environment for each stock in an industry, valuation biases are avoided that are sometimes caused by the application of inconsistent forecasts for the aggregate economy across different stocks.

For instance, if an institutional analyst values one stock based on a forecast of high aggregate economic growth, while another stock is analysed by another analyst at the same institution based on a forecast of low aggregate economic growth, sales and profit margin forecasts will be biased upward for the former stock compared to the latter stock, as will the stock valuation.

## USING DIFFERENT FORECAST INPUTS IN VALUATION MODELS

Guidelines on forecasting individual variables can be obtained from good documentation on good stock valuation software such as SIA. However, because many of the inputs into a valuation model are forecasted variables whose values must be predicted, the analysis is somewhat subjective and imprecise.

As a result, it is often useful to make several feasible scenario forecasts and obtain a value for each scenario. Scenarios can vary because of different operating

and competitive conditions for the firm as well as due to different assumed financial and operating policies. A simple framework for analysis here might be to value the firm using 3 scenarios: most likely, most optimistic, and most pessimistic (with each scenario having an equal chance of occurrence).

The scenario valuation process creates a range of possible values for the security. If the security's price is less than all prices in the feasible range, it should be purchased. If the security's price exceeds all prices in the feasible range, it is overpriced. If the security's price is within the feasible range, it is probably fairly priced. To estimate a single value for a security, the average of all values within the feasible range could be used (the average could be weighted by the probability of each forecasted scenario occurring if different probabilities of occurrence were estimated for each scenario).

In addition to a cash flow valuation of the firm, it is sometimes useful to evaluate the company's value if its assets were sold off in an orderly fashion. Here, the value of the company's assets would be estimated, assuming there was strong demand for such assets from other firms (such as other firms in the same industry). The maximum value that other firms would be willing to pay for such assets would be the current market value of such individual assets, which can be estimated by their replacement cost (which in turn can be estimated by multiplying the historical book value by some factor to allow for inflation in the price of those assets). After subtracting out the value of the liabilities, the net value to the shareholders would be the replacement cost book value. If this value exceeds the cash flow value of the firm, it might be deduced that the firm is mismanaging its assets, and that it should begin an orderly sale of such assets. Such a scenario should be considered when the present value of expected future cash flows is less than the replacement book value.

## P/E RATIO ANALYSIS

Many analysts value stocks relative to other stocks, in lieu of, or in addition to valuing stocks in absolute terms using a dividend discount model. In particular, many analysts compare the P/e ratios of stocks (often in the same industry) and determine which should have higher and lower P/e ratios, given the beta, ROE, and other factors that determine P/e ratios. These analysts attempt to determine whether any particular stock is under- or overpriced by observing whether it has a higher or lower P/e than other stocks that theoretically should have a lower or higher P/e.

For instance, if stock XXX has a forecasted ROE of 15% and a beta of 1, while stock YYY has a forecasted ROE of 14% and a beta of 1.1, then XXX should theoretically have a higher P/e. If YYY has a higher P/e, analysts would recommend buying XXX. Stocks can also valued in an absolute sense using P/e ratio analysis.

Although P/e ratio analysis is usually considered to be a rougher method of than discounting dividends with a pro forma model, it can be useful in providing additional insights on a stock's value. For instance, P/e ratio analysis can be used to second-guess (or double-think) a pro forma valuation analysis.

If P/e ratio analysis provides results that are inconsistent with pro forma valuations, it may be useful to reanalyze the forecasts in the pro forma model (or to double check the assumptions in the P/e ratio analysis model).

Analysts sometimes also examine ratios such as Price/ Sales Per Share, which may be evaluated like a P/e ratio within the context of an assumed "normal" profit margin in the future, and Price/Equity Book Value Per Share, which may be evaluated like a P/e ratio within the context of an assumed "normal" ROE in the future.

These ratios are especially important to consider for any firm whose reported profits are not believed to be representative of its true long-term earning power (like for firms with distorted or negative reported net). In all cases, investors prefer to pay lower prices per dollar of sales, book value, or earnings per share (all else being equal). A 1996 study by Haugen and Baker indicated that returns were indeed higher on stocks that had higher e/P, sales/price, and equity book/market ratios. Stocks which have such ratios that are relatively high are often referred to as value stocks to reflect the strong current fundamentals, whereas stocks with such ratios that are relatively low are often called growth stocks to reflect the potential growth in fundamental value for which the market appears to be paying.

## DUPONT ANALYSIS

Because of the importance of ROEs in determining stock values, this ratio is often decomposed into its component parts for further analysis. For instance, to assist in the evaluation and forecast of ROE, the ROE for a company can be computed as,

ROE = ROA/(1- Liabilities/Assets), where

ROA = Return on Assets = Net Income/Assets.

The ROA itself may be decomposed into its component parts of,

ROA = Asset Turnover × Profit Margin, where

Asset Turnover = Sales/Assets, and

Net Profit Margin = Net Income/Sales.

The decomposition of ROE into its component parts is often called Dupont analysis. This form of analysis may be used to pick up trends in the individual components of ROE that can assist in determining the cause of changes in ROE (and thereby assist in forecasting future ROEs).

For instance, assume that a rise in ROE is found to be the result of an increase in the net profit margin. It might be worth investigating whether the cause of the increased profit margin is the company overpricing its products relative to its competitors (which might eventually result in a decline in profitability), or whether the increased profit margin stems from reducing expenditures on quality control and R&D (which would probably force the company to eventually cut prices and profit margins). On the other hand, if the increase in the profit margin stems from improved efficiency, increased capacity utilization, or the development of new products, the increased margin might be sustainable (or could possibly even be increased further).

Alternatively, increases in ROE sometimes result from a rise in a company's Liability/Assets ratio. The Liabilities/Assets ratio can rise because the company took on more debt (perhaps issuing bonds to buy back stock). the benefits of a rise in ROE caused by an increase in financial leverage may be offset by the negative effects of an increase in required returns and an increase in the probability of bankruptcy. On the other hand, an increase in the Liabilities/Assets ratio may be caused by past write-offs that reduced equity while raising liabilities or decreasing asset values. An artificial rise in ROE caused by write-offs in prior years does not imply that the company can reinvest earnings at a higher rate and therefore cannot be expected to continue.

## THE EFFECT OF FOREIGN OPERATIONS ON RATIOS

Because of changes in currency exchange rates, the value of foreign revenue and costs translated into dollars fluctuates as the dollar rises and falls. For instance, a rise in the value of the dollar decreases the value of foreign sales, while a fall in the value of the dollar makes sales denominated in foreign currencies worth more in terms of dollars. Foreign exchange rate changes therefore clearly affect some of the important ratios that make up the ROE.

### *The Effect of Real Exchange Rate Changes on Turnover Ratios*

Changes in exchange rates affect turnover ratios for firms with foreign sales, through the effect on the numerator. Although the effect of expected domestic inflation can be incorporated into the nominal sales growth forecasts, the effect of foreign sales growth must be measured separately in the estimate of the change in the asset turnover ratios. In particular, nominal foreign sales measured in the domestic currency will grow at a rate that is different than for domestic sales to the extent that foreign inflation rates are different and to the extent that foreign currency exchange rates change. The exchange rates between two currencies can be expected to change by the difference in risk-free interest rates in the two countries (with the currency paying the higher interest being expected to depreciate). As a result, foreign sales translated into the domestic currency may be expected to grow at a rate above the domestic inflation rate by the amount of,

$$U = Rf - RF + MForeign - MUS, \quad (8\text{-}5)$$

where M is the expected future inflation rate in the subscripted country, and RF is the foreign risk-free interest rate in country F. The U calculation represents the difference in real interest rates in the two countries, which in turn forecasts the change in real exchange rates between the two currencies (i.e., the change in exchange rates not offset by differences in inflation rates in the two countries).

For example, 10-year interest rates in Japan were about 0.87%, while 10-year interest rates in the U.S. were 4.52% (with annual compounding). Given the lack of inflation in Japan currently, inflation in Japan might be expected to average 0% over the next 10 years, while the difference between the yields on fixed-rate U.S. Treasury bonds and inflation-indexed U.S. Treasury bonds indicates expected inflation in the U.S. to be 0.88% (with annual compounding).

In this case,

$$U = 4.52\% - 0.87\% + 0\% - 0.88\% = 2.77\% \quad (8\text{-}6)$$

and so nominal sales from a firm's Japanese operations translated into dollars might be expected to grow 2.77% more rapidly than the firm's U.S. sales (assuming the real growth in both the Japanese and U.S. economies were the same).

Thus, asset turnover ratios would rise to the extent of a company's sales exposure to Japan. For instance, if all of a company's sales were in Japan, the ratios would rise by 2.77% per year. However, if only 6% of a company's sales were in Japan, as was the case for Motorola, the turnover ratios would rise by only $2.77\% \times .06 = 0.17\%$ (e.g., a 0.17% rise in an asset turnover ratio of 1.09 would lead to an asset turnover ratio of $1.0017 \times 1.09 = 1.0919$).

To some extent, however, the existence of foreign capital (such as debt or preferred stock that makes payments in a foreign currency) can offset the effect of foreign exchange rate changes on sales. In particular, assets financed by foreign capital can negate some of the effect of the foreign exchange rate change on asset turnover ratios (because any turnover changes would be offset by an implicit changed cost for those assets financed by such capital). Therefore, an equation that more completely measures the total effect of foreign exchange rate changes is,

*Turnover Ratio Change = U[(foreign sales/total sales)-(foreign capital/capital)].*

These changes can be added across countries or areas to estimate the total turnover ratio change.

For example, U=0.21% for Motorola's European operations (based on 10-year bond yield differentials with no difference in forecasted inflation), European sales/total sales=19%, and European debt/capital=0%, so that there is a

Turnover Ratio Change = 0.21%(.19 -.00) = 0.04% related to the company's European operations. Adding Motorola's turnover ratio change for Japan (since Motorola had no Japanese yen capital, there would also be no foreign capital adjustment to the 0.17%. U estimated for its Japanese operations) indicates a total turnover change of 0.17% + 0.04% = 0.21%.

### *The Effect of Real Exchange Rate Changes on Profit Margins*

In addition to the effect on turnover ratios, real exchange rate changes as measured by U.also influence the ability of companies to compete and therefore affect their profit margins. For instance, if the real exchange rate of the U.S. dollar rises, the ability of U.S. exporters to compete against foreign firms

is impaired. In particular, a real rise in the value of the U.S. dollar means that dollar costs are rising more rapidly than the foreign currency costs of foreign companies translated into dollars. As a result, the profit margins of U.S. exporters tend to go down at such times (whereas export profit margins would tend to rise when the dollar fell in real terms). Similarly, U.S. companies that compete against foreign imports would be hurt by a real rise in the U.S. dollar as the foreign imports would become more competitive. The effect of exchange rate changes on profit margins is usually much stronger short-term than the effect on asset turnover ratios. However, for companies like Motorola that largely produce in the regions where they sell their products and that hedge much of their remaining currency risk with derivatives like currency options and forward/futures contracts, the effect of currency changes on profit margins are minimized.

# 7

# Fundamental Analysis of Real Asset Investments

The valuation of real assets is analysed. Both income-producing assets (which can be analysed using methods similar to those employed for equities) and non-income-producing assets (such as commodities) are evaluated.

## ANALYSIS OF INCOME-PRODUCING REAL ASSETS

Some equity investments in real assets, such as real estate, can produce income or cash flows. Examples of income-producing real assets are commercial real estate (which consists of office buildings, warehouses, retail outlets such as shopping centers, and guest quarters such as hotels and motels), industrial real estate (which includes industrial parks), residential real estate (which includes manufactured home and apartment complexes), and agricultural real estate (which consists of farms). Income is derived from these properties by renting or leasing them out to users. As with other income-producing assets, real estate may be analysed using the general cash flow model introduced in the *"General Discounted Cash-Flow Model"*

### *Valuing Real Estate*

Income from equity investments in real estate typically consists of rental or lease income less operating, financing, depreciation, and tax expenses. These revenue and expense streams are similar to those for equity investments in general business assets, and the equity valuation models.

*Capitalizing Real Estate Cash Flow:* Real estate is often valued using an income capitalization method that is similar to P/e ratio analysis. The process consists of estimating current income from the real estate and then dividing through by an appropriate capitalization rate.

Usually, however, real estate values are appraised by capitalizing income before depreciation, interest, and tax expenses (rather than net income after taxes). This income is often called net operating income or cash flow. Net operating income is often capitalized for real estate investments because depreciation is a noncash expense, often arbitrarily determined by using different accounting policies, and may not match the true replacement and repair costs of the fixed asset. In addition, interest expenses can vary widely depending on how much of a property is financed with debt. As a result of different depreciation and interest expenses, there can also be large differences in tax expenses. For instance, assume that a particular property is expected to generate net operating income of $10,000,000 per year. Assume that properties with similar risk and growth prospects have capitalization rates of 8% (e.g., assume that another property with similar risk and growth prospects had annual net operating income of $8,000,000 and a price of $100,000,000). The value of the property would b

Thus, this process of real estate valuation is similar to multiplying the adjusted earnings of a stock by an appropriate P/e ratio that is obtained from stocks with similar growth prospects and risk (with adjusted earnings for real estate being measured before depreciation, interest, and tax expenses).

Both operating income and cash flow growth prospects for real estate investments can be estimated using similar criteria as for stocks. However, for real estate investments, the primary focus is on rental increases net of cash operating expenses. As a result, real estate cash flow growth is often estimated by inflationary expectations that would permit rental increases. Higher inflationary expectations and growth prospects would result in lower capitalization rates, all else being equal, just as higher expected ROEs and dividend growth rates for stocks result in higher P/e ratios.

However, net cash flow growth prospects can be dampened by more than offsetting expectations of cash expense increases. In addition, cash flow growth expectations can also be affected by the possibility of changes in vacancy rates. In particular, the possibility of higher vacancy rates increases the chances of lower future net cash flows and thus results in a higher current capitalization rate. In fact, due to rising expenses, stagnant or failing rental rates, and higher vacancy rates, growth rate forecasts can be negative, resulting in very high capitalization rates. If the possibility of lower cash flows is related to the national economy (as opposed to being caused by a local or regional economic downturn, or being specific to the particular property or location), an even higher capitalization rate might be required by investors because of the higher systematic risk. The higher transaction costs typically incurred on real estate trades can also increase the capitalization rate.

Although growth prospects and risk determine the relative capitalization rate on different parcels of real estate for any moment in time, general changes in capitalization rates over time are largely caused by changes in risk-free interest rates, changes in market risk premiums, and changes in inflation Oust as changes in stock P/e ratios over time are largely determined by the same factors). In addition, general increases in capitalization rates can also result from past real estate building booms that often lead to widespread overbuilding and that can cause expectations of large rises in vacancy rates in the future (20% vacancy rates are often considered high).

Average and median capitalization rates for different property types are printed periodically in various different sources such as *Investment Property & Real Estate Capital Market Report* published by Institutional Real Estate, Inc. For instance, in the summer of 1998, the capitalization rate was 8.55% for office buildings, 8.70% for warehouses, 9.10% for retail outlets, and 8.50% for apartments. There may have been some fear on the part of investors of increased retail sales via the internet long-term, therefore causing more closures of retail outlets and higher vacancy rates for shopping centers and other retail real estate, and the resulting lower cash flow projected in the future from retail real estate investments made investors capitalize existing cash flow at the relatively higher average rate of 9.10%. However, despite the higher cap rate on retail real estate in general, there was also sentiment that some retail real estate would hold up fairly well in a recession, such as retail outlets that include grocery stores (people always need to buy food which can't easily be sold over the internet) and well-located malls with financially strong tenants and popular stores.

At this time, cap rates had been on the rise for virtually all real estate (especially for lodging and resorts, which had cap rates in excess of 10%, possibly because of investor fears that travel needs might be reduced by increased internet competition), as investors began to perceive that growth in revenue and operating cash flow in general were likely to slow.

### *Computing the Present Value of Real Estate Cash Flows*

Real estate can also be valued by forecasting future cash flows from the real estate and discounting at the required return using equation (4-1). The beta of unlevered real estate investments is generally fairly low because the value of unlevered real estate investments is not extremely volatile, and much of the volatility is related to local factors that are not a function of the aggregate economy. However, use of a large amount of debt in a real estate company can magnify the beta several times, as more debt magnifies systematic risk for the same correlation with the market portfolio.

As a result, discount rates for net real estate cash flows measured net of interest expenses would have to be set as a function of the debt/equity ratio of the company. As in the case for stocks in the same industry, betas for real estate investments could be estimated using the betas of publicly traded real estate stocks like equity Real Estate Investment Trusts (REITS) with similar leverage.

However, cash flows from real estate properties are often evaluated before considering the effect of debt financing. If that approach is utilized, it is necessary to estimate cash flows resulting from paying for the entire purchase price of the real estate in cash, assume therefore no debt service or interest payments, and use a very low discount rate (since the unlevered beta would be used). Often, though, it is difficult to separate the purchase decision from the financing decision (which typically has an important effect on after-tax cash flows), and so investors generally need to compute the present value of the cash flows that incorporate the effects of any debt financing (using software like SIA's PROJECT). Regardless of whether cash flows are measured with or without consideration of the effect of debt financing, it is important not to project the same income from a property into the far future. In particular, there is generally some justification for forecasting substantial changes in cash flows in the future. For instance, there is always the possibility of rising vacancy rates. High vacancy rates are more likely as a property ages, deteriorates, becomes obsolete relative to newer properties, and/or is negatively affected by demographic changes such as people and businesses moving out of an area.

It is also necessary to incorporate into the cash flow forecast the likelihood of increases in operating costs. For instance, maintenance expenses are likely to rise as a property ages. Increased marketing and management expenses (to attract and keep tenants) may also become necessary as a property becomes older, as may legal expenses and liabilities.

The probability of rental increases must also be considered. Although some long-term real estate lease payments are fixed, and many rental rates are controlled by government laws, the rental income on many properties is a function of the inflation rate. Even many long-term leasing contracts on real estate are specified to make rental payments as a function of inflation rate. For example, some lease contracts automatically increase the rental payment by the increase in the inflation rate.

When estimating the present value of real estate, a range of values often can be obtained using different scenarios (such as most likely, most optimistic, and most pessimistic). To maximize the probability of purchasing only underpriced properties, an investor might seek to acquire real estate only if it has a value that exceeds the present value under a most pessimistic scenario (one that has a feasible chance of occurrence).

In addition, real estate values can also be estimated under a best possible use criteria. If the value of the real estate under its current use (such as a shopping mail) is less than what it would be worth if it were converted to another use (such as a warehouse), the possibility of conversion should be taken into consideration (perhaps as one possible scenario, with the value computed net of conversion costs, just as the possibility of managing a company better should be considered when evaluating a stock investment).

As with stocks or any other asset, the final expected sales value of real estate should be a function of its expected final cash flow. To estimate that real estate values will go up in accordance with inflation or with past trends is as much a fallacy for real estate as for stocks. Similarly, to expect real estate values to appreciate forever because of limited supply is a further fallacy. Not all land has yet been used (especially in the United States), and new real estate projects are continually being built, while demand often slows or even falls due to economic and demographic changes. When more new real estate is available than demand, prices can fall. In addition, even with no increase in new real estate, prices of existing real estate can be bid up too high relative to cash flow value in a speculative boom, and a real estate depression with failing prices can result, as occurred nationally in the 1870s and 1930s (and as occurs locally and regionally very frequently).

For instance, as a result of economic factors related to speculation and overbuilding in the 1980s and demographic factors relating to declining population growth, several Harvard analysts predicted that, by the year 2007, residential real estate prices would fall about 50% in real terms (i.e., adjusted for inflation) from their 1990 level. The declining real estate prices of the early 1990s seemed to be consistent with that forecast, although prices recovered in the later 1990s.

The outlook for other types of real estate was also forecast to be poor in the 1990s. In particular, some analysts estimated that the excessive amount of office building construction in the 1980s had resulted in a situation where, even if there were no new office building construction, it would take over 10 years before demand for office space increased to the point where all vacant space could be placed into productive use. However, by the late 1990s, these types of real estate had also recovered from that situation.

Demand for both office and hotel space may be restricted in the future by the revolution in communication, which has made it less necessary for firms to maintain a physical presence in many different places and has reduced the need to travel. As a result, the outlook for real estate revenues and prices is uncertain, especially for lodging and retail real estate (as well as possibly for office space as more people are able to work from their own homes).

### *Cost Approaches to Valuing Real Estate*

In addition to the two methods of valuing real estate using expected cash flows (i.e., the present value and capitalization rate appraisal methods), some analysts also consider the replacement cost of the real estate. Replacement cost is often stated in the form of price per square foot of building floor space. The cost appraisal method is similar to using current cost book value to price stocks. If the real estate actually has a cash flow value in excess of the current cost book value, that value should performance as a floor for the price of the real estate. However, if cash inflows are low (perhaps because vacancy rates are high either locally or nationwide), the price of real estate may be far the replacement cost.

Often, it is possible to estimate the value of real estate by comparing it to the price per square foot of similar real estate in a nearby location. However, such a valuation method should be used with great caution because there are usually significant differences between two fairly similar parcels of real estate. In addition, quoted prices of other pieces of real estate may be only the prices at which other real estate owners are willing to sell, and there may be no buyers willing to pay such a high price. In addition, even where a transaction price is quoted, the price may be inflated by special financing subsidies and/or guarantees.

### *The Relationship Between Real Estate Values, Inflation, and Taxes*

Real estate is often glorified as an investment that has major tax advantages and is positively correlated with inflation. Although real estate investment can, in fact, have tax benefits, its reputation as an inflation hedge, at least short-term, may be undeserved.

### *The Relationship Between Real Estate Values and Inflation*

The values of many real estate assets frequently exhibit negative correlation with inflation. In particular, inflation tends to drive up interest rates. Higher interest rates not only increase the discount rate on real estate cash flows, but also often slow economic growth or even result in a recession that can cause an increase in vacancy rates and reduce cash flows from real estate (although higher interest rates may have a partially offsetting effect longer-term by limiting the number of new real estate projects that are begun and thereby reducing the supply of new real estate in the future).

In any event, to the extent that rents do not rise with inflation (sometimes because they are fixed by contract or by state rental laws, as well as for supply-and-demand or macroeconomic reasons), the effect of higher interest rates is not offset by growth in cash flows from real estate investments, and so the value of real estate investments has been found to be negatively correlated with inflation over short monthly or annual intervals.

*Tax Factors in Real Estate Investments:* When evaluating the value of real estate, depreciation tax shields should also be considered. These arise from noncash depreciation tax deductions on buildings and other properties. These tax deductions shelter from tax a portion of the cash flows from real estate investments and can therefore result in greater net cash flows after tax even while the real estate may be appreciating in price. However, in addition to real estate, depreciation tax shields exist on most fixed assets, including machinery, equipment, airplanes, and other assets into which productive enterprises invest. Although tax factors can enhance investment value, tax considerations alone cannot make real estate an attractive investment (taxes alone cannot make any asset an attractive investment).

Generally, when computing the value of real estate investments, it is only necessary to compute the present value of after-tax cash flows in order to incorporate the effect of depreciation on real estate values. As a result, it is especially useful to value real estate using the discounted cash flow approach.

*Real Estate Investors:* Because of the tax advantages associated with depreciation tax shields (which increase cash flow even while the underlying investment may be appreciating in value), real estate investments are very popular among individuals. For instance, Institutional Real Estate, Inc. reported in 1998 that private investors held 46.6% of the $687 billion that had been directly invested into large real estate properties in the U.S. A further 22.1% and 0.3% was held by REITs and public real estate limited partnerships, respectively, both of which are investment companies that are set up to pool investors' money into real estate so that investors only pay taxes on the income after the depreciation tax shields (investment companies are not subject to separate income taxation as long as they pay out all income to investors). U.S. institutional investors held only 26.8% of all real estate assets (with life insurance companies owning 5.0%, other financial institutions holding 1.8%, and pension funds owning 20.0%), while foreign investors held the other 4.2% of U.S. real estate.

*Real Estate Financing:* Because real estate ownership is publicly recorded, and because it is very difficult or impossible for the owner to carry it off with them, it represents very good collateral for loans. Loans with real estate as collateral are generally called mortgages.

Loans collateralized by assets that are expected to have a high value in case of default on the loan typically have relatively low interest rates. As a result, many investors finance their real estate holdings with large amounts of mortgage debt at a low cost. For instance, the $687 billion in large real estate holdings reported by Institutional Real Estate, Inc. in 1998 represented only the equity portion of the investment, which was measured net of $1.054 trillion that was financed with mortgage debt (i.e., of the total $1741 billion invested into large real estate property assets in the U.S., equity investors put up $687 billion while the other $1054 billion was financed with mortgages). Most of real estate financing is provided by financial institutions (e.g., of the $1054 billion in financing for the large real estate properties, 45.1% was provided by banks and mortgage companies, 8.8% by savings institutions, 17.1% by life insurance companies, 2.3% by pension funds, 9.8% by government agencies, and 16.9% by investment companies).

*Real Estate Transaction Costs:* While real estate investments are widely perceived to have tax and financing advantages, they are also recognized to entail significant transaction cost disadvantages. In particular, because there are so many individual properties, each of which is distinct and different from the others (unlike shares of stock of the same firm), and because real estate is not easily divisible (it is difficult to buy 1/10 of an office building), most real estate is not traded very frequently. As a result, investors may have to wait weeks or even months before being able to conduct a trade on a particular piece of real estate at a reasonable price, and, even after waiting, transaction costs tend to be higher than for other assets such as widely traded stocks of big corporations. Many investors therefore require higher returns on real estate investments because of a positive transaction cost premium in equation.

However, investment companies that invest into real estate provide some opportunity to invest into real estate with less transaction costs. The most important type of real estate investment companies are REITs. Individual shares in the REITs are widely traded each day for small transaction costs that approximate the expenses of trading the stocks of large corporations (with many REITs being traded on the NYSE like industrial stocks). As a result, there should be no transaction cost premium on such forms of real estate investment. As REITs continue to grow in size and buy up ever larger portions of the fixed amount of real estate in existence, they tend to bid up the prices and reduce the transaction cost premiums required on all real estate.

## VALUATION OF NON-INCOME PRODUCING REAL ASSETS

Many real assets like commodities (copper, lumber, wheat, etc.) produce no explicit cash inflows except from sale (either with or without further processing). These assets can be valued by taking the present value of the expected price of the asset, after deducting holding costs, which include warehousing or space costs, property taxes, insurance expenses, and loss related to spoilage, obsolescence, theft, fire, or other causes.

### *Determinants of Commodity Prices*

Estimating the expected sales price of a real asset can be very difficult. Long-term, prices tend to revolve around the cost of producing the asset. For instance, the price of copper fluctuates around the cost of mining copper, the price of lumber revolves around the cost of manufacturing lumber, and the price of wheat fluctuates around the cost of harvesting wheat, etc.

Supply shortages and surpluses can be influenced by a number of different factors. Supply surpluses may be caused by unanticipated declines in demand, such as due to recessions (especially worldwide ones), due to changes in consumer tastes (like a decreased preference for cattle and pork products because of their publicized contributions to human heart disease), and due to technological changes (like the replacement of sugar with corn syrup and chemical substitutes like Nutrasweet). Supply surpluses may also be related to increased production, which can result from favourable environmental conditions (such as favourable weather that makes bumper crops for agricultural commodities possible) and improved technology (such as agricultural genetic engineering and improved mining processes) as well as from government subsidies (and price support policies) that artificially encourage production (such as for many agricultural commodities).

On the other hand, short-term shortages can exist because of increases in demand and/or reduced production. Reduced production can be caused by unfavourable environmental conditions, such as weather-related droughts for agricultural commodities, as well as by artificial restrictions placed on production by national governments, such as international cartels like the Organization of Petroleum Exporting Countries (OPEC). Increases in demand can be caused by economic factors (such as booms), by shifts in consumer taste (such as an increased preference for oats over other foods because of its superior nutritional value), and by technological changes (such as the increased demand for palladium and platinum as chemical catalysts in high-technology production processes).

In many cases, the price of competing or substitute goods is a primary determinant for the floor or ceiling for prices. For instance, in addition to its usage in making bread, wheat can be utilized as animal fodder that has more nutrients per bushel than corn, and so the price of wheat tends to remain above that of corn. Similarly, palladium's price tends to hover below that of platinum because its industrial value (as a catalyst) is less than that of platinum.

### *Supply and Demand Factors Affecting Precious Metal Prices*

Precious metals and stones, which include gold, silver, platinum, palladium, and diamonds, represent the most popular form of investment commodity. The supply (or mining) of precious metals and stones tends to be concentrated in Russia (for gold, palladium, and diamonds) and South Africa (for gold, platinum, and diamonds—in addition, the worldwide distribution of diamonds is almost a monopoly that is controlled by DeBeers, which has historically been based out of South Africa).

Industrial uses of precious metals are highest for palladium and platinum (both of which are used in automobile catalytic converters, petroleum refining, and many high technology processes, as well as jewelry). Silver also has some important industrial use in camera film and electronics (as well as in jewelry). Gold and diamonds are largely restricted to jewelry use (and hoarding by investors), although low quality diamonds have some industrial use (as cutters). presents a brief summary of the percentage usage for each of the precious metals and stones.

**Table. Demand for Precious Commodities**

| Usage | Diamonds | Gold | Silver | Platinum | Palladium |
|---|---|---|---|---|---|
| Catalytic Converters | — | — | — | 33.5% | 7.5% |
| Chemical, Oil Industries | — | — | — | 17.5% | 9.5% |
| Electronics | — | 6.7% | 16.0% | 6.6% | 47.0% |
| Film | — | — | 46.1% | — | — |
| Dental | — | 2.7% | — | — | 24.0% |
| Jewelry, Other Uses | *100% | 90.6% | 37.9% | 42.4% | 12.0% |
| Total | 100% | 100% | 100% | 100% | 100% |

*An important component of the "other uses" is for investment. Most investments in precious metals occurs in the form of a large number of different coin types and bar sizes, especially for gold and silver, which once were used as money instead of paper currency.

Since commodity investments make no cash-flow payments, the purchase of a precious metal coin or bar represents speculation on a change in the supply-and-demand situation that would lead to an increase in the price of the commodity. Often, in addition to the effect of changes in industrial usage and changes in supply from mining operations, the price of a precious metal will be affected by increased hoarding demand during periods of political, economic, and inflation uncertainty.

For instance, during periods when investors begin to mistrust paper assets (such as during periods where there is substantial risk of hyperinflation or war), many purchase precious metals (mostly gold) because of their historical use as a form of money that holds its value well even when government-created paper money becomes worthless. As a result, during such times, the price of precious metals tends to rise. Nevertheless, the relationship between inflation and returns on precious metal investments is often found to be nonpositive from month to month, and the long-term return to precious metal assets is very low relative to security investments.

# 8

# Market Efficiency and Investment Performance

## AN OVERVIEW

Market efficiency is defined as Price=Value (i.e., where all information is incorporated into market price). Empirical tests of market efficiency are described within the context of investment performance, and the implications for investors are explained.

## MARKET EFFICIENCY IN INTERPRETING INFORMATION

Investors with different information sets may value an asset differently, and even investors with the same set of fundamental information may disagree on asset values because of different subjective interpretations of that information and different expectations about an uncertain future. Poor information interpretation and expectations can lead to some investors being willing to trade assets at prices much different from the intrinsic value that can be computed from the best or most efficient interpretation and set of expectations.

When transaction prices deviate from the intrinsic value, the opportunity for abnormal profits exists for investors who are operating with the best interpretation and set of expectations. Abnormal profits exist by buying assets below their intrinsic value and selling them above their intrinsic value, thereby earning returns above the required return.

Required returns are typically measured using the CAPM equation which indicates that, for any asset j:

$$i_j = R_f + (B_j [E(R_{m)}-R_{f]}), \quad (18\text{-}1)$$

where $R_f$ is the risk-free rate, $E(R_{m)}$ is the expected return on the market portfolio, and $B_j$ is the beta of asset j.

Investors with the best information, analysis, and set of expectations may not only be able to obtain abnormal profits for themselves but may also be able to sell investment advice for a fee that would enable other investors to also earn abnormal profits. Theoretically, they can continue to do so until the market prices approach intrinsic value (although it is often difficult to convince other investors that one has the best investment recommendations, since anyone, including poor analysts and even swindlers, can sell investment advice). This process can result in the price of assets selling below intrinsic value being bid up towards intrinsic value, while sales of assets selling above intrinsic value result in the price falling towards intrinsic value (although trading based on poor investment analysis can cause the opposite price reaction). When market prices approximately equal intrinsic value, there are no longer any opportunities for abnormal profits, and the market is defined to be efficient. In other words, market efficiency means that V=P, and $E(R_{j)}=i$.

There are two major degrees of market efficiency: semi-strong and strong. With semi-strong market efficiency, abnormal profits are not obtainable using all public information. With strong market efficiency, abnormal profits are not obtainable using any information, including inside information not made public. Differences between semi-strong and strong market efficiency are smaller when more information is made public (either voluntarily or due to government requirements of full disclosure) because less inside information then exists.

## TESTS OF MARKET EFFICIENCY AND INVESTMENT PERFORMANCE

Tests of market efficiency in interpreting information generally focus on the performance of some set of assets, portfolios, strategies, or managers to see if they generate abnormal profits. If these tests reveal that a set of assets is more likely to outperform the risk-return relationship in equation, the implication is that those assets are mispriced, and that the market for those assets is inefficient.

Similarly, if a test reveals that a portfolio or portfolios run by an investment managerare likely to outperform the risk-return relationship in, the implication is that the manager can find mispriced assets in what appears to be an inefficient market. That indeed is one of the goals of investment management..

## Measurement of Performance

The investment performance of an asset, strategy, or manager can be measured by several different criteria. These performance measures include the investment alpha, the Treynor ratio, the Sharpe ratio, and the geometric mean.

### *The Investment Alpha (Jensen Alpha)*

Computation of abnormal profits frequently employs an investment alpha, which is calculated using some form of the following regression equation:

$$R_j - R_f = a_0 + a_1 B_j [R_m - R_f] + z_j$$

where $a_0$, is the regression intercept often called the investment alpha, a 1, is the regression coefficient, $z_j$ is the regression residual, and actual periodic returns R for each investment are measured over some time interval (such as monthly returns over 60 months). Given the CAPM equation (18-1), a0 should equal 0, and a1 should equal I (and is often restricted to equal I in many tests). Tests of market efficiency focus on the a, term, which measures the abnormal return that exists that expected by CAPM equation (18-1). Using average returns, the investment alpha can also be written as

$$a_0 = R_j - R_f - B_j [R - R_f]. \quad (18\text{-}2b)$$

Although the $a_0$, term is often referred to as the investment alpha, it is also sometimes named the Jensen alpha after one of the earliest researchers in this field. If a, is found to be statistically significant from 0 for some set of assets or portfolios, there is evidence of abnormal profits. The abnormal profits can be earned by buying the assets if a $_{00}$> 0).

Because the regression factors out the return required on the asset for beta risk, the investment alpha evaluates the contribution of the asset to the performance of a diversified portfolio. As a result, the investment alpha may be used to evaluate the performance of both diversified and undiversified portfolios.

### *The Treynor Ratio*

A similar measure of performance is the Treynor ratio, which computes the average return the risk-free rate per unit of beta risk. In particular,

$$\text{Treynor Ratio} = (R_j - R_{f)}/B_j.$$

Like the investment alpha, the Treynor ratio may be used to evaluate the performance of both diversified and undiversified portfolios, although it suffers the problem of potentially being a meaningless performance measure when the beta is zero, very small, or negative.

### *The Sharpe Ratio*

Another measure of performance is the Sharpe ratio, which is named after another one of the earliest researchers in this area. This ratio measures return the risk-free rate per unit of total risk, i.e.,

$$\text{Sharpe Ratio} = (R_p - R_{f)}/S_{p'}$$

where s $_p$ is the standard deviation of return on portfolio p. Because much of the standard deviation of return on individual assets is diversified away in most portfolios, this measure of performance is not relevant for isolated parts of a portfolio (such as a single asset). Instead, this measure of performance is only relevant when applied to an investor's total risky portfolio p.

### *The Geometric Mean Return (Compounded Return)*

Other tests of market efficiency and performance also exist. For instance, some researchers (such as 1970 and 1971 research by Hakansson) have suggested simply measuring performance by the geometric mean or compounded return over time, which is computed as,

$$\text{Geometric mean} = [(1+R_1)(1+R_2)...(1+R_{T-1})(1+R_T)]^{1/T}-1. \quad (18\text{-}5)$$

If the geometric mean or compounded return on a portfolio exceeds that of the return on the market portfolio, the performance of the portfolio is deemed to be superior. Although risk and return variation do affect compounded returns are therefore implicitly incorporated into the performance criteria, the different risk aversion levels and diversification needs of many investors make the framework in more generally applicable (because it explicitly incorporates systematic risk).

### Use of the Performance Measures

Measures of investment performance may be used to evaluate whether a particular market for a particular set of assets is efficient or not. If a market is found to be inefficient, the implication is that opportunities for abnormal rates of returns exist, although it may take years, or even decades, to realise such abnormal returns if prices move towards value very slowly.

Measures of investment performance may also be used to evaluate investment managers. If the portfolio managed by an investment analyst earns abnormal returns, the implication is that the market in which the analyst invests is inefficient and that the analyst is skillful in picking out the mispriced assets. Individuals and institutions who decide not to make their own investment decisions should choose managers who can generate abnormally high rates of return.

When using the foregoing performance measures, it is usually wise to make comparisons with a peer group. Such a comparison is especially important when using the geometric mean compounded rate of return (which does not explicitly adjust for risk). For example, the compounded return of a bond mutual fund could be compared with the average compounded return of all bond funds, the returns of an international fund could be compared to that of the average international mutual fund return, the returns of a specialty mutual fund that invests into telecommunications stocks could be compared with other funds that specialize in that sector, etc.

## EMPIRICAL EVIDENCE OF MARKET EFFICIENCY

The overall evidence from empirical tests indicates that some markets may be inefficient and that opportunities for abnormal profits may exist. However, the pricing efficiency is fairly high in liquid markets, implying limited opportunities for abnormal profits there.

### Primary Markets

Pricing efficiency in the primary market is often a function of the amount and quality of analysis done by investors and issuers. A failure to properly conduct fundamental analysis can lead to substantial differences between value and price. Such mispricing can be especially large in negotiated and private placement markets where a limited number of investors may be involved on any one particular issue (such as in the case of a bank providing a loan).

Even in auction and underwritten markets where there are a large number of investors participating, the efficiency of the initial issue price in incorporating all public information can be low. For instance, prices of new stocks being issued to the public for the first time, called Initial Public Offerings (IPOs), tend to vary widely on the first day of trading in the secondary market. It is not totally unusual for prices of IPOs to rise more than 100% by the end of the first day, or to fall substantially.

Often, fundamental analysis of information on a new security can indicate the direction and magnitude of returns. One study has indicated that positive recommendations on an IPO by analysts at an investment bank not associated with underwriting the IPO are associated with returns that far exceed market returns. In addition, there are sometimes more subtle information clues in an IPO prospectus. For instance, when employees sell some of their own stock in conjunction with a new stock offering by the corporation, there is empirical evidence of investors suffering negative abnormal returns following issue. Although many employees (especially those in a closely held corporation) may sell stock of their corporation in order to reduce their portfolio concentration in one asset, employee stock sales may also indicate that they feel the price is greater than the value. Since employees may possess inside information not available to investors, their decisions to sell stock may have significant information content.

There is some evidence of underpricing in the primary issue market on average. For instance, for IPO stocks going public for the first time, abnormal returns average approximately 10% on the first day. This underpricing may represent compensation for the uncertainty of the pricing, as well as serve to facilitate floatation of the issue. Because of this average underpricing, there is usually an

excess demand from investors for an IPO (investors are also typically not charged a transaction cost for buying in the primary market, as this cost is borne by the issuer, as are the administrative costs of registering with the SEC and the implicit costs associated with underpricing). To ration the stock in the face of excessive demand at the IPO price, investment bankers generally give the first choice of an IPO purchase to their "best" customers (i.e., those who have paid them the most commissions in the past), who may also qualify for special non-public information. However, it should also be the "best" customers pass some IPOs by because they perceive them to be overpriced, and such IPOs that might therefore be available to other customers may be less likely to perform well. Moreover, there is some empirical evidence that, longer-term, the average IPO tends to underperform the average stock (especially after the first day).

## Secondary Markets

As has been summarized by 1970 and 1991 studies by Fama, tests of various secondary investment markets indicate a fair amount of efficiency in incorporating fundamental information into price, especially for liquid markets where there is a substantial amount of trading and investment advisory information. For instance, cosmetic changes in accounting procedures that do not affect cash flows, or stock splits that merely divide value into more pieces (without an increase in earnings or dividends), have not been found to result in abnormal returns. In addition, empirical evidence exists to indicate that stock prices already incorporate much fundamental information about stocks, and when there is an announcement that is different from expectations, a market price reaction occurs in the direction of the deviation from expectation within a few minutes of the announcement. For instance, a 1997 study by Kim, Lin, and Slovin indicated that professional purchase recommendations on a stock, on average, drive up the price by 4% on the NYSE and ASE and by 7% on the NASDAQ, with the movement taking place within 5 and 15 minutes, respectively.

However, there is also substantial evidence of stock returns being positively related to past returns and fundamental information announcements for months. There is also some evidence of a reversal from a trend after time periods of over one year. In a 1998 study, Daniel, Hirshleifer, and Subrahmanyam developed a psychological theory of investor behaviour to explain this phenomenon, whereby investors tend to become overconfident when stock prices and information reinforce their prior beliefs and trading decisions, so that they drive stocks in waves in one direction until they become so mispriced that they begin to move in an opposite trend, which itself feeds on a loss of confidence and pessimism that fuels further price moves in that opposite direction. In a 1998 study, Olson et al. have shown empirically that some of the technical trading signals advocated by are successful enough in picking up such trends to permit profitable trading strategies.

There are also other exceptions to market efficiency. For instance, research indicates that stocks with lower P/e ratios (and higher earnings yields) tend to outperform stocks with higher P/e ratios (and lower earnings yields) on a risk-adjusted basis. In addition, higher yielding bonds (junk) tend to outperform lower yielding bonds (investment grade and Treasury bonds) even over periods when general credit conditions are detrimental to bonds subject to high default, and even over periods when falling interest rates would cause greater appreciation on T-bonds with no call risk and on lower coupon bonds in general with longer durations. Such findings provide evidence that some yield information is not fully reflected in market prices. It is, however, possible that a portion of such abnormal returns reflect transaction cost premiums related to the illiquidity of trading many junk bonds and small company stocks.

Studies of the performance, of professional investment managers provide evidence that market prices do not fully incorporate all fundamental information. In particular, some tests have indicated that professional investors (like mutual fund managers, pension fund managers, and stockbrokers) in the U.S. are able to outperform the market average on a risk-adjusted basis by earning about a 1% higher return per year net of management fees and transaction costs over the long term. With annual management fees averaging about 1% of assets managed, with annual trading turnover averaging about 100% of the size of the portfolio being managed, and with transaction costs for institutions trading NYSE stocks ranging between 1% and 4%, the total expenses incurred by professional investment managers may be 2-5% (with higher transaction costs for more illiquid stock investments like in the OTC market).

The managers must be able to beat the market by 3-6% gross of expenses in order to beat the market by 1% net of expenses. In a 1996 study, Womack has reported results which indicate that investment banker recommendations are able to beat the market by such amounts (this finding is consistent with that reported by the *Wall. Street Journal* in its quarterly review of the leading brokerage house, recommendations that generally indicates virtually all of the investment banks make stock selections which greatly outperform the stock indexes over 5-year periods).

There also exists some evidence that investment managers who have outperformed the average over a fairly long past time interval (such as at least 4 years) tend to perform above average in the future.In particular, studies of mutual fund performance indicate that returns over one 5-year interval are positively related to the returns over a subsequent time interval. These results provide some support for the hypothesis that above-average performance over a past interval may not be due solely to luck. However, it should be emphasized that there are many cases of inconsistent performance among investment managers, and that past performance is no guarantee of future performance.There is also evidence that better-trained managers are able to outperform those that are not so well educated. For instance, a 1994 study by Shukla and Singh found that mutual funds managed by Chartered Financial Analysts (CFAs) outperformed those that were not run by CFAs.

Although some studies have found evidence that some sets of professional managers are not able to beat the market over some time intervals net of expenses, the general results indicate that some investment managers are able to beat the market before expenses. These results imply that good professional investment managers can identify securities whose values differ significantly from market prices, and that it is possible to profit from such opportunities. These findings compare favourably to those for investment clubs and discount broker customers who generally do not have access to professional investment management and whose average risk-adjusted returns are lower than for market indexes, both before and after transaction costs

In addition, some studies have found that managers with low operating costs are, net of expenses, able to outperform managers with high operating costs. Here, total costs include management expenses, turnover or transaction costs, and load fees. Thus, although net abnormal profit opportunities may exist in investments, the gains can be partially (if not fully) eaten up by high expenses. For example, for futures funds, whose annual expenses often exceed 20% of the value of the funds, returns net of expenses average no better than those obtainable from a buy-and-hold strategy, although gross returns are much higher. Even investors without professional investment management (such as customers of discount brokers) tend to perform better (but still worse than market indexes) when they trade less actively and have less transaction costs (e.g., in a 1998 report, Simon explains that female customers of discount brokerage firms tend to perform worse than male customers after transaction costs largely because they tend to trade less actively).

There is some evidence that the market for stocks of smaller companies are more inefficient than the market for stocks of larger companies that are more widely traded and analysed. Just for example, a 1998 report by Tam indicated that each of the largest 10 mutual funds which invest predominately into U.S. small company stocks earned higher risk-adjusted returns than an index of small stocks (the Russell 2000) over the last 10 years. This finding implies that it is possible to exploit the inefficiencies in market pricing of stocks of smaller companies even after the typically larger transaction costs and management fees (which compares very favourably to the studies that indicate even the average mutual that invests into U.S. large company stocks is not able to outperform an index of large company stocks net of management fees and transaction costs over some time intervals). The fairly illiquid OTC Bulletin Board and pink sheet markets are widely perceived as having the greatest market inefficiencies (and therefore the greatest potential for profitable trading and investment).

Even in the most liquid U.S. markets, lawyers frequently challenge the concept of value equaling market price, citing widespread evidence of market inefficiency there. In addition, the Internal Revenue Service (IRS) does not accept a market price as a conclusive appraisal. In particular, tax courts have accepted appraisals of securities at a value substantially different from market price when the market price was based on the sale of only a small portion of the total amount of a security outstanding, or when a sale occurs during special circumstances (including when the general market is considered to be greatly under- or overpricing securities, as often occurs just prior to or after stock market crashes).

In addition, even in the liquid markets where prices are fairly efficient in reflecting all public information, market prices are often fairly inefficient in reflecting inside information. As a result, although illegal in the U.S. (and in many other countries), it has been found that high abnormal returns (net of costs) are available from trading on nonpublic inside information (even in liquid markets). Decisions by insiders to buy or sell stock often provide clues to public investors concerning the fundamental value of the company given inside information. Similar information effects have also been found to occur when the corporation itself buys or sells its own stock, with a rise in price occurring following an announcement to repurchase stock and a fall in price occurring following an announcement to sell new stock.

Evidence of market inefficiency has also been found in some foreign markets. For instance, some evidence has been found of abnormal profits being available from trading stocks based on the existence of a positive or negative information announcement that has been public for several months. Following brokerage recommendations has also been found to result in abnormal profits in some foreign markets. As in the U.S., the more illiquid the market and the less sophisticated the investor, the more inefficient the market is in reflecting value

## INTERPRETATION OF MARKET PRICE

Although the market price of an investment may not represent a totally accurate or objective indicator of value, it does represent a sort of consensus view on the value of an asset. Many may feel the asset is worth more, while others may feel it is worth less, and the market price is the average of those valuation estimates weighted by the dollar amount of orders placed. For liquid securities that are widely and heavily traded, the market price represents the consensus value of a large number of investors. For illiquid securities that are infrequently traded, the market price represents the consensus value of a limited number of investors.

As a consensus estimate of value, the market price is often a reasonable indicator of value if one has no other information. It is thus similar to the expectations theory forecast of interest rates, which is based on a consensus forecast of interest rates and bond prices. The consensus estimate is invariably wrong and frequently by a large amount, but it is often difficult to produce a more accurate estimate.

## IMPLICATIONS FOR INVESTORS

The major implication for investors is that fundamental analysis may be useful (and necessary) in markets that are not totally efficient (whereas indexing may be appropriate in efficient markets). In addition, regardless of whether markets are efficient or inefficient, it is always necessary to analyse risk, taxes, and transaction costs.

### *Selecting Investments or Managers in Secondary Markets*

The analysis of market pricing efficiency indicates that market prices can deviate from value, even in the secondary market. As a result, it may be possible to locate underpriced investments, and, with sufficient skill, the time and expense associated with fundamental analysis may be justified. However, efficiency in analysis and trading is required to generate profits net of costs.

### *Choosing a Money Manager*

Many investors may feel that they do not possess the expertise to find prices that deviate from value (and thereby "beat" the market). In addition, many investors with smaller portfolios and/or with insufficient time (because of other job constraints) may not have the economies of scale and scope to earn abnormal returns in excess of the management and trading costs incurred in an active investment strategy. Such investors may optimally select investment managers and advisors, who do have the expertise and economies of scale and scope. For instance, such investors might consider investing through actively managed mutual funds, subscribing to an investment advisory newsletter, and/or investing through full service brokers and financial planners who can provide the necessary advice.

The choice of manager or advisor can be made using the performance criteria described If investors choose different managers or advisors for different portions of their portfolios, they may still need to determine how much to allocate to each investment category.

For instance, if an investor believes that she or he has superior skill in selecting between different investment categories, that investor can justify performing an analysis.if she or he wanted to let investment managers choose specific securities within each asset category. On the other hand, if an investor does not wish to make any investment decisions at all, it is also possible to let a single mutual fund allocate money across all asset categories by investing into a superior-performing asset allocation fund.

### *Indexing*

Some investors may not feel that they can pick out an honest investment manager or advisor who will sell services for a fee that is less than the value of those services. Such investors should consider investing into index mutual funds that track the market portfolio. In particular, if P approximates V, and if $E(R_j)=i$ after management and trading costs are subtracted from the gross returns that can be generated through fundamental analysis, the optimal portfolio p equals the market portfolio.

Because many index funds are indexed only within a specific asset category (such as a stock index fund or a bond index fund), investors following an indexing strategy would still have to allocate funds between stocks, bonds, foreign assets, and real assets. In order to attempt to match the return on the entire market portfolio, investors may allocate the risky portion of their portfolios to each investment category according to the weights in the market portfolio of all assets.Besides reducing the time and expense of evaluating investments, indexing also reduces the tax and transaction costs of trading. Nevertheless, indexing does incur some transaction costs and capital gains taxes, as securities that are replaced in the index must be sold and new securities in the index must be purchased. One study has indicated that the tax costs associated with tracking the S&P 500 index reduced after-tax returns by about 0.25% per year over the 1988-97 interval. While such costs could be reduced slightly by buying and holding the original stocks in the index, cash acquisitions would still result in some tax and transaction costs.

It should also be no matter how broad the index or set of indexes in which an investor takes a position, it is unlikely that all assets in the world will be purchased. As a result, the very many investors who do index their investments could drive up the prices of assets in the indices beyond their fundamental value, implying more lucrative investment opportunities on assets not included in major indices.

### *The Necessity of Security Analysis in Primary Markets*

Even if investors do not believe they can earn abnormal profits in the secondary market, it is still necessary for financial analysts to be able to analyse the value of new securities issued in the primary market. Poor security selection and poor pricing in the primary market can occur if either the seller or the buyer of the new security fails to analyse the value of the investment.

### *An Example of Mortgage Valuation*

Because the average homeowner is not equipped with computer models of mortgage pricing, and because the average homeowner is usually not able to monitor refunding opportunities on a daily basis, most homeowners are unable to determine the most appropriate time to prepay their mortgages. Some may prepay earlier than is optimal, but most tend to prepay later than is optimal. As a result, the prepayment right in a mortgage has less value to the average homeowner than it would to a more sophisticated mortgagor.

This lower value is typically incorporated into standardized residential mortgage pricing, as lenders usually price mortgages based on some expected prepayment pattern that is normally based on the past behaviour and evidence on average mortgagor prepayments. Thus, the lower value of the prepayment rights given an expectation of mortgagors suboptimally prepaying is passed on to all mortgagors in the form of a lower coupon rate.

For sophisticated mortgagors, this lender practice represents an opportunity to sell an asset for a price that is in excess of its value. In particular, sophisticated mortgagors, who will prepay their mortgages when it is optimal to do so, generally are offered the lower interest rate on their mortgages just like any other mortgage or (because the lenders cannot differentiate between sophisticated and other borrowers). By prepaying the mortgage only at optimal times, mortgagors obtain the full value of the prepayment rights in the mortgage but do not have to pay for them with a higher coupon rate.

Sophisticated mortgagors can also differentiate between different mortgage offers from different lenders. For instance, sophisticated mortgagors can determine whether a lender's offer to borrow at a specified fixed rate is better than another offer to borrow at a specified adjustable rate (that typically varies with some market interest rate like the T-bill rate).

In addition to being able to analytically compare fixed-rate mortgages (FRMs) and adjustable rate mortgages (ARMs), sophisticated borrowers can evaluate differences in other mortgage terms such as maturity, points, ARM teaser rates, and ARM caps. Points represent the percentage by which the mortgage is sold to the lender at a discount.

In addition to subtracting out points, the closing costs of entering into a mortgage (including title insurance, application fees, appraisal fees, and tax escrow waiver fees, together which average about 1% of the value of the mortgage) must also be subtracted from the face value of the mortgage in order to compute the net amount of cash received by the borrower. For ARMS, teaser rates represent an initially low coupon payment on an ARM, which is subsequently set to increase substantially even if interest rates do not change. Annual ARM caps represent the maximum percentage increase in ARM rates allowed per year. A lifetime ARM cap represents the maximum ARM rate that can be charged.

Let's take an example for October 19, 1998. Assume a homeowner has about 28 years in payments left on a 7.875% fixed-rate mortgage. The homeowner estimates his probability of default to be 0.2%, with a 50% expected value of the mortgage in default (because of the typical high value of the home used as collateral). The expected loss rate is therefore 0.2(1-.5)=0.10%. The homeowner also estimates a 5% chance of moving to a new home each year.

Plugging these numbers into the SIA software indicates the value of the homeowner's mortgage to be $1000 per $1000 in principal but to be $1016.55 if it were not currently callable (implying that the mortgage should optimally now be prepaid). Because the mortgage value exceeds the normal mortgage prepayment price of par value plus normal refunding costs of 1.2% of par value, the homeowner should consider refinancing the mortgage. By doing so, the borrower saves the difference between what the mortgage would be worth if it were not currently prepayable, 101.66%, and the prepayment price of 100% of par.

The difference here is 1.66% of par, which exceeds normal 1.2% refunding costs, and so prepayment of the bond should be considered. therefore enables the homeowner to evaluate the optimal time to prepay. Using intuition or rules of thumb such as "prepay whenever mortgage rates fall 2% below the mortgage coupon rate" generally result in prepayments that are later than optimal.

At this time, the homeowner shops around and finds a lender who is offering a 30-year fixed-rate mortgage with a 6.75% coupon and 1.5 points plus closing costs equal to 0.5% of the mortgage par value. The fixed-rate mortgage offer is valued using the SIA software as 97.46% of par. After deducting the 1.5+0.5=2% in points and closing costs for the fixed-rate mortgage, the borrower receives 98% of par in cash, which, compared to the present value for the obligation of

97.46% of par, represents a net present value gain of 0.54% of par.

In this example, the net proceeds to the borrower from the new loan (after deducting points and fees) exceeded the present value of the future loan payments, while the present value of the future payments on the old loan was greater than the prepayment price. As a result, it was clear that the mortgage should be refinanced. However, such a clear situation may not always exist, in which case a decision rule may be used. In particular, if the present value of the future payments on the new loan exceed the net proceeds to the borrower, it may still be optimal to refinance if the net gain from refinancing exceeds zero, i.e., if

Net Cashnew loan - Vnew loan + Vold loan - Prepayment Priceold loan > 0. (18-6)

Although this framework may not be necessary in obvious cases like the foregoing 30-year fixed-rate mortgage offer, the methodology can be useful for measuring the gain from the refinancing: Gain from refinancing with the fixed-rate = 98 - 97.46 + 101.66 - 100 = 2.20% of par > 0. (18-7)

In addition to helping to determine whether it is optimal to refinance, this type of analysis can also be used to choose from different refinancing alternatives. For instance, in the foregoing example, assume that lenders are also offering at this time a 30-year ARM with a coupon that equals the 1-year T-bill rate plus 1%, an initial rate of 4.75%, a 2% annual cap, an 10.75% lifetime cap and two points plus closing costs equal to 0.5% of the mortgage principal. For the ARM here, the cap restricts the coupon rate from going up more than 2% per year (i.e., the maximum rate is 6.75% in the second year) and restricts the coupon rate from going above 10.75% at any time. The SIA software, the value of this ARM is 97.74% of par.

The computer analysis indicates that the fixed rate mortgage is the better deal for the sophisticated mortgagor. In particular, after deducting 2.0+0.5=2.5% in points and closing costs for the ARM, the borrower receives 97.5% of par in cash, while the payments on the variable-rate debt have a present value of 97.74% of par, for a net present value loss of

0.24%. The borrower should therefore take the 30-year fixed-rate mortgage which provides the 0.54% gain.

Nevertheless, if the borrower had not found such advantageous terms on the 30-year fixed-rate mortgage, the ARM might have been acceptable, even though it has an estimated net present value loss before considering the benefits of refinancing.

In particular, even though the ARM results in the borrower receiving a cash amount that is lower than the present value of his debt, refinancing would still be optimal to doing nothing, as the loss on the ARM would be more than offset by the gain from prepaying the old 7.875% mortgage:

Refinancing gain with the ARM = 97.5 - 97.74 + 101.66 - 100 = 1.42%, (18-8) although it is clearly not as profitable as refinancing with the existing fixed-rate mortgage offer.

It should also be noted that, for different homeowners, the value and choice of mortgages may be different. For instance, for homeowners with a much greater probability of moving to a new home (which is a probability estimate that the SIA software incorporates into the valuation analysis), ARMs frequently have more favourable value-to-price ratios (as the ARM teaser rate is worth relatively more in such circumstances whereas the call option on the fixed-rate mortgage is worth relatively less).

Although the mortgage lender will often be losing on the sophisticated mortgagors who prepay optimally and choose the best mortgages, the lenders more than make up for the losses by lending to mortgagors who are not sophisticated, who do not prepay optimally, and who cannot choose the best mortgage offer. If more mortgagors become sophisticated, lenders will either begin to start earning lower profits, or mortgage rates will have to rise relative to treasury rates.

### *Analysis of Taxes, Transaction Costs, and Multiperiod Risk*

Regardless of whether investors believes they are capable of picking superior-performing investments or managers, it is still necessary for them to analyse transaction costs, taxes, and risk. Such analysis must be customised to meet the needs of each different investor.

**Tax and Transaction Cost Management**

To maximize net returns, the taxes on investment income and the transaction costs of conducting trades must be considered. Strategies that may maximize returns after transaction costs are discussed, which describes the markets with the lowest transaction costs. Guidelines for maximizing after-tax returns are provided, which shows how to select the optimal investment or type of account in which to make investments. Because each investor may have different cash inflows and outflows, different tax and trading strategies may be appropriate for different investors.

In all cases, a trade should be undertaken only if the gains from trading more than cover the transaction costs and taxes that arise from trading. For instance, assume an investor owns a stock with a price of $80 and assume that the investor would have to pay $2 per share in transaction costs and $15 per share in capital gains taxes if she sold it (because the investor had bought the stock at a much lower price of $4 fifteen months ago). The investor should generally hold onto this stock unless she believes that the stock's value is worth at least $15+$2=$17 less than the market price (i.e., only if the investor believed the stock was only worth less than $80-$17=$63 would it be optimal to sell the stock). Alternatively, if the investor could find another stock that was underpriced by enough to make up the difference, it might be optimal to sell the stock (e.g., if the investor found a stock selling for $70 that she thought was worth $95, she could justify selling the original stock just to be able to take advantage of the lucrative investment opportunity even if the original stock had a value equal to its $80 price).

**Multiperiod Risk Management**

The different cash needs and resources of different investors make evaluation of portfolio risk even more complex. many investors have complex needs and wishes, for which a

Multiperiod analysis is necessary. Such an analysis is similar to the single period analysis describe that merely attempted to maximize expected return for a given constraint on the maximum annual loss an investor could afford. The analysis involves choosing that level of leverage that maximizes the statistical probability of the investors having enough cash to achieve their personal consumption and financial needs and wishes. However, the existence of Multiperiod needs and wishes necessitates the use of a computer.

Regardless of whether individual assets are selected directly by the investor, whether active mutual funds are used to choose individual assets, or even whether index funds are employed, it is possible to utilize the PORTFOLIO portion of the SIA software to determine the optimal amount to be put into the risk-free asset. The PORTFOLIO programme makes the conservative assumption that the expected return on each asset in a portfolio will equal the naive expected return given by (3-2). If the market is efficient, this estimate is the actual expected return. On the other hand, if the market is inefficient, and if superior analysis is used, the expected return should actually be greater than this expected return (thus making it a conservative estimate).

# 9

# Government Securities for Investors

## INTRODUCTION

The government needs enormous amount of money to perform the following main functions: Provision of public services such as law and order; justice, national defence, and so on. Central banking and monetary regulation.

Creation and maintenance of physical infrastructure. The government generates revenue in the form of taxes and income from ownership of assets. Besides these, it borrows extensively from banks, financial institutions, and the public to finance its expenditure in excess of its revenues.

One of the important source of borrowing funds is the government securities market (GSM). The government raises short-term and long- term funds by issuing securities. These securities do not carry risk and are as good as the government guarantees the payment of interest and the repayment of principal. They are, therefore, referred to as gilt-edged securities. The government securities market is the largest market in any economic system and therefore, is the benchmark for other markets.

### Importance of the Government Securities Market

GSM constitutes the major segment of the debt market. It not only provides resources to the government for meeting its short-term and long-term needs but also acts as a benchmark for pricing corporate papers of varying maturities. The government securities issues are helpful in implementing the fiscal policy of the government.

It is critical in bringing about an effective and reliable transmission channel for the use of indirect instruments of monetary control. The working of the two of the major techniques of monetary control- Open Market Operations (OMOs) and Statutory Liquidity Ratio (SLR)- are closely connected with the dynamics of this market.

Government securities provide the highest type of collateral for borrowing against their pledge. They have the highest degree of security of capital and the return on each security depends on the coupon rate and period of maturity. They are traded for both long and short-term periods depending on the investment and liquidity preference of the investors. Switches between the short dated and long dated securities take place on the basis of difference in redemption yields. Issues, Investors, and Types of Government Securities

Government securities are issued by the central government, state governments and semi-government authorities which also include local government authorities such as City Corporations and Municipalities.

The major investors in this market, besides the Reserve Bank, are the national banks as they have to subscribe to these securities to meet their reserve requirements. The other investors are insurance companies, state governments, provident funds, individuals, corporates, non-banking finance companies, primary dealers, financial institutions and to a limited extent, foreign institutional investors and non-resident Indian (NRIs).

These investors can be classified into three segments.

- Wholesale market segment, namely institutional players such as banks, financial institutions, insurance companies, primary dealers, and mutual funds.
- Middle segment comprising corporates, providend funds, trusts, non-banking finance companies, and small cooperative banks with an average liquidity ranging from Rs. 7 crore to Rs. 25 crore.

- Retail segment consisting of less active investors such as individuals and non-institutional investors.

The government securities market is mostly an institutional investors market as standard lots of trade are around Rs. 1 crore and 99 per cent of all trades are done through the Subsidiary General Ledger (SGL) account, which is a kind of depository account held by the Reserve Bank. Individuals cannot open SGL accounts. They have to open SGL-II accounts with a bank or a primary dealer provided they have a huge balance and agree to trade on an ongoing basis.

Government securities are of two types: treasury bills and government dated securities. The latter carry varying coupon rates and are of different maturities. Sometimes, the Reserve Bank converts maturing treasury bills into bonds thereby rolling over the government's debt.

## GOVERNMENT SECURITIES MARKET IN THE PRE-1991 PERIOD

The Reserve Bank was established in 1935, after which it issued government securities on behalf of the government and sold them to various institutions and the public at large. In the 1930s, the government issued securities at interest rates as low as 2.5 per cent, as the cheap money policy was adopted. After independence, the Reserve Bank was nationalised; since then, it frames the monetary policy, structure of interest rates, programme of borrowing through government securities, and so on instructions from the government.

The programme of borrowing was gradually stepped up in the 1950s to finance development projects in various sectors of the economy. The rates of interest on government securities were also gradually stepped up to enable resource mobilisation. To facilitate this programme of higher borrowings, the Reserve Bank carried out open market operations which helped in creating a genuine market for government securities. Till the 1950s, government securities were more popular with individuals than with institutions.

Since the 1960s and until the 1990s, the government securities market remained dormant. The government was borrowing at preannounced coupon rates from banks which were the predominant group of investors. During the 1980s, the volume of both long-term and short-term debt expanded considerably, especially the latter due to automatic accommodation through the issue of ad hoc T-bills. The Reserve Bank had also little control over some of the essential facets of debt management such as volume and maturity structure of securities to be marketed and the term structure of interest rates. The maturity structure of market loans remained highly skewed in favour of a longer term of more than 15 years. Considering the significance of a vibrant government securities market and for activating an internal debt management policy, a number of measures were announced in the middle of 1991 to reform the government securities market.

### *Objectives of Reforms in the Government Securities Market*

*Reforms were undertaken in the government securities market to*:

- Increase the operational autonomy of the Reserve Bank;
- Improve institutional infrastructure;
- Improve the breadth and depth of the markets by introducing a variety of new instruments and bring about improvements in the market micro-structure such as yield-based and pricebased auctions, tap about improvements in the market microstructure such as yield-based and price-based auctions, tap loans, preannouncing notified amounts, reissues of dated secrities, announcing calendar of T-bills, liquidity support to primary dealers, and so on;
- Enable sound legal and regulatory framework by amendment to Securities Contracts (Regulation) Act and propose introduction of Government Securities Act;
- Bring in technology related improvements which include initiation of computerisation of Public Debt Offices (PDOs) of the Reserve Bank and of Real Time Gross Settlement System (RTGS);

- Improve transparency and introduce standardised codes for market practices for encouraging standardised accounting norms.

*Some Policy Measures Undertaken in the 1990s:* The auction system for the sale of medium and long-term securities was introduced from June 3, 1992. Some innovative instruments such as conversion of auction T-bills into term securities, zero coupon bonds, capital indemed bonds, tap stocks and partly paid stock were introduced.

From April 28, 1992, 364-days T-bills auctions were introduced and 91-day T-bills auctions from January 8, 1993. On June 6, 1997, 14- day T-bills were introduced but they were discontinued from May 2001.

Auctions of repurchase agreements (Repo) of dated government securities were introduced from December 1992.

To develop the market, Securities Trading Corporations of India (STCI) was set up in May 1994. it began its operations in June 1994. The most notable policy development in the government securities market during 1994-95 was the delinking of the budget deficit from automatic monetisation by initially limiting the creation of ad hoc Tbills and subsequently discontinuing them. The National Stock Exchange started trading in government securities from June 30, 1994. As a move towards greater transparency, the transactions of government securities through SGL accounts have been made public by the Reserve Bank on a regular basis from September 1, 1994.

A Delivery versus Payment (DVP) system for transactions in government securities was introduced with effect from July 17, 1995. The DVP system synchronises the transfer of securities with cash payment thereby reducing the settlement risk in securities transactions and also preventing the diversion of funds in case of transactions routed through the SGL accounts. In 1999, the computer networking between Reserve Bank's SGL and NSDL was completed, thus enabling electronic settlement for investors having depository accounts with NSDL. The Reserve Bank set up a strong regulatory system which required that every trade must settle with funds and delivery of securities. IOUs and netting were prohibited. Trade reporting of the negotiated deals was made compulsory at the WDM (Ways and means advances) segment of NSF.

In May 1995, the government, for the first time, issued guidelines for non-government provident funds, superannuation funds, and gratuity funds to earmark 25 per cent of their total corpus for investment in central government securities. A well developed government securities market enables other segments of the debt market to develop. As a step towards this, the government went for diversification of instruments-introduction of floating rate bonds indexed to yield on 364-day T-bills. Moreover, it reissued securities of two-year, three-year, five-year, and ten-year maturities at fixed coupon. Further, it permitted commercial banks to retail government securities with non-bank clients.

A plan of Ways and Means Advances (WMA) was introduced effectively from April 1, 1997, to accommodate temporary mismatches between government receipts and payments.

This plan replaced the practice of automatic monetisation of deficit. Foreign Institutional Investors, with a ceiling of 30 per cent investment in debt instruments, have been permitted to invest in government dated securities. In order to facilitate custodial and depository services to FIIs in government dated securities and T-bills, FII investments are now permitted through the SGL account of depositories, in addition to the SGL account of the designated banks, subject to certain conditions.

To encourage retail participation in the primary market for government securities, an allocation of upto 5 per cent has been provided to retail investors on a non-competitive basis.

The uniform price auction format for auctions which was confined to the auction of 91-days treasury bills was extended to the auction of dated securities. The central government issued two floating rate bonds on the basis of uniform price auction on November 21 and December 5, 2001, on an experimental basis. The trading entities have been allowed to sell government securities allotted to them in primary issues on the same day, thus enabling sale, settlement, and transfer on the same day. Some significant steps for further development of the government securities market which the Reserve Bank has taken in 2001-02 are as follows:

- Enhancing fungibility and liquidity through consolidation by re-issuance of existing loans.
- Promoting retailing of government securities and introduction of floating rate bonds.
- Elongation of the maturity profile of outstanding issuance including issuance of bonds with a maturity of 25 years.
- Development of new benchmark government securities by consolidating new issuance in key maturities.
- Setting up of an electronic Negotiated Dealing System (NDS) and Clearing Corporation of India Limited (CCIL) for facilitating trading and settlement in government securities. The NDS (Phase I) was operationalised from February 15, 2002 and CCIL too commenced its operations for clearing and settling of transactions in government securities including repos.
- The Electronic Funds Transfer (EFT) and Real Time Gross Settlement System are being put in force by the Reserve Bank.
- A road map for developing Separate Trading for Registered Interest and Principal of Securities (STRIPS) was prepared, and put on the Reserve Bank's website for comments and suggestions from the market participants.

The government also announced, on February 28, 2001, that comprehensive legislation will be introduced on securitisation and clarification will be issued by the Central Board of Direct Taxes (CBDT) to promote the issuance of Separate Trading Registered Interest and Principal Securities (STRIPS), zero coupon bonds, deep discount bonds, and the like. Retail trading in government securities at select stock exchanges commenced in January 2003.

*STRIPS in the Government Securities Market:* STRIPS is a process of stripping a conventional coupon bearing security into a number of zero coupon securities which can be traded separately. To emphasise, a 10-year government security can be stripped into a principal component and a set of 20 individual coupons/assuming half yearly coupon payments. Each of these 21 stripped securities can be treated as zero coupon bonds which can be traded at varying yields.

The conversion of one underlying security into a number of zero coupon securities called STRIPS increases the breadth of the debt market and provides a continuous market which ultimately helps in improving liquidity. The creation of securities of varied maturities from a single security satisfies the needs of different investors who have diverse risk profiles and investment horizons.

STRIPS benefits not only investors, but also issuers. STRIPS allows the issuer to issue securities with long-term maturity for any amount. These long-term securities can be stripped to meet the market needs for short-term securities. Moreover, the supply of securities increases with stripping and this boosts the secondary market activity. Further, banks can issue STRIPS against the securities held by them. Thus, STRIPS facilitates the management of the banks' asset-liability mismatches.

### Retailing of Government Securities

The existence of a strong retail segment is a prerequisite for the development of the government securities market. Individual can buy government securities from the Reserve Bank's public debt office during auctions. However, most investors are not familiar with the functioning of the government securities market and most of them perceive government securities as an instrument meant for institutional investors. Owing to this, the retail market of government securities did not develop. The Reserve Bank has made efforts to promote retailing of government securities.

Banks are allowed to freely buy and sell government securities on an outright basis at prevailing market prices.

They retail government securities to non-bank clients without any restriction on the period between sale and purchase. Further, the interest income on government securities was exempted from the provision of tax deduction at source with effect from June 1997, to facilitate genuine trading in the secondary market. With no TDS, government securities become an attractive investment for those interested in avoiding TDS, such as senior citizens. One of the major objectives of setting up the primary dealer system and satellite dealer system was to increase the distribution channels and encourage voluntary holding of government securities among a wider investor base.

The Reserve Bank has extended to them a plan for availing liquidity support and the facility of repos (as lenders) for increasing the retail network. With a view to enabling dematerialisation of securities of retail investors, the National Securities Depository Limited (NSDL), Stock Holding Corporation of India Limited (SHCIL) and National Securities Clearning Corporation Limited (NSCCL) were allowed to open SGL accounts with the Reserve Bank. The Reserve Bank allowed NSDL and CDSL to open a second SGL account for depository participants who, in turn, can hold in custody government securities on behalf of the ultimate investors. Retail investment in government securities has been made easy via demat accounts. The procedural hassels have been considerably reduced.

The Reserve Bank encouraged the setting up of mutual funds dealing exclusively in government securities called gilt funds with a view to creating a wider investor base for them. The Reserve Bank provides special liquidity support to the extent of 20 per cent of the investment in government dated securities. A primary dealer sells gilts with a minimum investment of Rs. 25,000 while gilt funds provide access to an individual investor with a low investment minimum of Rs. 5,000. The awareness about gilt funds is rising as they are offering good returns. PNB Gilts is using the Punjab National Bank branch network to popularise government securities with retail investors.

It has tied up with NSDL to work around the problem of physical transfers and has also launched an advertising campaign to inform the public about the advantages of investing in government securities. Gilt funds were managing more than Rs. 3,200 crore as on June 30, 2001.

### *The System of Ways and Means Advances (WMA) for the Centre*

The ad hoc treasury bills emerged as a popular mode of financing the central government's deficit in the mid-1950s. For the smooth conduct of the government's business, it was mutually agreed between the central government and the Reserve Bank that a minimum cash balance of Rs. 50 crore on Fridays and Rs. 4 crore on other days would be held by the central government.

To adhere to this administrative arrangement, it was agreed that whenever the cash balances fell Rs. 50 crore, the Reserve Bank would automatically issue fresh ad hoc T-bills of an amount that would restore the balance to Rs. 50 crore. This mechanism ensured an unlimited access to the Reserve Bank's resources. The ad hoc T-bills which were meant to be temporary, gained a permanent as well as a cumulative character. Indeed, it became an attractive source of financing government expenditure since it was available at an interest rate of 4.6 per cent per annum since 1974.

The Reserve Bank's credit to government is a source of reserve money generation and any investment in central government's securities by the Reserve Bank results in monetisation of government deficit. Monetised deficit is the increase in the Reserve Bank credit to the central government which is the sum of increase in the Reserve Bank's holdings of the government of India's dated securities, treasury bills, rupee coins, and loans and advances from the Reserve Bank to the centre since April 1, 1997, adjusted for changes in the centre's cash balances with the Reserve Bank. The Reserve Bank was expected to compulsorily finance ad hocs.

The increase in the central bank's credit to the government led to an increase in money supply and inflation. The Reserve

Bank had no way of containing monetisation of the budget deficit and effectively implementing its monetary policy. In order to restore the role of the monetary policy in the economy, the government entered into an agreement with the Reserve Bank to put an annual ceiling on the issue of treasury bills, to reduce that ceiling over time, and finally to eliminate ad hocs.

*The process of elimination of ad hocs was designed in three stages*:

- Through limits on creation of ad hoc T-bills which operated between 1994-95 and 1996-97.
- through a transition period of two years which began on April 1, 1997, when ad hocs were eliminated, and the new system of Ways and Means was introduced. However, overdraft Ways and Means was made permissible only beyond ten continuous working days; though at a cost.
- The full-fledged system of WMA has been operating effectively since April 1999.

*What is Ways and Means Advances (WMA)*:

- This plan has been evolved to accommodate temporary mismatches in government receipts and payments
  - The limit for WMA and the rate of interest on WMA will be mutually agreed to between the Reserve Bank and the government from time to time.
- Any withdrawals by the government from the Reserve Bank in excess of the limit of WMA would be permissible only for ten consecutive working days.
- When 75 per cent of WMA is utilized, the Reserve Bank would trigger fresh floatation of government securities. (v) Consistent with the discontinuance of ad hoc T-bills, the system of 91-day T-bills was also discontinued with effect from April 1, 1997. The outstanding ad hoc T-bills as on March 31, 1997, were funded into special securities without any specified maturity, at an interest rate of 4.6 per cent per annum on April 1, 1997.

- With the discontinuance of ad hoc T-bills and with the introduction of WMA, the concept of conventional budget deficit was no more relevant. Therefore, the practice of showing budgetary deficit was discontinued; the Gross Fiscal Deposit (GFD) is now the key indicator of deficit. Gross fiscal deficit is the excess of total expenditure including loans, net of recoveries over revenue receipts (including external grains) and non-debt capital receipts.

WMA is not a source of financing budget deficit and is not included in the budget estimates. It is only a mechanism to cover day-to-day mismatches in receipts and payments of the government. It is charged at market related interest rate. Hence, the use of WMA have to be periodically abandoned.

*Advantages of WMA*

- It is expected that WMA will not put an undue pressure on money supply as it is not a source of financing deficit. (ii) It would reflect the perceptions of both the issuer (the government) and the investors since the entire market borrowing programme of the government is an auction basis. This would lead to the deepening of the government securities market which, in turn, would facilitate the pricing of private corporate debt issues in relation to those of risk free government paper.
- The introduction of WMA is a major step towards the achievement of greater discretion. The Reserve Bank has larger flexibility in the choice of its assets which, in turn, provide it larger manoeuvrability over management of liquidity in the system.

WMA also entails important obligations. If the central government is not in a position to address its fiscal deficit suitably and if this results in a disproportionate rise in market borrowing, the rate of interest on government paper will start rising, affecting the entire interest rate structure.

### *WMA Limits*

The Reserve Bank is required to set the limits of WMA

for the government of India. For the year 1997-98, the limit for WMA was fixed at Rs.12,000 crore for the first half of the year (April- September) and Rs.8,000 crore for the second half of the year (October-March). These limits were revised in the year 1998- 99 and lowered to Rs.11,000 crore and Rs.7,000 crore respectively. Furthermore, the interest rates on WMA were delinked from the cut-off yield for 91 day treasury bills and linked to the bank rate. For 2001-02, the WMA limits were scaled down to Rs.10,000 crore during the first half of the year and Rs.6,000 crore during the second half of the year. When 75 per cent of the limit for WMA is utilized by the government, the Reserve Bank may trigger fresh floatation of market loans, depending on market conditions. The interest rate on WMA is the bank rate, and on overdrafts the interest rate is the bank rate plus two percentage points. The minimum balance required to be maintained by the government of India with the Reserve Bank is not less than Rs.100 crore on Fridays, as at the close of the government's financial year and on June 30, and not less than Rs.10 crore on other days. Overdrafts are limited to 10 consecutive working days.

**Table. WMA Limits of Government of India**

**(Rs in crore)**

| Year | Limit during April-September | Limit during October-March |
|---|---|---|
| 1997-98 | 12,000 | 8,000 |
| 1998-99 | 11,000 | 7.000 |
| 1999-2000 | 11,000 | 7.000 |
| 2000-01 | 11,000 | 7.000 |
| 2001-02 | 10,000 | 6,000 |
| 2002-03 | 10,000 | 6,000 |

## Primary and Secondary Market Segments of the Government Securities Market

- Primary Market of Government Securities

Debt instruments are issued in the primary market where initially they are subscribed by the various investors who may not trade in them subsequently in the secondary market. The Reserve Bank of India issues government securities on behalf of the government. The primary market operations of the Reserve Bank are mainly driven by the objectives of the debt management policy, which is to ensure funding of fiscal deficit from the market in a cost effective manner. The primary market instruments are treasury bills and government dated securities. The central government mobilises funds mainly through the issue of treasury bills and dated securities while state government do so solely through dated securities.

*Treasury Bills:* T-bills are short term obligations issued by the Reserve Bank on behalf of the Government of India through weekly and fortnightly auctions. Till 2000, there were 14-day T-bills, 91- day T-bills, 182-day T-bills, and 364-day T-bills. The 14-day T-bills were discontinued from May 14, 2001. The 91-day auctions seek to manage the cash position of the government whose revenue collections are typically bunched towards the year end whereas revenue expenses are more evenly dispersed. Since April 1998, the practice of the notifying amounts in case of all auctions including 364-day T-bills has been introduced.

The minimum denomination of 91-day T-bills is Rs.25,000 while that of 364-day T-bills is Rs.1,00,000. The 91-day auctions occur every Wednesday and the 364-day on Wednesday preceding the reporting Fridays (fortnightly). Auctions are open to all resident individuals and corporates. Settlement for the auction occurs on the following Friday for both 91-day and 364-day T-bills. In 2001-02, the dates of payment for both 91day T-bills, and 364-day treasury bills had been synchronised so that they could provide adequate fungible stock of treasury bills of varying maturity in the secondary market.

**Table. Calendar for Auction of Treasury Bills**

| **Type of Treasury Bill** | **Periodicity** | **Notified Amount (Rs. in crore)** | **Day of Auction** | **Date of Payment** |
|---|---|---|---|---|
| 91-day | Weekly | 250 | Every Wednesday | Following Friday |
| 364-day | Fortnightly | 1,000 | Wednesday preceding the reporting Friday | Following Friday |

*Competitive Report, 2001-02:* T-bills are issued through

bidding wherein the competitive bidders are primary dealers, financial institutions, mutual funds, and banks. Besides these, individuals, corporate bodies, institutions, and trusts have been allowed to bid in government securities auctions. Bids can also be routed through both banks and primary dealers. Non-competitive bids are conducted to encourage participants who do not have sufficient expertise in bidding. The non-competitive bidders are state governments, municipalities, non-government provident funds, and other central banks. Non-competitive bids are kept outside the notified amount so that the non-competitive bidders do not face any uncertainty in purchasing the desired amount. Non- competitive bidders are issued T-bills at the weighted average price determined in auction. The uniform price auction method is in use for selling T-bills. In such an auction, all successful bidders pay a uniform price, which is usually the cut-off price.

There exists a fixed calendars for auctions of all types of treasury bills and the auction is announced in advance through a public notification. Government Dated Securities The government of India securities are medium to long-term obligations issued by the Reserve Bank on behalf of the government to finance the latter's deficit and public sector development programme. Government securities are predominantly coupon bearing and the coupon is paid semi annually on a 30/360 days basis. However, there are floating rate or zero coupon securities also. No TDS is applicable. All government securities are SLR eligible. The central government securities are eligible for ready forward (Repo) facility, whereas state loans are not eligible for repos. These securities are highly liquid.

Primary Market Issuance of Government Securities Government securities are issued either through:

- Auction,
- Sale,
- Private placement with the Reserve Bank.

*Auction:* Auction is a form of allocative mechanism whereby commodities and financial assets are allocated to individuals and firms, particularly in a market-oriented economy. The government's preference for the auction system for selling securities stems from the ability of auctions to reveal more information about price determination and improve the allocation process. Auctions are designed to generate higher volumes for meeting the target market requirement without recourse to underwriting and/or devolvement, broaden participation to ensure that bids are not concentrated or skewed, and ensure efficiency through lowering the cost of borrowing for the government.

In June 1992, the government switched from the fixed price tender offer to the auction system for sale of government securities. The government, as a part of its annual budget exercise, announces the borrowing programme for the financial year. The Reserve Bank, acting in the capacity of merchant banker for the government's borrowing programme, raises money on behalf of the government by auctioning securities from time to time depending on the government's need for money, interest rates, and liquidity in the banking system.

The primary market for government securities starts with an auction. A brief outline of the auction: The Reserve Bank announces the quantum, maturity, and date of the auction. On the day of the auction, all the participants submit their bid to the Reserve Bank. The bid includes the quantum and the yield at which they are bidding.

The Reserve Bank decides the cut-off yield on the basis of the competitive bids it has received and as own view of the interest rates. Once the cut-off yield is decided, bids the cut-off yield are accepted and bids the cut-off yield are rejected. -If the amount for which the bids are received falls short of the total quantum for which the auction is conducted, the Reserve Bank devolves the shortfall on itself or on the primary dealers (to the extent of their underwriting commitments). -The cut-off yield becomes the coupon rate of that particular security.

Lately, in order to promote liquidity in a particular security and to reduce the number of different government securities, the Reserve Bank has started issuing further tranches of existing securities in price based auction. Since the coupon rate and the maturity of the security are decided earlier, the bids are for the price. The auction procedure remains the same except that the bids higher than the cut-off price are accepted. Successful bidders are those that bid at a higher price, exhausting the accepted amount at the cut-off price. The multiple-price auctions are predominantly used in selling government securities. Since 1999-2000, most of the current primary issues of dated securities are through re-issues and price-based auctions, instead of yield-based auctions, to enable the consolidation of securities. Such consolidation is necessary for ensuring sufficient volumes and liquidity in any one issue, to facilitate emergence of benchmarks, and development of Separately Traded Registered Interest and Principal of Securities.

The uniform price auction format for auctions, which are confined to the auction of 91-day treasury bills, was extended to the auction of dated securities in November 2001. The government securities auction held on April 4, 2002, was also based on uniform price auction.

The government auctioned for the first time on July 17, 2002, a bond with call and put features. The notified amount was Rs.3,000 crore and the bond had a maturity of 10 years. On any coupon date on or after five years, the government can call the bond with two months notice. The investor also has the right to put the bond on the same terms.

*Non-Competitive Bidding:* The Reserve Bank introduced non-competitive bidding with a provision for allocation of upto 5 per cent of the notified amount in specified auctions of dated securities for allotment to retail investors on a non-competitive basis at the weighted average rate. The plan was operationalized from January 14, 2002, with the auction of 15 year government stock.

Retail investors such as individuals, firms, companies, corporate bodies, urban cooperative banks, institutions, provident funds, trusts, and any other entity as may be prescribed by the Reserve Bank are allowed to participate in auctions as non-competitive bidders. These bidders are required to submit their bids through banks and PDs. Allocation for non-competitive bidding is within the notified amount and if the amount tendered by the non-competitive bidders is less than the reserved amount, all participants receive the full amount and the shortfall is transferred to a competitive position. If the amount received is more than the reserved amount, a pro-rata allotment is made to applicants. A non-competitive bidder is permitted to submit only one bid in the auction with a minimum amount of Rs.10,000 and a maximum of Rs.1crore, Non-competitive bidders are issued securities at the weighted average price determined in competitive auctions. There does not exist a fixed calendar for auctions of dated government securities. However, the auction of a dated security is announced in advance through a public notification. The securities are issued to successful bidders in the form of stock certificates or by cedit to their SGL account.

*Sale:* Earlier, the Reserve Bank used to adopt the sale route instead of auctions. Here, the coupon rate and maturity are predetermined and the securities are sold to investors at par. This approach is used predominantly for state loans. Of late, some states have tried the auction method successfully. As part of its open market operations, the Reserve Bank often sells outstanding securities (devolved or privately placed with itself earlier) through its sale window at preannounced prices.

*Private placement with the Reserve Bank:* There are times when there is very tight liquidity in the banking system or when investors expect very high yields on the one hand and on the other, the Reserve Bank to hold an auction/sale. The Reserve Bank then places the securities with itself and funds the government. These securities are later sold in the market through its sale window at an opportune time. In this way, the Reserve Bank also signals its view on the interest rate. The Reserve bank's ultimate objective is to move away from the primary market. Keeping this objective in view, a system of underwriting was oriented towards facilitating larger absorption by primary dealers.

## *Ownership Pattern of Central and State Government Securities*

The subscribers to government securities are the Reserve

Bank, commercial banks, insurance companies, mutual funds, provident funds and others. Ownership Pattern of Central and State Government Securities (Percentage to Outstanding Government Securities)

| Year | Subscribers | | | | |
|---|---|---|---|---|---|
| | RBI | Commercial Banks | LIC | Provident Funds | Others |
| 1990-91 | 20.3 | 59.4 | 12.3 | 1.7 | 6.3 |
| 1991-92 | 17.9 | 63.7 | 13.3 | 1.5 | 3.6 |
| 1992-93 | 8.2 | 66.4 | 14.7 | 1.5 | 9.2 |
| 1993-94 | 2.4 | 72.5 | 15.8 | 1.1 | 8.2 |
| 1994-95 | 2.0 | 69.6 | 16.2 | 1.0 | 11.2 |
| 1995-96 | 7.3 | 64.9 | 16.8 | 1.5 | 9.5 |
| 1996-97 | 2.8 | 67.3 | 18.7 | 1.9 | 9.3 |
| 1997-98 | 10.7 | 59.0 | 18.0 | 2.1 | 10.2 |
| 1998-99 | 9.1 | 59.5 | 17.8 | 1.8 | 11.8 |
| 1999-2000 | 7.0 | 60.9 | 18.1 | 2.0 | 13.0 |
| 2000-01 | 7.7 | - | 18.3 | 2.4 | - |

*Statistics on Indian Economy, 2001*: The market continues to be dominated by captive investors such as commercial banks and insurance companies. Banks have traditionally been the dominant investors the government securities due to SLR requirements.

The investment of commercial banks constitutes, on an average, 65 per cent of the stock of government securities even through the SLR of the banks was significantly lowered to 25 per cent in 1997. Banks have found it advantageous to invest in government securities beyond the statutory requirements due to attractive market related interest rates offered since 1992-93, zero- risk nature of these securities, and depressed commercial credit market.

The Reserve Bank's holding of government securities declined steeply in 1994-95 to 2.0 per cent from 20.3 per cent in 1990-91. This reflects that the government securities market has developed after reforms. However, this trend reversed in 1997-98 with the surge in the Reserve Bank's holdings to 10.7

per cent as special securities in the bank's portfolio were converted to marketable lots with a view to facilitating open market operations.

### *Maturity Structure of Central Government Dated Securities Outstanding*

With a move towards market related interest rates for meeting the borrowing requirements of the central government, there has been a significant shift in the maturity pattern of central government dated securities. The maturity structure of dated securities was highly skewed at the short end. The government's heavy dependence on short to medium-term securities for the mobilization of market borrowing was due to uncertainty in market conditions and investor preference for short-term maturities.

Moreover, it was a conscious policy on the part of the government to minimize the cost borrowing by placing a large part of the borrowings at the shorter end of the market. This maturity structure tilted towards short-term securities, which led to significant higher gross borrowings to adhere to the repayment schedule. To avoid such high cost borrowings and redemption pressure entailing refinance risk, a conscious decision was taken to lengthen the maturity profile of new securities. Since 1998-99, the government has avoided excessive maturities at the short end and the trend is towards issue of long-term securities.

**Table. Maturity Structure of Central Government Dated Securities Outstanding**

*(per cent of total primary issues)*

| Year | Over 10 years | Between 5 and 10 years | Under 5 years |
|---|---|---|---|
| 1995-96 | – | 36.5 | 63.5 |
| 1996-97 | – | 36.0 | 64.0 |
| 1997-98 | – | 63.1 | 36.9 |
| 1998-99 | 13.5 | 55.0 | 31.5 |
| 1999-2000 | 65.0 | 35.0 | – |
| 2000-01 | 52.5 | 35.0 | 12.5 |
| 2001-02 | 84.2 | 14.0 | 1.8 |

In view of the bunching of redemption liabilities in the medium-term, no securities with maturities of less than five years were issued during 1999-2000. About 65 per cent of the total primary issues was raised through securities of 10 years maturity in 1999-2000 as against 13.5 per cent in 1998-99. The market participants also found the long-term paper to be attractive due to low inflationary expectations and improvement in liquidity.

As a result, the weighted average maturity of dated securities during 1999-2000 increased to 12.64 years from 7.7 years in 1998-99 and 6.6 years in 1997-98. The weighted average maturity of debt dropped from 12.64 years to 10.6 years during 2000-01. This was due to the issue of short-term securities to accommodate the market's preference for short-term paper during the phases of market uncertainty. The weighted average maturity again rose to 14.3 years in 2001-02. The low inflation rate and development of the government securities market helped in the successful elongation of maturity.

### *Interest Rates in the Primary Market*

The interest rates in the primary market are influenced by the prevailing liquidity conditions, Reserve Bank's intervention by way of devolvement and private placement, and amount and frequency of issues during the year.

The weighted average interest rate of dated securities of the Centre progressively rose from 11.41 per cent in 1990-91 to 13.75 per cent in 1995-96 The increased recourse to borrowing from the market and spells of tight liquidity put pressure on interest rates. Since 1996-1997, the interest rates have declined; in the year 1999- 2000, the interest rates were very close to the interest rates in 1991- 92. Inspite of an increase in the market borrowing of the central government, the Reserve Bank was in a position to contain the interest rates. The Reserve Bank accepts the private placement of government stocks and releases them to the market when interest rate expectations become favourable. This policy of the Reserve Bank moderates the adverse impact. Weighted Average Coupon Rates on Government of India Dated Securities

*(Per cent per annum)*

| FiscalYear | Weighted average coupon rate | Range |
|---|---|---|
| 1990-91 | 11.41 | 10.50-11.50 |
| 1991-92 | 11.78 | 10.50-12.50 |
| 1992-93 | 12.46 | 12.00-12.75 |
| 1993-94 | 12.63 | 12.00-13.40 |
| 1994-95 | 11.90 | 11.00-12.71 |
| 1995-96 | 13.75 | 13.25-14.00 |
| 1996-97 | 13.69 | 13.40-13.85 |
| 1997-98 | 12.01 | 10.85-13.05 |
| 1998-99 | 11.86 | 11.10-12.60 |
| 1999-2000 | 11.77 | 10.73-12.45 |
| 2000-01 | 10.95 | 9.47-11.70 |
| 2001-02 | 9.44 | 6.98-11.00 |

## *Government Dated Securities-Secondary Market*

Secondary market in government securities can be categorised into two segments:

- Wholesale institutional segment and
- Retail segment.
- The wholesale institutional segment consists of active traders, mainly large banks, primary dealers, mutual funds, insurance companies, and others. The securities are traded in the SGL from and the market lot is Rs.5 crore. The secondary market for government securities is wholesale in nature, with most deals negotiated on telephone. The trades are generally closed on the telephone, which are then reported on the wholesale Debt Market segment of the National Stock Exchange. Trades are then settled through the Reserve Bank, which acts as a depositing-cum-clearing house.
- The retail segment includes cooperative banks, provident funds, non-banking finance companies, and others. The securities are traded in the SGL or physical form and the lots are odd, that is, less than Rs.1 crore. Trades are settled directly by the counter

parties and these trades may or may not be reported on the exchange. The high costs involved may not make it viable for the broker to report the transaction on the exchange.

With a view to promoting the retail market segment and providing greater liquidity to retail investors, banks were allowed to freely buy and sell government securities on an outright basis at prevailing market prices, without any restriction on the period between sale and purchase. Banks were permitted to undertake transactions in securities among themselves or with non-bank clients through the members of OTCEI in addition to NSE.

The interest income on government securities was exempted from the provisions of tax deduction at source with effect from June 1997 to facilitate quotations and trading in the secondary market. At present, the government securities market is predominantly institutional.

***Trading System***

Government securities do not have to be listed on an exchange. All government securities are deemed listed as and when they are issued.

The National Stock Exchange was the first stock exchange to introduce a transparent, screen-based trading system in the wholesale debt market including government securities in June 1994. Prior to the commencement of trading in the WDM segment of NSE, the only trading mechanism available in the debt market was the telephone. NSE provided, for the first time in the country, an online, automated, screen-based system known as National Exchange for Automated Trading across a wide range of debt instruments.

This system is an order-driven system which matches the best buy and sell orders on a price time priority and simultaneously protects the identity of the buyer and seller. Trading under this system leads to a risk-free, efficient price mechanism and transparency. The trades on the WDM segment could be outright trades or repo transactions with flexibility for varying days of settlement (T+0 to T+5) and repo periods (3-14 days). Order matching is carried out only between orders which carry the same conditions with respect to settlement days, trade type, and repo period, if any.

The OTCEI also started trading in government securities in July, 1997. The NSE and OTCEI members are authorised to transact business on behalf of commercial banks. Non-banking clients may also trade via brokers. In order to provide another platform for trading in government securities, the Reserve Bank permitted trading in government securities at the Bombay Stock Exchange in October 2000. The trading, however, commenced in June 2001. The Reserve Bank announced, in 2000-01, its decision to move over in due course to order-driven screen based trading in government securities on all stock exchanges.

*Settlements:* The government securities can be held and transacted in two forms- dematerialised SGL form and physical form. Registration of the participant with the Public Debt Office of the Reserve Bank is mandatory in case of holding and trading securities in the physical form.

### *Subsidiary General Ledger (SGL) Account*

The Reserve Bank acts as a depository-cum-clearing house settlement is through accounts maintained with the Reserve Bank called the Subsidiary General Ledger (SGL) accounts. The physical securities are dematerialised and the relevant holdings are in the form of book entries. Every participant in the government securities market maintains SGL and current accounts with the Reserve Bank. Those not eligible to maintain direct accounts with the Reserve Banks have the facility to open constituent SGL accounts or SGL II accounts with banks who have direct SGL accounts.

The Reserve Bank has permitted the National Securities Clearing Corporation Limited (NSCCL), banks, insurance companies, financial institutions, and primary dealers to offer constituent SGL account facility to an investor who is interested in participating in the government securities market. Any trade among participants are settled via this facility. The parties exchange the relevant SGL instruction receipts and the mode of transaction is delivery versus payment. The DVP system ensures settlement by synchronising the transfer of securities with cash payment.

The Reserve Bank settles only on DVP-I basis where both funds and securities are settled on a gross basis. For all transactions undertaken directly between SGL participants, the settlement period is of T+0 or T+1 days while for transactions routed through brokers of NSE, BSE, or OTCEI, the settlement period is upto T+5 days. Participants have the flexibility to decide the terms of settlement. Trades are settled by T+3, if desired by participants. This reduces settlement risks in securities transactions and also prevents diversion of funds through SGL transactions.

SGL accounts are maintained by the Public Debt Office (PDO). The PDO oversees the settlement of transactions through SGL and enables the transfer of securities from one participant to another. The seller fills up the SGL form, the buyer countersigns it, and the seller sends.

This form to the Reserve Bank. The buyer transfers funds towards payment. Inter-bank government securities trades are settled on the same business day while trades with non-bank counter parties settle either on the same day or upto five business days after the trade date. Secondary market trades in government securities between banks are carried on upto 1.00 p.m. on business days and settled on the same day. Trades after that are settled the next day.

The transfer of government securities does not attract stamp duty or transfer fee. Moreover, there is no tax education at source on these securities.

Trade in the physical form is settled by the parties directly. Securities are delivered in the form of a physical certificate along with the transfer deed duly executed by the authorised signatures of the transferor. The transferee has to lodge the certificates with the Reserve Bank for transfer.

### *Tools for Managing Liquidity in the Government Securities Market*

The Reserve Bank uses basically two tools to manage

liquidity in the government securities market. These are repos and open market operations.. The Reserve Bank manages short-term liquidity through repos and reverse repos and long-term liquidity through open market sales to absorb liquidity in conjunction with private placement/devolvement and open market purchases in tight liquidity conditions.

*Open Market Operations (OMO):* Open market operation is an important tool of liquidity management. OMOs are actively used to neutralise excess liquidity in the system and to contain wide fluctuations in the domestic money and foreign exchange markets.

It is an actively used technique of monetary control in developed countries such as the UK, and USA. OMOs directly affect the availability and cost of credit. Its two objectives are:

- To influence the reserves of commercial banks, in order to control their power of credit creation
- To affect the market rates of interest.

OMOs involve the sale or purchase of government securities by the central bank. When the Reserve Bank sells government securities in the market, it withdraws a part of the deposit resources of the banks, thereby reducing the resources available with the banks for lending. The bank's capacity to create credit, that is, give fresh loans, depends upon its surplus cash, that is, the amount of cash resources in excess of the statutory CRR stipulated by the Reserve Bank. The open market sale of securities reduces the surplus cash resources of banks as these resources are used to purchase government securities. Banks have to contract their credit supply to generate some cash resources to meet the CRR.

The supply of bank credit which involves the creation of demand deposit falls and money supply contracts. The reverse happens when the Reserve Bank undertakes open market purchase of government securities. The open market purchase of securities leads to reduction in the stock of securities of the seller bank and an expansion in the free surplus cash which augments the credit creation capacity of banks. The result is an expansion in the supply of bank credit and an increase in money supply.

Open market operations do not alter the total stock of government securities but change the proportion of government securities held by the Reserve Bank and commercial and cooperative banks. Open market sales result in a fall in net RBI credit to government (NRCG) and an increase in the other banks' (cooperative and commercial) credit to government (OBCG) without affecting the budget (fiscal) deficit in anyway.

The Reserve Bank resorts to private placement when market conditions for government securities is not favourable and conducts open market sales later when liquidity conditions turn favourable.

Thus, the Reserve Bank influences the resources position of banks, yields on government securities, and cost of bank credit through the open market sale and purchase of government securities.

The Reserve Bank can buy or sell or hold government securities of all maturities without any restrictions. The bank purchased and sold government securities upto 1991-92 out of the surplus funds of IDBI, Exim Bank, NABARD, and other institutions under a special buy back arrangement. Till 1991-92, the market of open market operations was quite narrow as interest rates were administered and the government securities market was not broad based either. However, with the initiation of several measures to promote both primary and secondary markets in government securities, the OMO market has become active and OMOs have emerged as an important tool of debt management.

Various steps have been taken to alter the composition, maturity structure, and yield of government securities. The Reserve Bank also introduced the sale of securities from its own account on the basis of repo. Besides this, the bank offers for sale only a select number of securities which it wishes to undertake in response to market conditions, instead of maintaining a list including all dated securities in its portfolio. The Reserve Bank has also put on its purchase list a couple of securities for cash with a view to providing liquidity to at least a few securities.

In a move to augment the stock of marketable securities for active OMOs, special securities of value aggregating Rs.15,000 crore at 4.6 per cent were converted into marketable securities of 10 year, 7- year, and 8-year maturities at 13.05 per cent, 12.59 per cent, and 11.19 per cent on June 3, June 18, and August 12,1997, respectively. The cost of additional interest on account of this conversion is fully borne by the Reserve bank and is paid to the government as part of transfer of profits from year to year. The Reserve Bank included treasury bills of varying maturities in the OMOs in 1998-99. The resort to OMOs epitomises the move from direct to indirect instruments of monetary control. OMOs have been successfully used by the Reserve Bank to groom or switch operations, that is, the sale of long-term scripts in exchange for short-term loans. This helps in lengthening the maturity structure of government securities which, in turn, becomes favourable for the working of the monetary policy.

The volume of Reserve Bank's net sales (salespurchase) increased over the years except in the year 1994-95 when tight money market conditions prevailed. Since 1996-97, OMOs have come into a sharper focus. The stock of marketable securities was augmented by conversion of special securities into marketable securities for conducting active OMOs.

During 1996-97, outright sale of securities came into prominence to absorb excess liquidity which was due to large capital inflows and to maintain domestic interest rate and exchange rate at reasonable levels. The Reserve Bank did not purchase any security during 1998-99 through its OMO window. The open market sale rose significantly by 290 per cent in 1998-99.

An important aspect in the OMO during 1998-99 was the inclusion of treasury bills of varying maturities. In 2000-01, due to uncertain foreign exchange market conditions and unfavourable market conditions for government securities, the Reserve Bank privately placed securities with itself. The securities were subsequently sold on-tap basis and through OMO auctions. The Reserve Bank's Open Market Operations in Central Government Securities

| Year | Purchases | Sales | Net sales (-)<br>Net purchase(+) |
|---|---|---|---|
| 1990-91 | 2,291.2 (14,287.1) | 2,238.1(13,725.2) | +53.1 (431.8) |
| 1991-92 | 3,244.8 (5,321.7) | 7,327.1(9.365.6) | -4,082.3 (-4,043.9) |
| 1992-93 | 6,273.4 | 11,792.5 | -5,519.1 |
| 1993-94 | 967.6 | 10,804.6 | -9.837.0 |
| 1994-95 | 1,560.98 | 2,309.03 | -748.05 |
| 1995-96 | 1,645.24 | 1,130.89 | +514.35 |
| 1996-97 | 633.95 | 11,097.55 | -10,463.60 |
| 1997-98 | 466.50 | 8,081.49 | -7,614.94 |
| 1998-99 | | 2,348.3 (GDS)<br>3,230.0 (T-bills) | -26,348.3<br>(Govt. securities)<br>-3,230.0 (T-bills) |
| 1999-2000 | 1,244.00 (GDS)<br>5,700.50 (T-bills) | 36,613.51 (GDS)<br>1,191.91 (T-bills) | -35,369.51 (GDS)<br>+4,508.59 (T-bills) |
| 2000-01 | 4,471.05 (GDS)<br>5.00 (T-bills) | 23,795.1 (GDS)<br>2,679.00 (T-bills) | -19,324.05 (GDS)<br>-2,674 (T-bills) |
| 2001-02 | 5,084 (GDS) | 35,418.59 (GDS) | -30,334.59 (GDS) |

The Reserve Bank conducted a series of open market purchases aggregating Rs.5,084 crore during September 18-October 10,2001, to support the government securities market in the face of the steep fall in the government securities prices due to adverse external developments after September 11, 2001. Subsequently, with stability in market conditions and easing of liquidity, it resorted to open market sales. These sales helped the Reserve Bank to absorb surplus liquidity on an enduring basis, stabilizing the prices of government securities, and offloading the securities privately placed with it.

### *Infrastructure Development of the Government Securities Market*

The government securities market constitutes the principal segment of the debt market. The development of any market requires the strengthening of the market infrastructure with large number of market players who have divergent perceptions about the market and who would continuously provide liquidity. One of the initiatives taken to develop the government securities market during the first stage of the reform process was the setting up of Securities Trading Corporation of India (STCI). The STCI together with Discount and Finance House of India (DFHI) had the task of developing an active secondary market in government securities.

The Reserve Bank introduced the primary dealer system and satellite dealer system to further strengthen the market infrastructure.

*Primary Dealer System*

A system of primary dealers was introduced in 1996, to further strengthen the market infrastructure and to make it more liquid and broad based.

*The objectives of the introduction of this system were*:

- To strengthen the government securities infrastructure;
- To bring about improvements in the secondary market trading, liquidity and turnover in government securities;
- To encourage a voluntary holding of government securities amongst a wider investor base; and
- To make PDs an effective conduit of open market operations.

The major focus of PDs would be on increasing the turnover of government securities rather than becoming a mere repository of this system. Hence, their role would be to performance as market makers by providing two-way quotes in the secondary market, thereby ensuring liquidity and support to the primary market operation. In the long run, this system would facilitate the transfer of market-making activities from the Reserve Bank to primary dealers.

PDs can be subsidiaries of scheduled commercial banks, subsidiaries of all-India financial institutions, companies under Companies Act, 1956 engaged predominantly in government securities market, and subsidiaries of foreign banks/securities firms. Every PD has to maintain minimum net owned funds of Rs.50 crore deployed daily in the government securities market. PDs institutional entities fall in the category of non-banking finance companies. PDs are registered with and regulated by the Reserve Bank of India, irrespective of whether they accept public deposits or not.

*Obligations upon PDs Facilities Extended to them:* In order to enable PDs to perform their role effectively, the Reserve Bank has cast certain obligations upon PDs which include an annual minimum bidding for dated securities and treasury bills with a minimum success ratio and commitment to underwrite the shortfall (gap) between the subscribed accepted amount and the notified amount. PDs have to achieve an annual turnover of not less than five times of average month-end stocks during the year in dated securities and ten times in treasury bills, within which outright transactions should be three and six times respectively.

To strengthen this system and to make PDs fulfil their obligations, the Reserve Bank extends to them various facilities like access to SGL and current account facility with the Reserve Bank, liquidity support through reverse repos linked to both bidding commitment and performance of PDs in the primary and secondary markets, freedom to deal in money market instruments, facility of transfer of funds from one centre to another under the Reserve Bank's Remittance Facility Plan, exclusive access to open market operations in treasury bills since February 2000 and a switch facility Plan, exclusive access to open market operations in treasury bills since February 2000 and a'switch facility' to swap their medium to long-term dated government securities with 364-day treasury bills during August 2000. Routing operations in the call money market are allowed through all PDs to increase their profitability. PDs are allowed to issue commercial papers (CPs) to raise resources.

The Reserve Bank provides liquidity support to PDs through repos/ refinance against central government securities under three levels. At the first level, normal refinance at bank rate is provided upto a specified amount. A backstop refinance at a variable rate upto a fixed amount is provided at the second level. Finally, discretionary support is extended through Liquidity Adjustment Facility (LAF). The total assured liquidity support for all PDs together is about Rs.4,500 crore for 2002-03 as against Rs.6,000 crore during 2001-02, of which two- third is under the normal facility and one-third under the backstop facility. If any PD in any auction of treasury bills, fails to submit the required minimum bid or submits a bid lower than its commitment, the Reserve Bank will reduce liquidity support to the extent of shortfall/failure in submission of bids for a period of three months from the date so specified by the Bank. For instance, if a bid is short by an amount of Rs.10 crore, liquidity support will be reduced by an amount of Rs.10crore for 3 months.

Act, 1934, the borrowings by commercial/cooperative banks from them is netted for reckoning their demand and time liabilities for computation of cash reserves.

PDs are expected to substantially underwrite the primary issues of government securities and treasury bills. In view of the increasing trend in government borrowings, the role of PDs in enhancing the market for government securities is becoming crucial. PDs give two- way quotes in the Press/Reuters screen and bid in the auctions of 91-day/364-day treasury bils and in the floatation of new loans. PDs are permitted to participate in the call/notice money market, term money market, and bill rediscounting plan both as lenders and borrowers. The system of payment of commission on purchase of securities was replace in 1997-98 by a system of underwriting fees on the amount underwritten by them through competitive bids. The uniform pricing approach is used in accepting bids for underwriting.

The system of underwriting facilitates larger absorption by PDs, keeping in view the Reserve Bank's ultimate objective of moving away from the primary market. The underwriting commitment of each PD is broadly decided on the basis of its size, in terms of its net owned funds, its holding strength, committed amount of bids, and volume of turnover in government securities. In case of auctions of treasury bills, PDs are no longer required to undertake devolvement. Hence, the payment of commission for treasury bills was withdrawn with effect from June 5, 2001-02, a revised plan for bidding and underwriting was announced. PDs are also given a favoured access to the Reserve Bank's OMOs.

Number of PDs DFHI and STCI were accredited as dealers on March 1, 1996. ON June 1, 1996, four more PDs-SBI gilts, PNB gilts, Gilts Securities Trading Corporation Limited, and ICICI Securities -became operational. As on March 31, 2002, there were 18 approved PDs in

the gilts market. The initial six PDs constitute the subsidiaries of RBI/nationalized banks/financial institutions, while the remaining new PDs represent private sector participants. These 18 PDs have net owned funds of over Rs.4,000 crore and total assets of Rs.15,658 crore out of which government securities constitute Rs.12,236 core (78 per cent of total assets).

### *Primary Dealers Association of India (PDAI)*

PDs formed an autonomous, self-regulatory organisation (SRO), Primary Dealers Association of India (PDAI) in 1996. The role of PDAI is

- To promote a liquid debt market and set common standards for market participants;
- To achieve a harmonious integration of different segments of markets;
- To build a healthy relationship between different segments of market participants; and
- To remove some legal, procedural, and administrative bottlenecks in the efficient functioning of the market.

Banks and PDs together formed another autonomous self-regulatory body. Fixed Income Money Market and Derivatives Association of India (FIMMDAI), in 1997.

These two SROs have been proactive and the closely involved in contemporary issues relating to the development of the money market and government securities market. The credit for upgrading the technological infrastructure in these two markets goes to these two SROs. The representatives of the PDAI and FIMMDAI are members of the Technical Advisory Group on Money and Government Securities

Markets of the Reserve Bank. The FIMMDAI has now taken over the responsibility of publishing the yield curve in the debt markets. The FIMMDAI prepared the guidelines for standard procedures and documentation to be followed by the participants in the commercial paper market and certificate of deposit (CD) market. Currently, the FIMMDAI is working towards the development of uniform documentation and accounting principles of repo market.

*Satellite Dealers:* In order to widen the scope for organised dealing and distribution arrangement in the government securities market and to support the system of primary dealers, the Reserve Bank introduced a supporting infrastructure in the form of satellite dealers. SDs form the second tier of trading and distribution of government securities.

The guidelines for registration of satellite dealers in government securities market were announced on December 31, 1996. The guidelines, subsidiaries of scheduled commercial banks and all-India financial institutions (AIFIs) and companies incorporated under Companies Act, 1956 with minimum net owned funds of Rs.5 crore were eligible to be SDs. In pursurance of these guidelines, the Reserve Bank granted approval to 16 entities for registration as SDs in the government securities market. SDs were permitted to issue commercial papers for raising resources and could avail of liquidity support from the Reserve Bank and the facility of ready forward transactions. Some of the satellite dealers were promoted as primary dealers. The network of satellite dealers was created to promote the retailing of government securities but the performance of the satellite dealers was not found to be satisfactory. The Reserve Bank decided to discontinue the system after obtaining the view of the Primary Dealers Association of India. No new SDs will be licensed and existing SDs were required to make action plans satisfactory to the Reserve Bank for termination of their operations as SDs by May 31, 2002.

### *Measures to Strengthen the Government Securities Market Infrastructure*

For bringing about an improvement in trading and

settlement in the money market and government securities market, the Negotiated Dealing System (NDS) and Cleaning Corporation of India Limited (CCIL) have been setup.

Negotiated Dealing System: The Reserve Bank introduced NDSE with a view to reforming the secondary market in government securities and money market operations, introducing transparency, and facilitating electronic bidding in auctions. Test turns on the NDS started in November 2001 and phase I was operationalised from February 15, 2002 with 41 participants.

The NDS provides an on-line electronic bidding facility in the primary auctions of central/state government securities, OMOs/LAF auctions. It enables screen -based electronic dealing and reporting of transactions in money market instruments including repo, secondary market transactions in government securities, and dissemination of information on trades with the least time lags.

The NDS is integrated with the Securities Settlement System (SSS), of the Public Debt Office as also with the CCIL to facilitate paperless settlement of transactions in government securities and treasury bills and bring about improvement in services to investors in government securities. Once a trade is done/reported over NDS, it can be settled either through CCIL or directly through RBI-SGL. Settlement through CCIL is on Delivery versus Payment (DVP-II) mechanism. DVP-II refers to settlement of securities on gross basis (trade by trade basis) while funds will settle on net basis.

Banks, primary dealers, and financial institutions having SGL accounts and current accounts with the Reserve Bank are eligible to participate in NDS. It provides an electronic dealing platform for these participants in government securities. It enables the execution of deals in both the computer matching mode or a chat mode for negotiating deals on the system itself. Members are expected to report all the trades negotiated outside the system for settlement. If facilitates member participation in the primary auctions of government securities and treasury bills by submitting their bids/applications for auctions/ floatation through their own terminals or pooled terminals. The pooled terminal facility is provided at all regional offices for use by SGL account holders not having member terminals. NDS is used by the Reserve Bank for extending the liquidity adjustment facility to eligible members. All entities having SGL accounts with the Reserve Bank were advised to become members eligible members of the NDS by May 31, 2002. Till Agusut 5, 2002, 138 SGL account holders were members of NDS. On an average, 526 deals were reported daily on NDS, of which 473 deals for Rs.11,688 crore were ready for settlement during the quarter ended June 2002. These deals comprised money market deals (109 deals for Rs. 8,762 crore), outright government securities trades (344 deals for Rs.2,080 crore) and repo transactions among member participants. The settlement of the government securities transactions through the CCIL constituted 91.3 per cent of the total government securities trades dealt/reported on the NDS.

The NDS has brought about significant improvements in secondary markets also. It has helped in increasing the level of transparency of the dealings in government securities, T-bills, and other instruments. The system has facilitated screen-based trading, provision of on-line trade information, and reporting through trade execution system for settlement.

Clearing Corporation of India Limited: The Clearing Corporation of India Limited (CCIL) was registered on April 30, 2001 under the Companies Act, 1956. The State Bank of India is the chief promoter of CCIL. Its other promoters are banks, financial institutions, and primary dealers. It has been set up as an ordinary, limited liability, non-government company under the Companies Act, 1956 with an equity capital of Rs.50 crore. It functions like a business entity that is subject to corporate tax on its business profits.

It acts as the central counterparty in the settlement of all trades in government securities, treasury bills, money market instruments, repos, inter-bank foreign exchange deals, and derivatives of any kind where the underlying instrument is a security or money market instrument. CCIL is the clearing and settling agency in respect of all trades by institutional players such as banks, DFIs, primary dealers, mutual funds, corporates, and NBFCs who account for more than 98 per cent of the total trades.

In foreign exchange transactions, CCIL resorts to loss allocation mechanism to manage credit and market risk and restricts the membership to authorised dealers only.

To ensure liquidity for uninterrupted settlements, CCIL has arranged rupee securities through member contributions to the SGF, rupee funds through line of credit with various banks, and US dollar funds by way of a fully collateralised line of credit with the settlement bank.

To deal with operational risk, CCIL is developing a fully automated system for processing trades. A Disaster Recovery Site is being set up at the Institute for Development and Research in Banking Technology (IDRBT), Hyderabad, to ensure business continuity in case of a disaster.

The government raises short-term and long-term funds by issuing securities. These securities do not carry no risk and are as good as the government guarantees the payment of interest and the repayment of principal. The government generates revenue in the form of taxes and income from ownership of assets. Besides these, it borrows extensively from banks, financial institutions, and the public to finance its expenditure in excess of its revenues. Government securities are of two types: treasury bills and government dated securities. The latter carry varying coupon rates and are of different maturities. Sometimes, the Reserve Bank converts maturing treasury bills into bonds thereby rolling over the government's debt. The interest rates in the primary market are influenced by the prevailing liquidity conditions. Reserve Bank's intervention by way of devolvement and private placement, and amount and frequency of issues during the year. With a view to promoting the retail market segment and providing greater liquidity to retail investors, banks were allowed to freely buy and sell government securities on an outright basis at prevailing market prices, without any restriction on the period between sale and purchase.

Banks were permitted to undertake transactions in securities among themselves or with non-bank clients through the members of OTCEI in addition to NSE. The Reserve Bank manages short-term liquidity through repos and reverse repos and long-term liquidity through open market sales to absorb liquidity in conjunction with private placement/devolvement and open market purchases in tight liquidity conditions. A system of primary dealers was introduced in 1 9 9 6, to further strengthen the market infrastructure and to make it more liquid and broad based.

In order to widen the scope for organised dealing and distribution arrangement in the government securities market and to support the system of primary dealers, the Reserve Bank introduced a supportinginfrastructure in the form of satellite dealers. SDs form the second tier of trading and distribution of government securities. For bringing about an improvement in trading and settlement in the money market and government securities market, the Negotiated Dealing System (NDS) and Cleaning Corporation of India Limited have been setup.

# 10

# Efficient Market Theory

## INTRODUCTION

The fundamental approach, the security analyst or prospective investor is primarily interested in analyzing factors such as economic influences, industry factors, and pertinent company information such as product demand, earnings, dividends, and management, in order to calculate an intrinsic value for the firm's securities. He reaches an investment decision by comparing this value with the current market price of the security.

Technical analysts believe that they can discern patterns in price or volume movements, and that by observing and studying the past behaviour patterns of given stocks, they can use this accumulated historical information to predict the future price movements in the security. Technical analysis,, comprises many different subjective approaches, but all have one thing in common- a belief that these past movements are very useful in predicting future movements.

Financial Markets are influenced by money flows and information flows. In free and highly competitive markets, demand and supply pressures determine the prices or interest rates. In a theoretical sense, markets are said to be efficient, if there is a free flow of information and market absorbs this information fully and quickly. James Lorie has defined the efficient security market as follows:

"Efficiency...means the ability of the capital market to function, so that prices of securities react rapidly to new information. Such efficiency will produce prices that are appropriate in terms of current knowledge, and investors will be less likely to make unwise investments."

What will happen is that market making mechanism is free and unfettered. There are no pockets with holding information or interested parties making undue gains by insider information by manipulation of supply and demand forces. There will be no monopoly elements and malpractices or corruption etc. are not prevalent. Information flow is free and costless. In the normal course, capital or money flows into areas which are most profitable which in turn depends on their efficiency and competitiveness.

Money flows also from less profitable to more profitable avenues if information flow is free, fast and costless. In such market scenario, all investors will have the same information, which is immediately reflected in the stock prices and nobody can gain extra profits. Al instru- ments in the market will be correctly priced, as all the available infomration is perectly absorbed and any investor entering the market any time will have the same advantage or returns. No excess profits are possible in this scenario. As the demand and supply forces are playing their role freely, the emerging prices are fair and move in a randon manner.

Prices of today are no more a function of the prices in the past as the day-to-day forces move in an independent and random manner. This concept of randomness has led to the theory of random Walk in the determination of prices. This Random Walk hypothesis is thus a special case of the Efficient Market Theory.

*Assumptions*

For the capital market efficiency theory to operate, the following assumptions are made

- Infomration is free and quick to flow.
- All investors have the same access to information.
- Transaction costs, taxes and any bottlenecks are not there and not hampering the free forces of market.
- Investors are rational and beahve in a cost effective competitive manner for optimization of returns.

- Every investor has access to lending and borrowing at the same rate.
- Market prices are not stickly and absorb the market information quickly and the market responds to new technology, new trends, changes in tastes, habits of consumers etc., efficiently adn quickly.

In essence, the technician says that it is somewhat an exercise in futility to evaluate accurately a myriad of detailed information as the fundamentalist attempts to do. He chooses not to engage in this type of activity, but rather to allow others to do it for him. Thus, after numerous analysts and investors evaluate this mountain of knowledge, their undoubtedly diverse opinions will be manifested in the price and volume activity of the shares in question. As this occurs, the technician acts solely on the basis of that price and volume activity, without cluttering his mind with all the detail that he feels is superfluous to his analysis. He also believes that his price and volume analysis incorporates one factor that is not explicitly incorporated in the fundamentalist approach-namely, the psychology of the market.

## RANDOM WALK THEORY

Random walk theory poses a question- Can a series of historical stock prices or rates of return be an aid in predicting future stock prices or rates of return?

As per this theory, changes in stock prices are independent of each other. The prices of today are independent of the past trends. The present price is randomly determined and only information flow can influence prices. As information is free and independent, the resulting prices are free and independent.

A word of caution is necessary here. This Random walk hypothesis was postulated by researchers on the basis of empirical work on the market price behaviour. It does not therefore tantamount to the same theory as the capital market efficiency theory. Only market efficiency promotes randomness and is therefore not a necessary condition. The fact that prices move independently has been found empirically and the analysts found an explanation for this in the efficient function- ing of the markets and the market absorption of the information quickly and efficiently. The equilibrium price of a stock is determined by demand and supply forces, based on the available information. Quickly as the fresh information becomes available, a new equilibrium point is reached and the resultant price is thus independent of the part. This Random walk hypothesis contradicts the Chartist and Technical School which believes that the present prices are the result of the past trends and that averages discount all fluctua- tions and that the average trends move in a predictable manner as the history of trends repeats itself. On the other hand, fundamental school postulates that the prices are a function of the intrinsic value pf the stock and prices result from changes i the intrinsic value and information relating to fundamental factors influence the equilibrium prices. Random walk hypoth- esis is an offshoot or a phase of the capital market efficiency theorem. The market efficiency theory postulates that prices are the result of free flow of information which the market absorbs quickly and efficiently.

## Assumption of Random Walk Theory

- Market is supreme and no individual investor or group can influence it.
- Stock prices discount all information quickly.
- Markets are efficient and that the flow of information is free and unbiased.
- All investors have free access to the same information and nobody has superior knowledge or expertise.
- Market quickly adjusts itself to any deviation from equilibrium level due to the operation of free forces of demand and supply.
- Market prices change only on information relating to the fundamentals, when the equilibrium level itself may shift.
- These prices move in an independent fashion, witin undue pressures or manipulation.
- Nobody has better knowledge or insider information.

- Investors behave in a rational manner and emand and supply forces are the result of rational investmnt decisions.
- Institutional investors or any major fund managers have to follow the market and market cannot be influenced by them.
- A large number of buyers & sellers and perfect market conditions of competition will prevail;

## Random Walk and Efficient Market Theory

Random Walk hypothesis is considered as restatement or a form of Efficint Market Theory by some Analysts. The EM - (Efficient Market Hypothesis) is based on the flow of free and correct information and the market absorption of it. This information flow and its absorption by the market are the critical elements of this theory. There are three types of informa- tion affecting the market, namely, pst Prices and trends, other public information and inside information. If all these types are not absorbed perfectly by the market, there is a possibility of some gaining above average returns, from the investments. Based on the three types of information, the analysis have placed the market absorption and the related theory under three heads; namely:

- Weak Form of EMH, which absorbs only market price information,
- Semistrong Form which absorbs price information and also all other public information and
- Strong Form which absorbs all types of information including insider information.

Weak form of EMH is closely related to the Random Walk Hypothesis, as the past prices are already absorbed by the market and the present prices move therefore independently of the pat, which is the same as the Random walk hypothesis. The present trends are thus random variables, and past data cannot be used to predict the future. All the information on the past data on price trends and volumes was already absorbed earlier. As prices have no memory of the past, yesterday prices have nothing to do with today's prices. To give an example from BSE quotation Dr. Reddy Labs has yearly low of Rs. 190 and a high of Rs. 333; its price at close on Oct. 15, 1996 was Rs. 215, but it opened on Oct. 16, at Rs. 212 and closed at Rs. 210. A day later it opened again at a higher price, independent of the last closing. It is futile exercise that the, present day price can be derived by any past data, at least in short run. If that is proved empirically, then prices move in a random fashion like the walk of a Drunkard, each move independent of the other. It is anybody's guess or the result of a toss of coin of what will be the price of TISCO today or Dr. Reddy Labs tomorrow. Thus the Random Walk hypothesis states that prices move in random manner, independent of the past prices.

In the real world, the weak form of market efficiency may exist, as prices do move in an independent manner which the empirical evidence has shown as the past prices are already absorbed by the market. However, it is to be canceded that market imperfections, costs of information and blocks to the free flow of information may stand in the way of free play of market forces. Speculators and groups of interested parties or even brokers may manipulate the prices through corneing of shares and reducing the flating stock of the market The empirical evidence in the random-walk literature existed before the theory was established. Empirical results were discovered first, and then an attempt was made to develop a theory that could possibly explain the results. Both the Random walk hypothesis and weak form of EMH, state almost the same thing, namely, that knowledge of the past stock price does not aid the investors to gain any improved performance.

The prices move independent of the other; although they may move in a random manner they move around a trend line decided by the anticipated real earnings of the company and its fundamentals. Both EMH in weak form and the Random Wal;k Theory thus postulate that analysing the past does not improve the forecasting ability of stock prices and new information and prices that result from them cannot be predicated. After these initial occurrences, more results and more theory were uncovered. This has led then to a diversity of theories, which are generically called the random-walk theory. A good deal of confusion resulted from the diversity of the literature; and only recently has there been some clarification of the proliferation of empirical results and theories.

## Empirical Tests

There were several empirical tests on the Random Walk Theory. The question tested was whether the security prices follow a "Random Walk, whether today's prices are in any way a function of the past prices. Similarly weak form of Market efficiency also states that no investor can use the price information of the past to earn superior return on investment. Investors who analysed the past fundamentals involving price behaviour of the past did pick up good blue chips in their portfolio, but that did not give them superior portfolio Empirical tests were conducted both in the past and the present and in India and abroad on the validity of Random Walk hypothesis. These tests to some extent support the hypothesis that price changes of today are independent of the past price changes. But the evidence is not conclusive and results varied with the time period's chosen and the data used. Cowles (1934) and JOnes (1937) and Kendall (1953) etc. have shown in their research that security prices moved in a random fashion.

## Filter Tests

Filter tests are based on the principle of fixing a filter level varying from 0.5% to 5%, and then examine how well pick up both trends and reversals.Thus, if a stock moves up a filter point say 5%; then buy it and hold it long; when it reverses by the same filter point, 5%, sell it and take a short position in it. A short position is one where on sells even without holding shares to deliver. When the stock price reverses again at the filter point, cover the short position by buying the shares in the market. By this process, the contention of chartists that prices and volume data of the past are supposed to tell the entire story and our approach is to forecast the trends and reversala only. Filterig is the screening of the important information affecting the prices from unimportant and see how well the price changes pick up the trends and reversals. The results of tests conducted by Fama, Blume and Alexander on the basis of filter points also did not gie conclusive proofs. If the filter level is low, the market swings capture these levels, but if the filter level is taken to be large, then results did not prove the hypothesis. Even in case of smaller filters, if transaction costs and other charges are taken into account the investors did not profit by using the filter tests. In sum, the results of filter tests did not prove the chartist school's validity. Stock prices do not move in a predictable fashion of movement and reversals and one cannot make return in excess of the results warranted by the risks assumed by the investors. These reults prove that the weak form of market efficiency holds good as it is not possible to gain more from the price infomration of the market.

## Serial Correlation Tests

Mr. Moore tested the movement of stock prices through serial correlation tests. Serial correlation is used to measure the extent of association of one series of security prices with a series in the past. Moore measures the correlation coefficient of price changes of one week with the price changes a week later and so on down the line. Its results showed that the correlation coefficient is very low indicating that a price rise did not show the tendency to the price fall and vice versa in any predictable manner. The price changes of this week do not therefore depend on the past price changes to any significant extent.

Fama did the same correlation tests on daily price changes in 1965. He studied the companies included in the Dow Jones Industrial average for five years.

His research showed low correlation and this proved that there is no significant relation between price changes in successive periods. Serial correlation or auto correlation of price data of different time periods did not show significant positive results. This proves that prices move in an independent fashion to a large extent.

## Run Tests

A run is a set of consecutive price changes in the same direction. The time series data on price changes of stocks are used to test whether there are dependencies among these series in terms of signs and reversal of signs. Fama made Run Tests to examine whether the price changes were likely to be followed by further price changes in the same direction. Run tests are conducted by the following method:

### *Example Elecon Engi*

*Suppose the price changes are as follows:* Rs. 40, 40.5, 41.50, 41.5, 45.0, 44.0, 44.0, 44.5, 46.0, 45.0 - 10 observations for ten days, then count the number of consecu-tive signs in the same direction which will have (+) sign.

Then count the number of signs with no change with a zero sign and those with consecutuve price declines (with Minus sign). In the example we have two positive, two zero sign and then one positive, one negative sign, two with zero sign and two again the positive sign and the last with a negative sign. These data show that there are no price dependencies. Yesterday's prices neither tell us of today's price nor today's price of to- marrow's price.

There is no consistency in the price changes. This cease also gives support to Random Walk hypoth- esis. Hagerman and Richmand made a similar study for prie changes observed on securities traded on O.T.C. (Over the Counter). The efficiency of options Market was tested by Black and Scholles. Their research showed that the market was not perfect and that the transactions costs are so high that those tradign in the market could not make abnormal returns. Granger and Morgenstern used a method known as Spectral Analysis in 1963 to test the Random nature of the stock prices. They did not notice any worthwhile relationship between the returns of security in one period and the returns in the previous periods.

Most of these research results proved that security prices moved in a random manner and are not amenable to any precise forecast.

### *Other Testsher*

Brownian motion in physics is a kind of Random Walk. The research conducted by Osborne showed that stock prices moved in a Brownian fashion. This means that simulation tests conducted by some authors showed that the mechanism of Random Walk generated variables which are similar to movement of stock prices. Robert's research in simulation tests in particular confirmed that price changes in the present period are independent of the past trends. Research conducted by Levy in 1967 and be Jensen and Bennington in 1970 and many others did not find any signifi- cant abnormal returns due to a study of past price and volume data used in portfolio selection.

### Mutual Fund Performance

Similarly mutual fund performance based on insider information is also not found to bear any superior returns. Friend in 1972, Sharpe in 1966 and Jensen in 1969 studied relative performance of mutual funds. It was for that their results are no better. The hypothesis tested and found void is that mutual funds could earn extra ordinary returns and constantly achieve a higher average performance, because they have better access to insider information. Research studies made by Blume, Williamson and others in this line proved that the mutual-fund performance was not extra ordinary or superior to average market performance. They have probably no insider information or their expertise is not superior or their administrative costs are higher than for individuals.

### Misconceptions of the Random Walk Model

Our generalisation of the random-walk model, then, says that previous price changes or changes in return are useless in predicting future price or return changes. That is, if we attempt to predict future prices in absolute terms using only historical price-change information, as suggested, not be successful.

Note that random walk says nothing more than that successive price changes are independent. This independence implies that prices at any time will on the average reflect the intrinsic value of the security. (Often one will find this intrinsic worth referred to as the present value of the stock's price or its equilibrium value). Furthermore, if a stock's price deviates from its intrinsic value because, among other things, different investors evaluate the available information differently or have different insights into future prospects of the firm, professional investors and astute non-professionals will seize upon the short-term of random deviations from the intrinsic value, and through their active buying and selling of the stock in question will force the price back to its equilibrium position.

It is unfortunate that so many misconceptions of the random-walk model exist. It is, in point of fact, a very simple statement. The random-walk model says nothing about relative price movements that is, about selecting securities that may or may not perform better than other securities. It says nothing about decomposing price movements into such factors as market, industry, or firm factors. Certainly, it is entirely possible to detect trends in stock prices after one has removed the general market influences or other influences; however, this is no way would refute the random-walk model, for after these influences have been removed, as suggested, in fact be dealing with relative prices and not with absolute prices, which lie at the heart of the random-walk hypothesis. Furthermore, these 'trends' provide no basis for forecasting the future.

In addition, it should be reemphasized that the empirical results came first, to be followed by theory to explain the results; therefore, discussions about a competitive market, or instantaneous adjustments to new information, or knowledgeable market participants, or easy access to markets, are all in reality not part of the random-walk model, but rather possible explanations of the results we find when performing our empirical investigations.

Also, there seems to be a misunderstanding by many to the effect that believing in random walk means that one must also believe that analyzing stocks, and consequently stock prices, is a useless exercise, for if indeed stock prices are random, there is no reason for them to go up or down over any period of time. This is very wrong. The randomwalk hypothesis is entirely consistent with an upward or downward movement in price, the hypothesis supports fundamental analysis and certainly does not attack it.

## THE EFFICIENT MARKET HYPOTHESIS (EMH)

Efficient market theory states that the price fluctuations are random and do not follow any regular pattern. Fama suggested that efficient market hypothesis can be divided into three categories.

*They are*:

- The weak form,
- The semistrong form, and
- The strong form. The level of information being considered in the market is the basis for this segregation.

There are three forms of the Hypothesis, namely, weak form of EMH discussed under Random Walk Theory, semi strong from and strong form. In the words of Fama, efficient market is defined as the market where there are a large number of rational profit maximisers actively competing with each trying to predict the future market and where the current information is almost freely and equally available to all participants.

Analysis of the Research studies done so far confirm partly the weak form of EMH. But the other two forms of the Theory are found not really realistic in the Practical Market Scene

### Weak form of EMH

The weak form hypothesis says that the current prices of stocks already fully reflect all the information that is contained in the historical sequence of prices. Therefore, there is no benefit in examining the historical sequence of prices forecasting the future. This weak form of the efficient market hypothesis is popularly known as the random-walk theory. Clearly, if this weak form of the efficient market hypothesis is true, it is a direct repudiation of technical analysis. If there is no value in studying past prices and past price changes, there is no value in technical analysis. As we saw in the preceding, however, technicians place considerable reliance on the charts of historical prices that they maintain even though the efficient-market hypothesis refutes this practice.

Now, as suggested, analyse statistical investigations of this weak form of the efficient-market hypothesis.

### *Semi Strong Form of EMH*

This form of EMH postulates that the market absorbs quickly and efficiently not only the price information but all publicly available information. Examples of this public information are found in the Financial reports, Balance Sheets and Profit and Loss Accounts, Earnings and Dividend Reports, financial results etc.

In addition to financial data, any material informa- tion affecting the financial position, such as financial structure, liquidity, solvency etc. is also found relevant and absorbed by the market in the price formation. Some data and information may be contradictory and biased information, rumours etc. would also flow in as news affecting the market.

Revision of data or changes in conditions of the company also affect the price. Studies on the time lag involved in the impact of any change of fundamentals on the company share price showed varied time lags, some being discounted even before the event is announced and some before the event took place. Such matters like earnings reports, bonus, rights affect the market even in anticipation before the formal announcement.

The studies on the semi strong form of market efficiency related to the effect of any public information released, on the share price. The tests are invariably based on pricing models, as under the CAPM or some economietric models. These studies showed that the absorption of this information on share prices was inefficient and varied from scrip to scrip, and the time period studied.

The inefficiency in the market mechanism absorbing this data is found to be corrected over a time period as investors take time to analyse and conclude the effect of any public information. Thus, the semistrong form is empirically not well supported, but in many foreign markets, the semi strong form is foudn to be applicable and markets quickly absorb all published informa- tion. This is possible in those markets due to strict law enforcement, bu the market authorities, instantaneous display of all market information through electronic media and investor awareness of their impact and their quick absorption of the data.

The revoluion in informatics and communication technologies has made it possible for the application of the semistrong form of the EMH to these markets in developed countries. Strong Form of EMH Under this hypothesis markets are so perfect that all informa- tion including private information, insider information and unpublished data, affecting the market are absorbed in the stock prices. Any investor can then gain the same average returns, whenever he entres the market.

The information of all types is flashed to all investors simultaneously and all players ahve the same information at the same itme. This means that only supeiror analysis and interpretation can give better market returns. This is possible for inside traders, floor brokers and institutional investors who have highly efficient market research component. The acumen with whch prie movements can be forecast can only result in superior return and not otherwise.

Studies made in developed markets have showed that strong form of efficiet market does not exist there also. Investors have not shown consistently higher returns een with all the informa- tion available to them. It was also found that average investor could do better by picking up securities in a random fashion.

**Markets in India**

It will thus be seen that the EMH in its strong form is not realistic in the actual markets. In India, in particular, despite all best efforts of SEBI, market prices are rigged up, and it is comon to notice various price behavioural patterns and manipulation of prices. Information is costly and time consuming. No unqualified empirical support is found for efficient market hypothesis, even in its weakest form in India. In the case of institutional investors, equity market research is a tool used for forecasting prices and identification of underval- ued scrips through fundamental analysis and determining the timings for purchase asnd sale by technical analysis, Although the followers of Technicals or Chartist methods are very few in India, the major component of market research revolves around both fundamental and technical factors.

In practice, therefore many of these Theories, including the random walk theory are inapplicable to Indian conditions. Speculation is as high as 70-80% in Indian markets and markets are not perfect and the absorption of all types of information is also not timey and efficient.

The investors in India go by research into fundamentals and select the scrips on the basis of their assessment of the extent of overvaluation and under valuation Investment analysis therefore only involves the market research, fundamental analysis to a great extent and technical analysis to lesser extent with a view to select the undervalued scrips in the context of market conditions, reflect in the sentiment and psychology of the market

**Empirical Tests of the Weak Form**

Over the years an impressive literature has been developed describing empirical tests of random walk (Paul H. Cootner, 1967). This research has been aimed at testing whether successive or lagged price changes are independent. In this part as suggested, review briefly some of the major categories of statistical techniques that have been employed in this research, and as suggested, summarize their major ceases. These techniques generally fall into two categories: those that test for trends in stock prices and thus infer whether profitable trading systems could be developed and those that test such mechanical systems directly. Although certain of these studies were conducted many years ago, they are the basis upon which research on the efficient-market theory has been based, and are included here to provide the necessary conceptual basis for the theory and its evolution.

Simulation tests: In the year 1959, Harry Roberts produced some graphs as part of an interesting experiment. The essence of this experiment was to examine the appearance of the actual level of the Dow Jones index expressed both in levels and in terms of weekly changes, and to compare these graphs with a simulated set of graphs. A series of price changes was generated from random-number tables and then these changes were converted to graphs depicting levels of the simulated Dow Jones index.

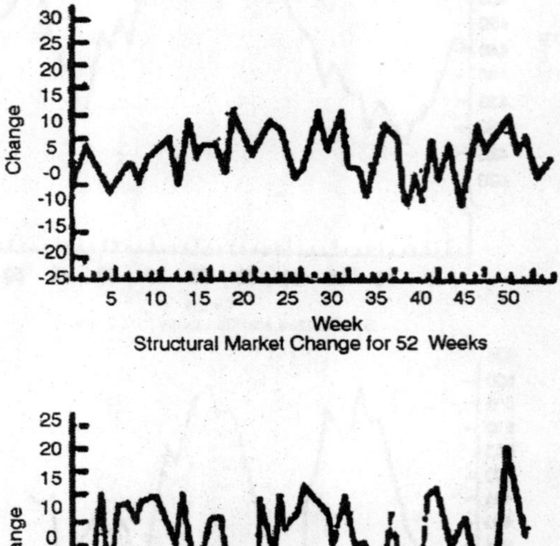


Structural Market Change for 52 Weeks

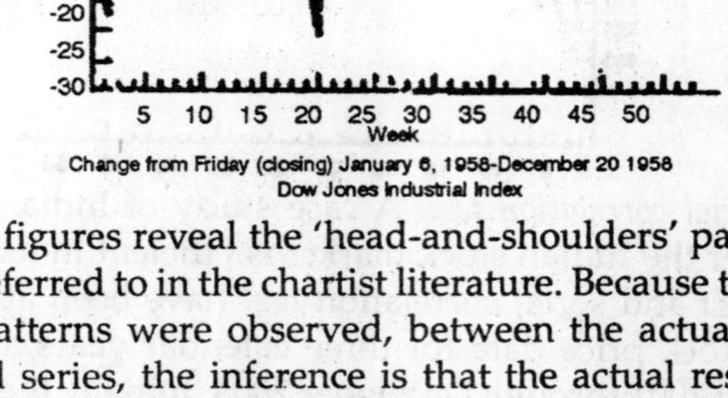


Change from Friday (closing) January 6, 1958-December 20 1958
Dow Jones Industrial Index

Both figures reveal the 'head-and-shoulders' pattern that is often referred to in the chartist literature. Because these very similar patterns were observed, between the actual and the simulated series, the inference is that the actual results may well be the result of random stock price movements.

Another way to test for randomness in stock price changes is to look at their serial correlations (also called auto-correlations).

That is, whether the price change in one period correlated with the price change in some other period? If such auto-correlations are negligible, the price changes are considered to be serially independent.

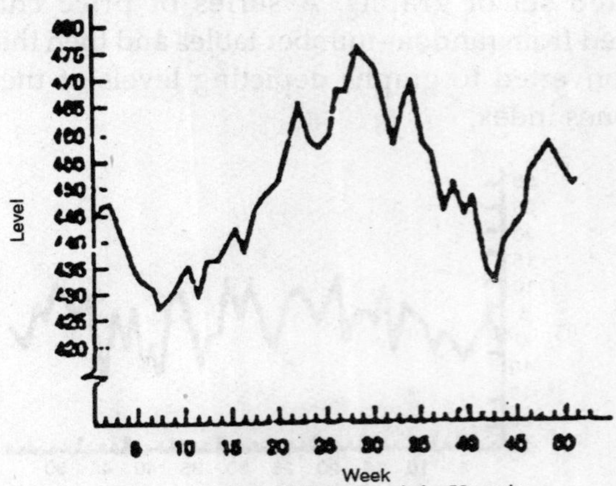


Structurized Market Levels for 52 weeks

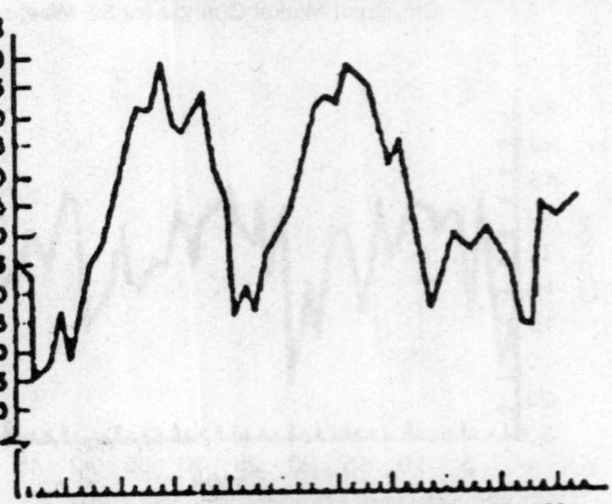

*Serial correlation test:* A case study of India. To examine whether the Indian stock market is efficient in its weak form, runs test and serial correlation test have been applied to the daily stock price data for three calendar years, commencing January 2001 through December 2003. Initially the sample size consisted of all the 50 scrips of S & P CNX Nifty which is considered as the most representative index in India. However, due to non-availability of data on three scrips, we had to rely on daily closing price data of only 47 scrips obtained from website of NSE

As the period covered under study includes both bearish phase (March 2001 to March 2003) and bull phase (March 2003 to Dec. 2003), it is expected that the results of the study would offer a true picture of the efficiency of National Stock Exchange.

In order to test the null hypothesis that share prices follow the random walk behaviour or that successive price changes are linearly independent, the Log Random Walk (LRW) model has been applied in this study. This is a suitable data transformation procedure, which is used to make the original series stationary. Mathematically, the testable form of LRW model is,

In(Pt)/Pt-1 = et

Where E $(e_t) = 0$, Covariance $(e_t, e_{t-s}) = 0$, all s '" 0; $P_t$ and $P_{t-1}$ are the prices at time t and time t-1 respectively, and $e_t$ is the residual of the time series data at time t. On computing the daily stock returns based on this model, the weak form of efficient market hypothesis has been tested with the help of 'runs test' and 'serial correlation test'.

In the present study the auto-correlation of return series has been examined for the period 1st January 2001 to 31st December 2003.

The auto correlation coefficients are computed by the inbuilt programme for the purpose using SPSS package. For testing the joint hypotheses that all the auto correlation coefficients are simultaneously equal to zero, Box-Ljung (BL) statistics which is defined as,

$$BL = n(n+2)\sum_{k=1}^{m}\left(\frac{\rho^{\wedge 2}}{n-k}\right) \sim \chi^2_m$$

has been applied for 16 lags.

Where,

n = sample size

m = lag length and degree of freedom ñ^ k = Serial correlation coefficient

BL statistics follow the chi-square distribution with 'm' degree of freedom.

## The Runs Test

After computing the stock returns as per the LRW model, the runs test was applied. The runs test is a statistical technique used to detect if a time series is random or not. The computational procedure of runs test is that it ignores the absolute values in a time series and deals only with the signs, plus or minus.

The test is essentially concerned with the direction of changes in a given time series. Since it is a non-parametric test, there is no need to predefine the nature of probability distribution of the time series data.

A runs test is performed by comparing the observed number of runs (O) in the sample against its sampling distribution under the random walk hypothesis. In other words, we compare the observed number with the expected number of runs.

If the observed number of runs is not significantly different from the expected number of runs (E), then it may be concluded that the successive price changes are independent and the series is characterized by mean reversion. On the other hand, if this difference is statistically significant, then the price series would be regarded as dependent, and the series is characterized by trends. This cease will indicate that the future share prices may be predicted using historical information. When each observation is assumed independent and identically distributed, and the null hypothesis of randomness is true, then the mean or expected number of runs can be calculated as:

$$E(R) = \frac{2n_1n_2}{n_1 + n_2} + 1$$

The standard error of the number of runs can be calculated as,

$$SE(R) = n2(n - 1)$$

To test whether the time series is random or not, we use the statistic Z:

$$Z = \frac{R - E(R)}{SE(R)} - N(0,1)$$

Where,

R = Number of actual runs in the sample, Z = Standard normal variate,

SE(R) = Standard error of the number of runs, and E(R) = Expected number of runs.

In this study, the null and alternative hypotheses that were tested with the help of runs test are as follows-

Under $H_0$: The stock price series are random.

Against $H_1$: The stock price series are not random.

***Results of Runs Test***

It is evident from the table that z statistics, which have been computed to test the significance of the difference between the number of actual runs and the expected runs, are significant at.01 level in case of only 4 stocks out of 47 (8.5%). While 3 values (6.38%) are so at 0.10 level of significance.

Thus only 14.89 per cent of the z-values turn as significant upto 5 per cent level of significance.

The table further pinpoints that of the 47 values of standardized variable z, 27 (i.e. 57.45%) reveal negative signs.

The negative signs of z values indicate that actual number of runs have fallen short of the expected number of runs, but the differences between the two is not significant except in the aforesaid cases. Thus, the runs test confirms randomness in about 85 per cent of the companies.

To determine whether day-to-day price changes follow a random walk, we have also applied runs test to the daily closing S & P CNX Nifty Index for the period January 1, 2001 to December 31, 2003.

The results of runs test, as shown at serial number 48 in Table, reject the null hypothesis of independence, since the standardized variable z is found significant at 1 per cent level in this case.

Thus, the market index hints that the market is not efficient.

**Table. Results of runs test**

| S. | Scrip (Company) Name | Actual No. of Runs | Expected. No. of Runs | Z Value | 2 tailed distribution (Sign) |
|---|---|---|---|---|---|
| 1 | Asia Brown Boverital | 386 | 376.78 | 0.659 | 0.510 |
| 2 | Associated Cement Co. Ltd. | 361 | 376.98 | -1.166 | 0.244 |
| 3 | Bajaj Auto Ltd. | 365 | 376.26 | -0.874 | 0.382 |
| 4 | Bharat Heavy Electricals | 385 | 375.94 | 0.584 | 0.559 |
| 5 | Bharat Petroleum Corp. Ltd. | 365 | 375.38 | -0.873 | 0.383 |
| 6 | Britannia Industries Ltd. | 393 | 373.93 | 1.17 | 0.242 |
| 7 | BSES Ltd. | 387 | 377 | 0.733 | 0.464 |
| 8 | Cipla Ltd. | 367 | 376.93 | -0.73 | 0.466 |
| 9 | Colgate Palmolive (India) Ltd. | 390 | 376.4 | 0.949 | 0.343 |
| 10 | Dabur India Ltd. | 385 | 375.27 | 0.6 | 0.549 |
| 11 | Digital Equipment Ltd. | 375 | 376.32 | -0.146 | 0.884 |
| 12 | Dr. Reddy's Labouratories Ltd. | 353 | 375.59 | -1.751 | 0.080 |
| 13 | Gas Authority of India Ltd. | 308 | 310.01 | -0.424 | 0.611 |
| 14 | Glaxo Consumer | 62 | 55.28 | 1.252 | 0.211 |
| 15 | Glaxosmithkline | 366 | 376.01 | -0.803 | 0.422 |
| 16 | Grasim Industries Ltd. | 358 | 376.73 | -1.387 | 0.166 |
| 17 | Gujarat Ambuja Cements Ltd. | 337 | 376.93 | -2.915 | 0.004 |
| 18 | HCL Technologies Ltd. | 353 | 376.93 | -1.747 | 0.081 |
| 19 | HDFC Bank | 378 | 375.83 | 0.076 | 0.939 |
| 20 | Hero Honda Motors Ltd. | 364 | 376.99 | -0.949 | 0.343 |
| 21 | Hindustan Lever Ltd. | 367 | 376.48 | -0.729 | 0.466 |
| 22 | Hindustan Petroleum Corporation Ltd. | 375 | 376.45 | -0.143 | 0.886 |
| 23 | Housing Development Finance Corporation Ltd. | 378 | 376.99 | 0.076 | 0.939 |
| 24 | ICICI Banking Company | | | | |

| | | | | | |
|---|---|---|---|---|---|
| | Ltd. | 380 | 376.68 | 0.224 | 0.823 |
| 25 | Indian Hotels Co. Ltd. | 352 | 376.78 | -1.81 | 0.070 |
| 26 | Indian Petroleum Corporation Ltd. | 349 | 376.04 | -2.039 | 0.041 |
| 27 | ITC Ltd. | 382 | 376.62 | 0.366 | 0.715 |
| 28 | Larsen & Toubro | 342 | 376.14 | -2.55 | 0.011 |
| 29 | Mahindra & Mahindra | 327 | 376.68 | -3.645 | 0.000 |
| 30 | MTNL Ltd. | 371 | 376.62 | -0.429 | 0.668 |
| 31 | National Aluminium Co. Ltd. | 381 | 376.96 | 0.295 | 0.768 |
| 32 | NIIT Ltd. | 383 | 377 | 0.438 | 0.661 |
| 33 | Oriental Bank of Commerce | 380 | 373.55 | 0.224 | 0.823 |
| 34 | Ranbaxy Lab. Ltd. | 360 | 375.27 | -1.24 | 0.215 |
| 35 | Reliance Ind. Ltd. | 385 | 376.47 | 0.585 | 0.559 |
| 36 | Satyam Computers Ltd. | 381 | 376.23 | 0.292 | 0.770 |
| 37 | Shipping Corp. of India | 377 | 376.78 | 0.003 | 0.998 |
| 38 | State Bank of India | 379 | 376.4 | 0.147 | 0.883 |
| 39 | Steel Authority of India Ltd. | 351 | 369.24 | -1.36 | 0.174 |
| 40 | Sun Pharmaceuticals (I) Ltd. | 388 | 376.87 | 0.803 | 0.422 |
| 41 | Tata Chemicals Ltd. | 359 | 376.93 | -1.309 | 0.191 |
| 42 | Tata Power Ltd. | 331 | 375.83 | -3.346 | 0.001 |
| 43 | Tata Tea Ltd. | 340 | 376.96 | -2.699 | 0.007 |
| 44 | TISCO Ltd. | 347 | 376.32 | -2.175 | 0.030 |
| 45 | VSNL Ltd. | 359 | 376.5 | -1.313 | 0.189 |
| 46 | Wipro Ltd. | 380 | 376.4 | 0.219 | 0.827 |
| 47 | Zea Telefilms Ltd. | 374 | 376.78 | -0.219 | 0.827 |
| 48 | S & P CNX Nifty | 333 | 374.28 | -3.211 | 0.001 |

## Results of Serial Correlation Test

The results of serial correlation test are presented and summarised in Tables. The autocorrelation coefficients were computed upto 16 lags from the return series using SPSS. It is evident from the results that out of the 752 autocorrelation coefficients computed, only 61 (8.11%) and 19 (2.53%) are significant at 5 per cent and 1 per cent level, respectively. Thus this test gives supportive evidence for the weak form of efficiency. However, the Box-Ljung statistics are significant at 1 per cent and 5 per cent level for 10 (21.28%) and 9 (19.15%) series respectively.

This suggests that successive daily price changes are independent of previous day price changes in case of approximately 60 per cent price series. These results of serial correlation test are, by and large in keeping with the results obtained under runs test. Putting again, both the tests indicate that successive daily price changes are independent of previous day price changes.

A perusal of serial correlation coefficients according to number of lags shows that out of 47 coefficients for price changes with one day lag, 7 are significant at 1 per cent level and 9 at 5 per cent level. With two days lag, 4 coefficients out of 47 are significant at 1 per cent and 15 coefficients at 5 per cent levels.

However, only 6 coefficient with lag 3 are found significant upto 5 per cent level of significance. In aggregate, 41 (29.08%) coefficients from lag 1 to 3 are significant. A close look at the coefficients upto 3 lags indicates that 67 coefficients (47.5%) have negative signs. The finding also conforms to the random walk theory. Further, it is noteworthy that merely13 (3.95%) serial correlation coefficients are significant at 5 per cent level with a lag 10 to 16. It indicates that prices during the days of successive week are independent of the price changes during the days of previous week.

We have tested the weak form of market efficiency with the two tests, namely the runs test and serial correlation test using daily data for three years period commencing January 2001 through December 2003. The results of the runs test have given a clear-cut inkling of the existence of weak form market efficiency in the Indian securities market. Similarly, the serial correlation analysis based on its coefficients confirms the weak form hypothesis of efficient market.

**Table Serial Correlation Coefficients**

| Companies | Lags 1 | 2 | 3 | 4 | 5 | 6 | 7 | 8 | 9 |
|---|---|---|---|---|---|---|---|---|---|
| Asia Brown Boverital | -0.016 | -0.039 | -0.017 | 0.024 | 0.004 | -0.029 | 0.011 | -0.053 | 0.028 |
| Associated Cement Co. Ltd. | 0.007 | -0.09* | -0.029 | 0.033 | -0.028 | 0.028 | 0.006 | 0.068 | -0.013 |
| Bajaj Auto Ltd. | 0.07 | -0.024 | -0.029 | -0.021 | 0.056 | 0.023 | 0.042 | 0.019 | 0.04 |
| Bharat Heavy Electricals | -0.009 | -0.066 | 0.036 | 0.01 | -0.032 | -67 | 0.044 | 0.075* | -0.04 |
| Bharat Petroleum Corp. Ltd. | 0.037 | -0.019 | 0.019 | -0.052 | 0.02 | 0.002 | -0.024 | -0.025 | 0.033 |
| Britannia Industries Ltd. | -0.112** | 0.004 | 0.045 | 0.012 | -0.007 | 0.067 | 0.012 | 0.006 | 0.039 |
| BSES Ltd. | 0.031 | -0.121** | -0.026 | -0.01 | 0.073* | 0.055 | -0.03 | 0.006 | -0.052 |
| Cipla Ltd. | 0.062 | 0.004 | -0.066 | 0.023 | 0.052 | -0.04 | 0.012 | 0.002 | 0.041 |
| Colgate Palmolive (India) Ltd. | 0.011 | 0.096* | -0.055 | -0.072* | -0.055 | -0.035 | 0.049 | 0.001 | 0.033 |
| Dabur India Ltd. | -0.016 | -0.055 | -0.003 | 0.027 | -0.027 | -0.075* | 0.043 | 0.066 | 0.009 |
| Digital Equipment Ltd. | 0.1 | -0.072* | 0.022 | 0.029 | 0.032 | 0 | 0.026 | -0.004 | -0.023 |
| Dr. Reddy's Labouratories Ltd. | 0.021 | -0.0565 | -0.017 | 0.005 | 0.001 | -0.037 | -0.086* | -0.006 | 0.062 |
| Gas Authority of India Ltd. | 0.069 | 0.012 | 0.086* | 0.08* | 0.018 | 0.023 | 0.026 | -0.009 | -0.041 |
| Glaxosmithkline | 0.06 | 0.049 | -0.026 | -0.019 | -0.071 | 0.017 | 0.031 | 0.04 | -0.012 |
| Glaxo Consumer | -0.126** | -0.027 | 0.159** | -0.06 | 0.123** | 0.0531 | -0.025 | 0169** | -0.166** |
| Grasim Industries Ltd. | 0.034 | -0.129** | 0.025 | -0.003 | -0.005 | 0.052 | -0.04 | 0.004 | 0.023 |
| Gujarat Ambuja Cements Ltd. | .073* | .163** | 0.054 | 0.06 | 0.026 | -0.039 | 0.001 | 0.031 | 0.021 |
| HCL Technologies Ltd. | 0.083* | -0.029 | -0.048 | -0.012 | -0.096* | -0.036 | 0.118** | 0.008 | -0.029 |
| HDFC Bank | -0.085* | -0.098* | 0.03 | -0.015 | 0.021 | -0.013 | 0.007 | -0.036 | 0.003 |
| Hero Honda Motors Ltd. | 0.007 | 0.004 | 0.004 | 0.006 | 0.009 | -0.004 | 0.007 | -0.011 | -0.031 |
| Hindustan Lever Ltd. | 0.043 | -0.103* | -0.065 | -0.034 | -0.034 | 0.004 | 0.013 | -0.004 | 0.105* |
| Hindustan Petroleum Corp. Ltd. | 0.044 | -0.04 | 0.007 | -0.017 | 0.044 | 0.052 | 0.011 | 0.014 | 0.054 |

| Companies | Lags | | | | | | | | |
|---|---|---|---|---|---|---|---|---|---|
| | 1 | 2 | 3 | 4 | 5 | 6 | 7 | 8 | 9 |
| Housing Devel. Finance Corp. Ltd. | -0.061 | -0.034 | 0.007 | -0.016 | -0.019 | 0.005 | 0.011 | 0.034 | 0.009 |
| ITC Ltd. | -0.055 | -0.075* | -0.054 | 0.002 | 0.038 | 0.018 | -0.032 | 0.047 | 0.008 |
| ICICI Banking Company Ltd. | 0.061 | -0.075* | 0.025 | 0.022 | 0.005 | 0.024 | -0.034 | -0.05 | -0.049 |
| Indian Hotels Co. Ltd. | 0.095* | -0.002 | 0.048 | 0.033 | 0.093* | 0.022 | -0.006 | -0.007 | -0.002 |
| Indian Petroleum Corp. Ltd. | 0.108** | 0.064 | 0.102* | 0.084* | 0.054 | 0.019 | 0.063 | 0.038 | 0.028 |
| Larsen & Toubro | 0.086* | -0.095* | 0.072* | 0.058 | 0.023 | 0.002 | 0.029 | 0.039 | -0.022 |
| MTNL Ltd. | 0.087* | -0.095* | -0.015 | 0.039 | -0.081* | -0.005 | 0.052 | 0.043 | -0.075* |
| Mahindra & Mahindra | 0.155** | -0.049 | 0.096* | -0.01 | 0.012 | 0.024 | 0.037 | 0.081* | 0.038 |
| National Aluminium Co. Ltd. | 0.006 | -0.042 | 0.047 | -0.022 | -0.027 | -0.019 | -0.01 | 10.006 | 0.018 |
| NIIT Ltd. | 0.088* | -0.074** | 0.021 | 0.095* | 0.063 | 0.041 | 0.01 | 0.025 | 0.096* |
| Oriental Bank of Commerce | 0.038 | -0.084* | 0.05 | 0.004 | -0.047 | 0.002 | 0.082* | -0.019 | 0.007 |
| Ranbaxy Lab. Ltd. | 0.055 | -0.003 | -0.02 | -0.03 | -0.049 | -0.013 | 0.00 | -0.015 | -0.033 |
| Reliance Ind. Ltd. | 0.026 | 0.068 | -0.021 | -0.048 | 0.043 | -0.106* | 0.01 | -0.027 | 0.009 |
| Satyam Computers Ltd. | 0.046 | -0.081* | -0.004 | 0.02 | -0.005 | -0.054 | -0.041 | 0.052 | -0.028 |
| Shipping Corp. of India | 0.02 | 0.009 | 0.006 | 0.037 | 0.029 | 0.045 | 0.01 | 0.047 | -0.015 |
| State Bank of India | 0.047 | -0.074* | 0.055 | 0.007 | -0.011 | -0.079* | 0.048 | 0.07 | 0.013 |
| Steel Authority of India Ltd. | 0.105* | -0.092* | 0.037 | 0.061 | 0.004 | 0.042 | 0.048 | 0.078* | 0.043 |
| Sun Pharmaceuticals (I) Ltd. | -0.011 | -0.021 | 0.03 | 0.003 | 0.024 | -0.022 | -0.003 | 0.012 | 0.013 |
| Tata Chemicals Ltd. | 0.07 | -0.077* | -0.002 | 0.036 | 0.162** | -0.016 | -0.088* | 0.053 | 0.01 |
| TISCO Ltd. | 0.034 | -0.047 | 0.012 | 0.059 | -0.009 | -0.008 | 0.018 | 0.008 | 0.026 |
| Tata Power Ltd. | .133** | -.149** | 0.01 | 0.049 | 0.071 | 0.002 | -0.015 | -0.001 | 0.016 |
| Tata Tea Ltd. | .134** | -.084* | -0.05 | 0.046 | .085* | -0.043 | -0.06 | -0.01 | 0.109* |
| VSNL Ltd. | 0.055 | -0.014 | -0.004 | -0.027 | -0.017 | 0.006 | 0.039 | 0.036 | -0.051 |
| Wipro Ltd. | .087* | -0.047 | -0.024 | 0.017 | 0.001 | -0.01 | -0.005 | -0.008 | 0.029 |
| Zea Telefilms Ltd. | .123** | -0.032 | 0.024 | -0.048 | -0.031 | -0.034 | -0.068 | 0.034 | 0.047 |
| S & P CNX Nifty | .136** | -0.062 | 0.013 | 0.069 | 0.076* | -0.019 | -0.018 | 0.015 | 0.042 |

| Companies | Lags 10 | 11 | 12 | 13 | 14 | 15 | 16 | BL |
|---|---|---|---|---|---|---|---|---|
| Asia Brown Boverital | 0.031 | 0.022 | -0.029 | 0.009 | 0.054 | 0.023 | -0.028 | 10.569 |
| Associated Cement Co. Ltd. | -0.051 | -0.035 | -0!007 | -0.023 | 0.007 | 0.04 | 0.006 | 17.162 |
| Bajaj Auto Ltd. | 0.021 | 0.006 | 0.009 | 0.01 | -0.007 | 0.013 | -0.04 | 12.702 |
| Bharat Heavy Electricals | -0.009 | -0.066 | 0.036 | 0.01 | -0.032 | -0.067 | 0.044 | 0.075 |
| Bharat Petroleum Corp. Ltd. | 0.006 | -0.045 | -0.017 | -0.009 | 0.015 | 0.029 | -0.076* | 22.678 |
| Britannia Industries Ltd. | -0.053 | -0.029 | 0.027 | -0.054 | -0.017 | 0.006 | 0.044 | 23.251 |
| BSES Ltd. | -0.008 | 0.025 | 0.004 | -0.016 | -0.0465 | -0.0415 | 0.066 | 29.068** |
| Cipla Ltd. | 0.017 | -0.06 | -0.013 | 0.012 | -0.009 | -0.025 | -0.017 | 15.269 |
| Colgate Palmolive (India) Ltd. | 0.014 | 0 | 0.027 | -0.06 | -0.002 | 0.032 | 0.004 | 19.295 |
| Dabur India Ltd. | 0.05 | 0 | -0.064 | 0.044 | -0.017 | 0.006 | 0.043 | 20.83 |
| Digital Equipment Ltd. | 0.036 | 0.038 | -0.041 | 0.023 | 0.063 | -0.065 | -0.067 | 27.768** |
| Dr. Reddy's Labouratories Ltd. | -0.002 | -0.014 | -0.029 | 0.008 | 0.049 | 0.005 | 0.025 | 15.79 |
| Gas Authority of India Ltd. | -0.02 | -0.105 | -0.026 | -0.054 | 0.053 | -0.021 | -0.043 | 26.77** |
| Glaxosmithkline | -0.015 | 0.039 | 0.011 | -0.021 | 0.021 | 0.02 | 0.016 | 21.138 |
| Glaxo Consumer | -0.083* | 0.057 | 0.014 | 0.017 | 0.014 | -0.062 | 0.059 | 16.381 |
| Grasim Industries Ltd. | -0.011 | 0.05 | -0.027 | -0.124 | -0.014 | 0.069 | -0.038 | 36.717* |
| Gujarat Ambuja Cements Ltd. | -0.029 | -0.009 | 0.002 | -0.04 | -0.068 | 0 | -0.069 | 40.833* |
| HCL Technologies Ltd. | 0.006 | 0.041 | -0.065 | -0.005 | 0.025 | -0.024 | -0.027 | 32.995 |
| HDFC Bank | -0.024 | 0.017 | -0.014 | -0.028 | 0.008 | 0 | 0.047 | 18.225 |
| Hero Honda Motors Ltd. | -0.007 | -0.005 | 0.023 | 0.015 | -0.001 | 0.009 | -0.012 | 1.827 |
| Hindustan Lever Ltd. | -0.011 | -0.014 | 0.005 | -0.066 | 0.022 | 0.032 | -0.035 | 28.615** |
| Hindustan Petroleum Corp. Ltd. | -0.061 | 0.024 | -0.054 | -0.02 | 0.074* | -0.012 | 0.006 | 19.128 |
| Housing Devel. Finance Corp. Ltd. | 0.006 | -0.016 | 0.007 | 0.011 | -0.012 | -0.022 | 0.002 | 7.341 |
| ITC Ltd. | -0.027 | -0.098* | 0.026 | 0.003 | 0.051 | -0.057 | -0.032 | 25.674*** |

| Companies | Lags 10 | 11 | 12 | 13 | 14 | 15 | 16 | BL |
|---|---|---|---|---|---|---|---|---|
| ICICI Banking Company Ltd. | -0.032 | 0.053 | 0.016 | 0.009 | 0.01 | 0.090* | 0.023 | 23.399*** |
| Indian Hotels Co. Ltd. | 0.033 | 0.067 | 0.088* | 0.018 | -0.037 | -0.042 | 0.031 | 30.177** |
| Indian Petroleum Corp. Ltd. | -0.02 | 0 | 0.042 | 0.048 | 0.017 | 0.033 | 0.042 | 36.827* |
| Larsen & Toubro | 0.012 | 0.052 | 0.027 | -0.052 | -0.033 | 0.07 | -0.002 | 30.946** |
| MTNL Ltd. | -0.034 | 0.01 | -0.045 | -0.009 | 0.003 | -0.02 | 0.011 | 29.789** |
| Mahindra & Mahindra | 0.06 | 0.015 | -0.056 | -0.015 | -0.008 | 0 | -0.016 | 40.415* |
| National Aluminium Co. Ltd. | -0.053 | -0.028 | -0.088* | 0.008 | 0.05 | -0.042 | -0.005 | 16.628 |
| NIIT Ltd. | 0.052 | 0.014 | 0.036 | 0.032 | 0.064 | -0.027 | -0.048 | 38.613* |
| Oriental Bank of Commerce | -0.016 | 0.026 | 0.043 | -0.056 | -0.027 | 0.011 | -0.041 | 21.834 |
| Ranbaxy Lab. Ltd. | -0.001 | 0.01 | 0.026 | 0.016 | 0.015 | -0.017 | -0.013 | 7.537 |
| Reliance Ind. Ltd. | -0.007 | 0.035 | 0.052 | 0.022 | 0.017 | -0.046 | 0.013 | 22.09 |
| Satyam Computers Ltd. | 0.043 | 0.043 | -0.031 | 0.034 | 0.024 | -0.069 | -0.05 | 23.549*** |
| Shipping Corp. of India | -0.031 | -0.011 | 0.01 | 0.006 | -0.014 | 0.028 | -0.074* | 11.456 |
| State Bank of India | 0.017 | -0.026 | -0.055 | -0.011 | -0.009 | 0 | -0.014 | 21.926 |
| Steel Authority of India Ltd. | 0.018 | -0.029 | -0.004 | 0.036 | 0.062 | 0.054 | -0.077* | 39.426* |
| Sun Pharmaceuticals (I) Ltd. | -0.005 | -0.02 | -0.006 | 0.008 | -0.035 | -0.009 | -0.001 | 3.778 |
| Tata Chemicals Ltd. | -0.004 | -0.007 | -0.113** | -0.011 | 0.005 | -0.042 | -0.046 | 50.251* |
| TISCO Ltd. | 0.048 | -0.007 | -0.013 | 0.042 | 0 | -0.01 | -0.001 | 10.121 |
| Tata Power Ltd. | 0.031 | -0.049 | 0.041 | 0.046 | -0.042 | 0.024 | 0.009 | 43.45* |
| Tata Tea Ltd. | 0.043 | -0.031 | -0.042 | -0.009 | 0.06 | -0.003 | -0.025 | 47.915* |
| VSNL Ltd. | -.083* | -0.018 | -0.049 | 0.009 | -0.009 | 0.025 | -0.025 | 15.752 |
| Wipro Ltd. | 0.067 | .113** | -0.008 | 0.032 | 0.056 | -.078* | -0.049 | 31.721** |
| Zea Telefilms Ltd. | 0.025 | -0.01 | -0.03 | 0.015 | 0.059 | 0.047 | -0.039 | 29.103** |
| S & P CNX Nifty | 0.014 | 0.019 | -0.023 | 0.022 | 0.058 | -0.019 | -0.029 | 31.772** |

*Significant at 0.05 level, **Significant at 0.01 level
Box-Ljung Statistics Significant at 0.01, 0.05 and 0.10 level for *, ** and *** respectively.

However, the Box-Ljung (BL) statistics gives mixed ceases as forty per cent of the BL values are significant, rejecting the joint hypothesis that all the serial correlation coefficients are simultaneously equal to zero. As, the hypothesis is accepted in case of majority (60%) of the series, we may conclude that successive price changes are independent of the previous day price changes. Although, a few lower order serial correlation coefficients of daily price changes as well as S & P CNX Nifty disclosed some departure from random walk hypothesis, the results of runs test conforms to the results in favour of random-walk theory. Thus,, the existence of efficient market reduces the likelihood of continuously earning extra returns by forecasting the security prices.

Filter tests: Filter test examines the random-walk hypothesis from a different, but more direct, approach. Categorized as filter tests, they have been developed as direct tests of specific mechanical trading strategies. In other words, no inferences about such strategies need be made, for the approach is to examine directly the validity of specific systems.

One such test is based on the premise that once a movement in price has surpassed a given percentage movement, the security's price will continue to move in the same direction. Thus the following rule, which is similar to the famous Dow theory:

If the daily closing price of a security moves up at least X%, buy the security until its price moves down at least X% from a subsequent high, at which time simultaneously swell and go short. The short position should be maintained until the price rises at least X% above a subsequent low, at which time cover and buy.

As the reader has undoubtedly observed, the selection of a high filter will cut down his number of transactions and will lead to fewer false starts or signals, but it will also decrease his potential profit because he would have missed the initial portion of the move. Conversely, the selection of a smaller filter will ensure his sharing in the great bulk of the security's price movement, but he will have the disadvantage of performing many transactions, with their accompanying high costs,as well as often operating on false signals. As we see in Table only when the filter was at its smallest did this mechanical procedure outperform a simple buy-and-hold strategy, and even then, only before transactions costs were considered.

**Table. AVerage Annual Rates of Return Per Stock**

| Value of x (%) | Return with trading strategy (%) | Return with buy-and-holdstrategy (%) strategy | Total transactions with trading | Return with trading strategy, after commissions (%) |
|---|---|---|---|---|
| 0.5 | 11.5 | 10.4 | 12,514 | -103.6 |
| 1.0 | 5.5 | 10.3 | 8,660 | -74.9 |
| 2.0 | 0.2 | 10.3 | 4,784 | -45.2 |
| 3.0 | -1.7 | 10.3 | 2,994 | -30.5 |
| 4.0 | 0.1 | 10.1 | 2,013 | -19.5 |
| 5.0 | -1.9 | 10.0 | 1,484 | -16.6 |
| 6.0 | 1.3 | 9.7 | 1,071 | -9.4 |
| 7.0 | 0.8 | 9.6 | 828 | -7.4 |
| 8.0 | 1.7 | 9.6 | 653 | -5.0 |
| 9.0 | 1.9 | 9.6 | 539 | -3.6 |
| 10.0 | 3.0 | 9.3 | 435 | -1.4 |
| 12.0 | 5.3 | 9.4 | 289 | 2.3 |
| 14.0 | 3.9 | 10.3 | 224 | 1.4 |
| 16.0 | 4.2 | 10.3 | 172 | 2.3 |
| 18.0 | 3.6 | 10.0 | 139 | 2.0 |
| 20.0 | 4.3 | 9.8 | 110 | 3.0 |

An Introduction to Risk and Return from Common Stocks

## *Semistrong form of EMH*

The semistrong form of the efficient-market hypothesis says that current prices of stocks not only reflect all informational content of historical prices but also reflect all publicly available knowledge about the corporations being studied. Further-more, the semistrong form says that efforts by analysts and investors to acquire and analyse public information will not yield consistently superior returns to the analyst. Examples of the type of public information that will not be of value on a consistent basis to the analyst are corporate reports, corporate announcements, information relating to corporate dividend policy, forthcoming stock splits, and so forth.

In effect, the semistrong form of the efficient market hypothesis maintains that as soon as information becomes publicly available, it is absorbed and reflected in stock prices. Even if this adjustment is not the correct one immediately, it will in a very short time be properly analysed by the market. Thus the analyst would have great difficulty trying to profit using fundamental analysis. Furthermore, even while the correct adjustment is taking place, the analyst cannot obtain consistent superior returns.

### *Empirical Tests of the Semistrong Form*

We have learnt that the semistrong form says that current stock prices will instantaneously reflect all publicly available information. The tests that will be summarized briefly in this part test whether in fact all publicly available information and news announcements, such as quarterly earnings reports, changes in accounting information, stocks splits, stock dividends, and the like, are quickly and adequately reflected in stock prices. Furthermore, these tests attempt to analyse if an analyst using such data when they become available to him can successfully use this information to obtain superior investment results. Fama, Fisher, Jensen, and Roll made a major contribution with their study of the semistrong-form hypothesis. They tested the speed of the market's reaction to a firm's announcement of a stock split and the accompanying information with respect to a change in dividend policy. The authors concluded that the market was efficient with respect to its reaction to information on the stock split and also was efficient with respect to reacting to the informational content of stock splits vis-à-vis changes in dividend policy.

Ball and Brown conducted another test in this area by analyzing the stock market's ability to absorb the informational content of reported annual earnings per share information. In their study the authors examined stock price movements of companies that experience 'good' earnings reports as opposed to the stock price movements of companies that experienced 'bad' earnings reports. A 'good' earnings report was a reported earnings per share figure that was higher than the previously forecast earnings per share, and conversely a 'bad' earnings report was a reported earnings per share figure that was lower than had been forecast previously. They found that those companies with 'good' earnings reports experienced price increases in their stock and those with 'bad' earnings reports experienced stock price declines. The interesting result was that about 85 per cent of the informational content of the annual earnings announcement was reflected in stock price movements prior to the release of the actual annual earnings figure.

Joy, Litzenberger, and McEnally conducted another stock priceearnings report test in this area. In their study the authors tested the impact of quarterly earnings announcements on the stock price adjustment mechanism. Some of their results somewhat contradicted the semistrong form of the efficient-market hypothesis. In some of their subtests, the authors found that favourable information contained in published quarterly earnings reports was not instantaneously reflected in stock prices.

*Basu also conducted a test of the semistrong form:* In his study, Basu tested for the informational content of the price-earnings multiple. He tested to see whether low P/E stocks tended to outperform stocks with high P/E ratios. If historical P/E ratios provided useful information to investors in obtaining superior stock market returns, this would be a refutation of the semistrong form of the efficient market hypothesis.

Because if historical publicly available P/E information led an investor to buy a particular type of stock and this in turn led to abnormal returns, this would be a direct contradiction of the semistrong form. His results indicated that the low P/E portfolios experienced superior returns relative to the market and high P/E portfolios performed in an inferior manner relative to the overall market. A similar anomaly to the semistrong form of the efficient-markets hypothesis-namely, the size effect was also tested by researchers. These studies attempt to test whether smaller firms tended to experience larger returns than the larger firms experienced over the same time period. These studies indicated that small firms did provide the investor with significantly larger risk-adjusted returns than did the larger firms examined. However, other researchers have pointed out that this apparent anomaly results more from inappropriate risk measurements, the amount of attention analysts pay to the securities, volume of trading, frequency of trading, and transaction costs, rather than the size differential alone.

By way of summary, of the semistrong efficient tests, we have reviewed here, the great majority provide strong empirical support for the hypothesis; however, there have been some notable exceptions to this support. Most of the reported results demonstrate that stock prices do adjust rapidly to announcements of new information about stocks. Some of the studies indicate further that investors are typically unable to utilize this information to earn consistently above-average returns.

## Critique of EMH

Opinion is divided as to the validity of the EMH particularly in the strong form. In weak form Random Walk hypothesis holds good, as per some studies. The semi strong form has found less support from the empirical studies. The perfect markets do not exist, as the stocks as a rule do not sell at the best price based on intrinsic values. Many times, speculative fervour sentiment and expectations play a greater role on the stock prices than the fundamental factors.

Similarly news does not spread evenly among all segments of the market and among all investors. Institutional investors gain through market equity research and through economic of scale and better expertise. But individual investors do not gain by speedy spread of information and the absorption of the same by market. To gain, superior advantage, there was no adequate evidence from any of the empirical studies, based on prices or information. There is thus a controversy on the validity of Efficient Market Theory. In real market operations, this theory did no find support, as portfolio managers did not perform better based on the results of this theory.

This theory posed a challenge to both the chartist school and the fundamentalist school. If Random Walk or Weak Market Efficiency holds good, chartist school finds its tools are not of real value to gain superior returns. Similarly if random walk holds good, chartist school finds its tools are not of real value to gain superior returns. Similarly if random walk holds good, following the study of fundamentals will not secure better returns, unless additional information and insights into the company or better insider knowledge are available to investors

We have seen that the weak form of the efficient-market hypothesis maintains that past prices and past price changes cannot be used to forecast future price changes and future prices. Semistrong form of the efficient-market hypothesis says that publicly available information cannot be used to earn consistently superior investment returns. Some studies that tend to support the semistrong theory of the efficient-market hypothesis were cited. Finally, the strong form of the efficient-market hypothesis maintains that not only is publicly available information useless to the investor or analyst but all information is useless. Specifically, no information that is available, be it public or 'inside', can be used to earn consistently superior investment returns.

The semistrong form of the efficient-market hypothesis could only be tested indirectly- namely, by testing what happened to prices on days surrounding announcements of various types, such as earnings announcements, dividend announcements, and stock -split announcements. To test the strong form of efficient-market hypothesis, even more indirect methods must be used. For the strong form says that no information is useful. This implies that not even security analysts and portfolio managers who have access to information more quickly than the general investing public are able to use this information to earn superior returns.

Therefore, many of the tests of the strong form of the efficient market hypothesis deal with tests of mutual-fund performance. As suggested, review some of the findings of these tests of mutual-fund performance in part

Tests of the trading of specialists on the floor of the stock exchanges and tests of the profitability of insider trading suggest that the possibility of excess profits exists for these two very special groups of investors who can use their special information to earn profits in excess of normal returns.

It should, however, be emphasised that these two examples of market inefficiencies represent very minor inefficiencies when compared with the market as a whole. The strict form of the efficient-market hypothesis states that two conditions are met: first, that successive price changes or changes in return are independent; and second, that these successive price changes or return changes are identically distributed- that is, these distributions will repeat themselves over time.

In a practical sense, this seems to imply that in a random-walk world, stock prices will at any time fully reflect all publicly available information, and furthermore, that when new information becomes available, stock prices will instantaneously adjust to reflect it.

The reader will note that the random-walk theorist is not interested in price or return levels, but rather in the changes between successive levels. The more general efficient-market model, when interpreted loosely, acknowledges that the markets may have some imperfections, such as transactions costs, information costs, and delays in getting pertinent information to all market participants; but it states that these potential sources of market inefficiency do not exist to such a degree that it is possible to develop trading systems whose expected profits or returns will be in excess of expected normal, equilibrium returns of profits. .

Generally, we define equilibrium profits as those that can be earned by following a simple buy-and-hold strategy rather than a more complex, mechanical system. Thus, we see that the random-walk model represents a special, restrictive case of the efficient-market model.

## The Efficient-market Hypothesis and Mutual-fund Performance

It has often been said that large investors such as mutual funds perform better in the market than the small investor does because they have access to better information. Therefore, it would be interesting to observe if mutual funds earned above-average returns, where these are defined as returns in excess of those that can be earned by a simple buy-and-hold strategy. The results of such an investigation would have interesting implications for the efficientmarket hypothesis.

Researchers have found that mutual funds do not seem to be able to earn greater net returns (after sales expenses) than those that can be earned by investing randomly in a large group of securities and holding them. Furthermore, these studies indicate, mutual funds are not even able to earn gross returns (before sales expenses) superior to those of the native buy-and-hold strategy. These results occur not only because of the difficulty in applying fundamental analysis in a consistently superior manner to a large number of securities in an efficient market but also because of portfolio overdiversification and its attendant problems- two of which are high book-keeping and administrative costs to monitor the investments, and purchases of securities with less favourable risk-return characteristics. Therefore, it would seem that the mutual-fund studies lend some credence to the efficient-market hypothesis.

There are three broad theories concerning stock price movements. The fundamentalists believe that by analyzing key economic and financial variables, they can estimate the intrinsic worth of the security and then determine what investment action to take. The technical or chartist school maintains that fundamental analysis is unnecessary; all that has to be done is to study historical price patterns and then decide how current price behaviour fits into these. Because the technician believes that history repeats itself, he can then predict future movements in price based on the study of historical patterns. The random-walk school has demonstrated to its own satisfaction through empirical tests that successive price changes over short periods, such as a day, a week, or a month, are independent. To the extent that this independence exists, the random-walk theory directly contradicts technical analysis; and furthermore, to the extent that the stock markets are efficient in the dissemination of information and that they have informed market participants and the proper institutional setting, the random-walk school poses an important challenge to the fundamentalist camp as well.

If the markets are truly efficient, then the fundamentalist will be successful only when

- He has inside information, or
- He has superior ability to analyse publicly available information and gain insight into the future of the firm, and
- He uses– and/or – to reach long-term buy-and-hold investment decisions.

The empirical evidence in support of the random-walk hypothesis rests primarily on statistical tests, such as runs tests, correlation analysis, and filter tests. The results have been almost unanimously in support of the random-walk hypothesis, the weak form of the efficient market hypothesis. The results of semistrong-form tests have been mixed.

# 11

# Investment Companies

Investment companies collect investors' money for purposes of investing it into various specified assets. Investment companies are often restricted by their organizational charter to holdings of only certain types of assets. Most investment companies are organized as corporations, although some are set up as limited partnerships for tax reasons, and others are organized as real estate investment trusts (REITs). Generally, investment companies are required to pay out all net income (both interest and dividends received plus all realised capital gains net of investment company expenses and realised capital losses) to the shareholders or owners of the pool (or else the investment companies themselves are subject to tax).

Investment companies can be either passively managed or actively managed. A passively managed investment company does not attempt to evaluate whether the assets in its portfolio should be replaced with superior investments. An actively managed investment company seeks out superior investment opportunities and may change its portfolio holdings by buying and selling different assets when it finds superior investments. In all cases, the investment company's managers and administrators charge the investment company a fee for their investment services. This fee is often quoted on an annualized basis as a per cent of the investment company's assets, although it is typically levied daily.

Investment companies can be categorized into two major types: asset-backed securities and mutual funds. Both types are analysed in subsequent parts.

## ASSET-BACKED SECURITIES

The simplest form of investment companies are asset-backed securities, which are claims on a share of a group of assets passively held by a closed-end pool. The assets in the pool are initially chosen from a group of fairly homogenous assets, and the asset holdings are fixed over the life of the pool. All interest and principal payments from the assets in the pool are passed through to the investment company shareholders as they are made (after deducting the pool's fees at the end of each month), and the pool's life terminates with the final principal payment on the pool's assets. Asset-backed securities are often therefore called pass-through securities.

Asset-backed securities usually have some form of credit guarantee from the issuer or seller of the pool. These credit enhancements frequently take the form of a blanket guarantee of full payment of principal on any asset in the pool that defaults on a payment (after a typical 90-day grace period). However, some credit enhancements only guarantee up to a certain amount of the pool's assets (such as 5%), in which case losses from defaults over that amount would have to be borne by the pool's shareholders. In all cases, the value of such guarantees is only as good as the credit quality of the guarantor.

### *Mortgage-Backed Securities*

The largest amounts of asset-backed securities are mortgage-backed securities, sometimes called mortgage pass-throughs. Most mortgage pass-throughs represent pools of residential mortgages with similar payments and credit characteristics. The similar credit characteristics are usually defined by the issuer in terms of loan-to-value ratios (such as including into the pool only mortgages whose par value is less than or equal to 80% of the appraised value of the home collateral). The similar payments generally consist of regular monthly payments that amortize the principal over 30 years (or over 15 years for 15-year mortgage pools). In addition, each pool is usually somewhat homogenous in terms of having a narrow range of coupons for fixed-rate mortgage pools, or similar characteristics for adjustable-rate mortgage (ARM) pools, and a narrow range of time remaining to maturity (such as 28-30 years).

Payments on most mortgage pools are 100% guaranteed against default, often by the issuer of the pool (or sometimes by a separate private insurance company). For instance, Government National Mortgage Association (GNMA) pass-throughs represent pools of a particular type of residential mortgages that are issued by GNMA, which is an existing U.S. agency. The mortgages issued by GNMA are FHA and VA mortgages (for lower-income families on lower-priced houses) that are guaranteed against default by the U.S. government.

The primary other large mortgage pool issuers and guarantors are privatized government agencies. Because these agencies have been privatized, the guarantees are not risk-free. For instance, FHLMC participation certificates are conventional residential mortgage pools 100% guaranteed against default by a privatized government agency called the Federal Home Loan Mortgage Corporation. Another privatized government agency that issues guaranteed mortgage pools is the Federal National Mortgage Association (FNMA). Both these private (but governmentregulated) organizations have very high leverage ratios (over 90% liabilities/assets ratios) and can default on their guarantees if they become bankrupt.

Many mortgage pools have more than one class of shareholder and are called Collateralized Mortgage Obligations (CMOs) because the mortgages serve as collateral for each of the shareholder claims. CMOs divide claims on the payments from a pool into several classes or tranches. An example of a simple CMO is a pool that passes through all mortgage interest payments to an IO (interest-only) tranche and all mortgage principal payments to a PO (principal-only).

Many CMOs create tranches with different priority claims on both interest and principal. For instance, a first tranche may receive all principal payments from the pool until its total principal claim is paid off, the second tranche may receive only a specified monthly amount of interest until the first tranche is paid off and thereafter receive all principal passed through until its principal claim is also paid off, and similarly for successive tranches. However, some CMOs have special Principal Amortization Class (PAC) tranches which have a prior claim each month on only a portion of its total claim on principal.

Except for IOs and POs, each CMO tranche typically receives a monthly cash coupon interest payment on the amount of principal not yet paid (in some CMOs, tranches called *floaters* exist that have the coupon rate float with a specified market interest rate, while the coupon rate floats inversely with market interest rates on *inverse floater* tranches). However, some CMOs have a *Z bond* tranche that only accrues interest until all the other tranches are paid in full, after which it receives all cash passed through the CMO until a specified coupon rate is earned. CMO positions generally have substantial risk related to changes in the level and volatility of interest rates (that can be evaluated with SIA mortgage valuation software).

### Other Asset-Backed Securities

Other publicly traded debts are also gathered into pools. The most typical types are pools of auto loans and pools of credit card loans. Like mortgage pools, these pools pass through the payments from the indebted individuals (or other revenue streams). These pools often have some type of credit enhancement from the private issuer of the pool, but the guarantee is usually restricted to a certain per cent of the assets. There also exist asset-backed securities issued on corporate debt, such as pools of account receivables and commercial real estate mortgages. More exotic sorts like securities passing through Italian cemetery revenues and pools backed by money grams from Mexican workers in the U.S. have also been created. In addition, some of these other asset pools have several classes of shareholders or participation certificates like CMOs do.

Although there was over $1 trillion in mortgage-backed securities in existence at the end of the 1980s (which represented a securitization of about 1/3 of all U.S. residential mortgages), there were only $10 billion in auto loan pools and $12 billion in credit card pools in the U.S. By 1998, however, the amount of nonmortgage asset-backed securities outstanding had risen to over $600 billion (while the amount of mortgage-backed securities had risen to almost $2 trillion, of which over $500 billion were CMOs). The amount of securitized foreign debt is much smaller, although some countries such as England have begun to develop mortgage-backed securities markets.

### *Unit Investment Trusts*

Another type of investment company is a unit investment trust. Unit trusts are similar to other asset-backed securities, except that the initial assets put into the pool are professionally selected by the issuer of the pool (instead of being issued on a fairly homogenous class of assets with similar characteristics in the case of asset-backed securities). Once chosen, the assets in the pool are not sold or changed over the life of the trust (the life of the trust is specified in the pool charter before its creation). The pool passes through all payouts and principal payments from the assets in the pool, after subtracting out an administrative fee. Most unit trusts are closed-end, and the assets in the trusts are often not guaranteed against default.

Most unit trusts are issued on a group of municipal bonds that have been selected as good investments by the issuer. The termination of these trusts generally coincides with the final principal payment on the municipal bonds.

However, some unit trusts have also been issued on a portfolio of other bonds and/or stocks. The trust is specified to terminate in a number of years, after which the securities in the pool are sold and the cash proceeds are paid to the shareholders.

There is another type of investment company with a similar name called a *unitrust*. A unitrust differs from a unit trust insofar as a unitrust can permit changes in the portfolio holdings of the investment company whereas the assets held by a unit trust are static. In addition, instead of paying out only the principal, interest, and dividend payments from the assets of the investment company, a unitrust may pay out a portion of capital before its expiration. In that sense, a unitrust is more like a mutual fund..

## INVESTMENT COMPANIES WITH VARYING PORTFOLIOS

Other investment companies such as mutual funds differ from asset-backed securities insofar as their investment holdings can change over time, as the investment company manager is allowed to buy and sell assets for the pool. Mutual funds are the most widely known of this type of investment company. Mutual funds sell shares to the public and use the money to invest primarily into assets for which there is an active resale market (i.e., into assets that can be easily and quickly sold).

Other investment companies with varying portfolios either raise money privately from specified investors (such as unitrusts, private money management companies, and hedge funds) and/or invest primarily into assets for which there is no active resale market (such as REITs that invest into real estate and venture capital firms that invest into the stock of very small companies).

Some investment companies (such as private money management companies and hedge funds) tend to cater tend to cater to larger investors, while others are offered only to specific tax-exempt investors (e.g., unitrusts are sold to endowment funds and trusts, whose tax-exempt status and desire to spend a stable amount of money each year motivates most unitrusts to be set up to pay out to unitholders a fixed annual percentage of NAV regardless of capital gains and other investment income).

Most such investment companies can be evaluated just as mutual funds are (although there may be less public information available about them). For investment companies with large holdings of illiquid assets, however, it is generally not possible to compute NAV (one exception is a real estate investment company offered by the Teachers Insurance and

Annuity Association, or TIAA), and so somewhat different methodologies must be used to analyse these investment companies.

## General Characteristics of Mutual Funds

mutual funds are organizations that pool investors' money into various investments, of which 85% must be liquid marketable securities for which there is an active resale market. Most mutual funds are members of a family of mutual funds with a single administrative organization (such as Vanguard), which offers many mutual fund choices under the same umbrella, address, and phone number (allowing for ease in transferring money between funds in the same mutual fund family).

Most mutual funds require each new shareholder to initially invest a minimum amount (such as $1000) into the fund (over 25% of all funds in existence in 1997 required minimum initial investments of over $1000). However, many funds have smaller initial minimums for Individual Retirement Accounts (IRAs). Smaller investors can sometimes circumvent any such restrictions by borrowing an amount to meet the initial minimum and then redeeming fund shares to repay the loan. Mutual funds generally allow accounts that have been set up to have less than the initial minimum if the investor enters into an automatic investment plan where some small amount (such as $25 monthly) is periodically invested into the account. Alternatively, it is possible to buy mutual funds through some brokers such as Accutrade (1-800-228-3011) that permit (in return for an initial brokerage fee of about $27) investing as little as $100 into any of over 7600 different mutual funds as long as the investor pledges to invest at least $100 per quarter thereafter (without brokerage fees).

Once the money is raised from investors, the managers of the mutual funds buy and sell assets within a prespecified category of investment as they see fit. Such buying and selling of assets represents portfolio turnover. Turnover is often measured as the total dollar amount of asset sales in a fund divided by the total dollar amount of assets in the fund (so that 200% annual turnover on a fund with $10 million in assets indicates that the fund has sold $20 million in assets over the year, implying that the fund, on average, replaced its assets twice over the year by selling existing security holdings and buying new ones).

Mutual funds can offer expertise in investment selection and diversification within a stated category of permitted investments as well as other services. In return for these services, mutual fund managers levy expense fees on the pool of money in the fund. These expenses are typically levied or accrued daily, although the funds usually quote these expenses on an annualized basis as a per cent of assets. Besides a normal fee levied as a percentage of assets, some funds (such as hedge funds and futures funds) also charge funds a fee equal to a percentage of the profits of the fund.

The expense ratios of mutual funds normally do not include much of the transaction costs of trading. The transaction costs caused by portfolio turnover are typically included in the total prices paid for purchases and in the net prices received for asset sales. As a result, such costs are frequently difficult to measure although they can be approximated by applying 1998 Keim and Madhavan data on institutional trading costs to fund turnover figures.

As mutual funds receive interest and dividends from their investments and earn profits from the sale of investments at prices in excess of the amount paid, they generate income that usually exceeds the expenses they charge their funds. All such net income must generally be paid out to their shareholders in the form of a dividend (and the mutual fund thereby avoids being taxed on the net income). Although such dividends can be paid at any time over the course of the year, mutual fund dividends from regular interest and dividend income are typically paid monthly or quarterly, while gains from the sale of securities are normally paid out only at the end of the year.

### *Open-end Funds*

Some mutual funds called open-end funds also offer an additional service of offering to buy or sell any shares requested at the net asset value per share (NAV) at the end of any business day. NAV is computed as:

NAV = (Market Value of Fund Assets - Fund Liabilities)/ Shares, where the fund's estimate of fair value is used for any non-trading assets held.

Requests to buy or sell shares may be made directly to the fund, often via a toll-free 800 number, or through brokers and financial planners who agree to trade the mutual fund shares for investors (typically for a fee that is charged either to the investor or to the mutual fund).

Payment for fund share redemptions can be made via wire, electronic funds, or mailed check at the request of the shareholder. In addition, many funds (especially those that invest into fixed-income securities) permit shareholders to write checks on their investments (writing a check on a fund results in automatic share sales at net asset value when it clears through to the mutual fund). Regardless of how redemptions are made, open-end mutual funds provide a substantial amount of liquidity to investors by agreeing to redeem shares at net asset value.

Some open-end mutual funds levy an explicit sales fee on purchases and/or sales of shares of the fund. This sales fee is called a load (which can't exceed 8.5% of the investment by U.S. law). Sales fees levied on purchases of open-end mutual fund shares are often called front-end loads. Funds that levy such a front-end fee are normally called load funds. Sales fees that are levied by some mutual funds on share redemptions at the NAV are called back-end loads. Some funds levy only a front-end load or only a back-end load, while other funds levy both. Although the entire load is kept by the mutual fund administrator if the transaction is made directly with the mutual fund, many transactions are made through financial planners and brokers who are paid a portion of the load (typically half).

Some load funds give investors the choice of how they would like to pay their load by offering several different types of shares. For instance, some mutual funds allow investors to purchase A-class shares that levy only a normal front-end load but also permit investors to buy B-class shares that levy no front-end load but instead charge the investor an annual load. In the latter case (the B shares), the load must be paid by the investor directly just for holding the shares (and it is not charged to the mutual fund, so it does not increase the mutual fund's expense ratios). The shares with an annual load would be preferred by more active traders, while the front-end loaded shares might be preferred by long-term investors.

Many back-end loads are reduced or even eliminated for investors who hold the shares for a specified minimum length of time. For instance, many back-end loaded funds levy a 7% fee to sell if the fund is held less than one year, 6% if the fund is held less than 2 years, 5% if the fund is held less then 3 years, etc., until the backend load disappears for investors who have held the shares at least 7 years. Other mutual funds have small back-end loads (like 1%) that disappear if an investor holds the shares just three months.

Many funds do not levy any load and are called no-load funds. However, in practice, any fund without a front-end load is often called a no-load fund if any back-end load is eliminated for investors who hold onto the fund shares long enough.

Some funds pay salespeople (such as brokers and financial planners) for soliciting new shareholders but do not levy any load (neither front-end, back-end, or annual load) directly on investors owning or trading shares. Instead, many of these funds pay the sales fee or commission out of the fund itself in the form of higher daily expenses. Such sales fees (as well as other marketing and distribution costs) charged to the fund as a whole are called 12b-1 expenses and must be disclosed by the mutual fund. These funds are technically no-load funds although they frequently have higher than average annual fees charged to the fund because of the 12b-1 expenses. In 1998, 40% of open-end mutual fund transactions were made directly with the mutual funds. Another 36% were made through full-service brokers, 12% through commercial banks, 7% through financial planners, and 5% through insurance companies and discount brokers (in the future, an increasing share of trades was expected to be made through financial planners and directly with the mutual funds, while a declining share of mutual transactions were forecast through banks and full service brokers).

### *Closed-End Funds*

Open-end mutual funds contrast with closed-end funds which are not required to redeem shares at the net asset value. Although closed-end funds are not obligated to redeem shares, these fund shares may usually be sold to other investors in the market at whatever price the other investors are willing to pay. the price investors are willing to pay for closed-end funds is different from NAV. Some closed-end funds buy up some of their own shares in the market when the price falls far below NAV.

### *Types of Mutual Funds*

Many mutual funds restrict themselves to only one category of investments such as domestic equities. However, some funds have the freedom to invest in a mixture of asset categories.

For instance, balanced funds can invest in both domestic equities and bonds, while asset allocation funds can invest in most any type of asset (and these latter funds typically diversify into stocks, bonds, real asset investments, and foreign assets).

Other funds are restricted to only a specific subsection of an asset category, such as investment-grade bonds. Some mutual funds even invest in other pools, such as GNMA funds. In 1991, there was $1.347 trillion invested into mutual funds in the U.S. (including $368 billion in equity funds, $439 billion in bond and other fixed-income funds, and $540 billion in money market funds) and $1.375 trillion invested into foreign mutual funds (including $396 billion in French mutual funds, $349 billion in Japanese mutual funds, and $175 billion in German mutual funds, with fixed-income and money market funds making up over 50% of the total). By 1997, there was about $4 trillion invested into U.S. mutual funds, of which over half was invested into stock funds.

There are two general categories of mutual funds: actively managed funds and passively managed funds. Actively managed funds have substantial discretion as to which assets will be purchased by the fund. Passively managed funds are typically restricted to only specified securities with specified weights.

The typical passively managed fund is an index fund, which is constrained to investments in an index of assets (such as the S&P 500) in proportions that approximate the weightings of the index. The purpose of an index fund is to approximately match the performance of the index. Because the assets in the index change from time to time (due to acquisitions and bankruptcies, for instance), the investments of the index fund must be periodically rebalanced.

Such portfolio rebalancing differentiates them from unit investment trusts, which are otherwise very similar insofar as both index funds and unit trusts are passively managed. Another difference between index funds and unit trusts is that some active selection may go into choosing the initial investments for the unit trust, whereas an index fund blindly buys the stocks in an index.

In addition, unit trusts typically have a specified termination date, whereas index funds do not. Although most unit trusts and open-end mutual funds are open-end (agreeing to redeem assets at NAV), there are a few closed-end index funds such as Spiders (an abbreviation for S&P Depository Receipts), which invest into the S&P500, and such as over a dozen different Webs, each of which invests into the equity index of a specified foreign country (like Germany).

Regardless of whether a mutual fund is passively or actively managed, most funds have only one class of stock that shares equally in all the investment income and capital gains of the fund. However, some mutual funds have several classes of stockholders.

For instance, dual funds have one class of shareholders with a claim on the fund's investment income (dividends and interest payments) while another class of shareholders has a claim on the capital gains of the fund.

More recently, a new type of mutual fund has been developed whereby one class of preferred shareholders has a prior claim on the interest income of the fund up to a specified amount that varies with a specified money market interest rate, while the common shareholders of the mutual fund have a claim on all remaining investment income and capital gains. This latter capital structure is especially useful for municipal bond funds, as it gives the preferred shareholders a fairly secure money market interest rate that exceeds high-grade municipal money market rates, while allowing the common shareholders of the fund to obtain a leveraged investment in municipal bonds by essentially "borrowing" at a low tax-advantaged rate (because municipal securities are exempt from federal tax, they tend to have negative terms with yields below the risk-free Treasury rate.

There has been a great deal of discussion about the optimal size of a mutual fund. Although larger mutual funds tend to have lower administrative expenses due to economies of scale, they also often have higher trading costs because of the need to buy so much of a security to obtain a meaningful position. In addition, larger funds find it especially difficult to take significant positions on smaller companies without substantial trading costs. Overall, although it is nearly impossible to start a mutual with less than $1 million in assets, and administrative costs tend to be extremely high for funds with even $10 million in assets, there are many fund managers who believe that it is so counterproductive to be too large that they close their funds to new investors once they reach several billion dollars in assets.

There also exists a type of fund called a fund of funds that pools investors' money for purpose of investing into other mutual funds. Many of these fund of funds are offered by the administrator of a family of mutual funds to invest only into a portfolio of mutual funds in that family. Many funds of funds generally add an extra layer of annual expense (often called a wrap fee) for the service of determining for investors the mutual funds into which they are to invest (as little as 0.08% per year for Fidelity but closer to 2% for others, which is in addition to the annual expenses charged to the funds themselves into which the money is invested). However, some fund administrators (such as Vanguard, Scudder, and T. Rowe Price) do not charge for this service. There was $29 billion invested through such funds of funds in 1998.

**Types of Mutual Funds and Similar Investment Companies**

- A listing follows for many different types of mutual funds and other investment companies with varying portfolios that exist. Unless otherwise specified, each type may be either closed-end or open-end, depending on the individual investment company.
- Domestic Bond Funds - invest in domestic fixed-income securities (some of the funds may have a specified concentration in bonds with short, medium, or long maturities, while others may have a specified concentration in bonds with either low or high default risk —bond funds specified to invest into debt with higher default risk are often called "high income funds" or "high yield funds").
- *Money market funds**: Invest in money market instruments.
- *Corporate bond funds*: Invest in corporate bonds.
- *Municipal bond funds*: Invest in bonds issued by state and local governments. *government bond funds* - invest in bonds issued by the federal government and/or federal agencies. *mortgage REITs* (real estate investment trusts) - closed-end investment companies that invest into mortgages.
- *Domestic Stock Funds*: Invest in domestic equities
- *Balanced funds*: Invest in stocks and bonds *preferred*
- *Stock funds*: Invest into preferred stocks (usually high-yielding investment grade preferred).
- *Income funds*: Invest in stocks (and/or bonds) with high current yields.
- *Growth funds*: Invest in stocks with low current yields.
- *Small cap funds*: Invest in stocks of companies with

smaller market capitaliza-tions (as measured by the market value of all equity, which is computed as the market price times the number of shares outstanding) large cap funds-invest in stocks of larger companies *specialized funds*-invest in stocks of a particular industry (such as health care).

- *Index funds*: Invest into a specified index of stocks (such as the S&P 500).
- *Option funds*: Invest in stocks and options *R&D*
- *Partnerships*: Closed-end investment companies that invest directly in research and development projects (especially related to drug development).
- *Venture capital companies:* Closed-end investment companies that invest in the stock of small companies for which there is no secondary market.
- *Real Asset Funds:* Invest in real assets or companies that produce real investment assets.
- *Real estate funds:* Invest in a portfolio of real estate equities.
- *Precious metals funds:* Invest in companies that mine gold and other precious metals.
- *Equity REITs* (real estate investment trusts) - closed-end investment companies that invest directly into real estate properties.
- *Rreal estate partnerships:* Closed-end investment companies that invest directly into real estate properties.
- *Oil and gas partnerships:* Closed-end investment companies that invest directly into projects that explore for or pump petroleum.
- *Commodity funds or pools:* Funds that invest in commodity futures contracts.
- *Futures funds or pools:* Funds that invest in commodity and financial futures contracts.
- *Intemational Funds:* Invest in foreign securities
- *International bond funds*: Invest in foreign fixed-income securities.
- *International stock funds*: Invest in foreign equities.

- *Specialized country funds:* Invest in the assets (mostly stocks) of a single foreign country (such as Ireland).
- *Specialized regional funds:* Invest in the stocks of a singly region (such as Europe or Asia).
- *Emerging market funds:* Invest into less developed countries (such as Latin America and Southeast Asia).
- *Total Asset Management Funds:* Invest into several categories of assets (often into all four categories: stocks, bonds, real assets, and foreign assets).
- *Asset allocation funds*: Actively invest into stocks, bonds, and foreign assets, as - well as often into real assets.
- *Hedge funds*: Invest into any assets (including derivatives), taking both long and - short positions (with the positions often being fairly balanced or hedged in order to reduce exposure to systematic risk). The number of investors is usually restricted for regulatory purposes to be under 100, with each investor generally being required to invest at least $250,000 (since 1996, hedge funds have been allowed to have as many as 500 investors if each investor in the fund has a minimum of $5 million in marketable security investments).

  Most hedge funds are closed-end except on specific dates, such as the first business day of the year when redemptions may be made at net asset value. By 1998, there were several thousand hedge funds in existence (including many funds of funds that diversify into different hedge funds) with over $200 billion in assets (some limited empirical evidence indicates that, despite very high management fees, the surviving funds have generated double- digit rates of return on average while having low betas or correlation with the aggregate market portfolio of all assets). -
- *One special note on money market funds: these generally value securities at - cost and thereby maintain a constant NAV of $1 per share. Interest on the funds' investments are accrued to shareholders

daily and paid at the end of the month. If there were ever a run by investors to redeem shares of a money market fund after interest rates had risen, the fund might have to sell assets at less than cost, and the NAV could fall below $1. However, despite frequent large gyrations in interest rates, only one money market fund in the U.S. has ever failed to redeem shares at a $1 NAV. As a result, money market funds are often considered to be virtually risk-free investments (as are most diversified portfolios of money market instruments).

- A large number of international mutual funds are also offered in foreign - countries. However, unlike many mutual funds in the U.S., most mutual funds in foreign countries charge an upfront load. For instance, until recently in Germany, there was a typical load of 5% for stock funds, 3% for bond funds, and 1% for - money market funds. Increasing financial integration, deregulation, and competition are changing that situation, however.

### *Evaluating Investment Companies with Varying Portfolios*

An analysis of mutual funds requires an examination of the most important characteristics of each fund. One of the most important functions of mutual funds is to provide diversification, and it is important to ensure that the selection of funds meets the investors' needs. Because most funds concentrate their investments in some particular category of assets (such as stocks), it is generally necessary to choose more than one fund. For instance, to achieve the diversification guidelines, an investor might need to invest into at least 4 different mutual funds: one for domestic equities, one for domestic bonds, one for real assets, and one for foreign assets (with more than these four funds being required if any of the funds has concentration in any individual securities, industries, or foreign regions). Although an investor with limited knowledge could blindly assign equal weights to each category (i.e., 25% into each investment category), or according to the approximate weights of the market portfolio of all securities as estimated i.e., about 20% into U.S. bonds, 20% into U.S. equities, 5% into U.S. real estate, and 55% into foreign bonds and equities), the per cent of wealth allocated to each fund concentrated in an investment category should optimally be set as a function of the type of aggregate fundamental analysis On the other hand, it is also possible to allow professional managers to determine the optimal allocation to each investment category. For instance, if one invested in a balanced fund, there would only be a need for a minimum of 3 different funds, as a balanced fund includes both domestic stock and bond holdings. It is actually possible to select just one fund, if it is an asset allocation fund that diversifies across all investment categories.

When choosing which funds, it is also important to exercise judgment with respect to various other criteria besides diversification. Among the most important information to examine on any fund are the fee or load charged directly to investors for buying or selling shares of the fund, the annual operating expenses charged to the fund for its administration, and the fund's historical performance in maximizing long-term returns net of those expenses. Guidelines for analyzing, researching, and choosing mutual funds and other investment companies with varying portfolios are provided.

### *Analysis of Mutual Fund Investments*

For purposes of selecting a fund for each investment category, it is often useful to investigate 4 fund characteristics: long-term past performance, annual expenses charged to investors, portfolio turnover, and the existence of a load. Generally, it is thought that, if a fund manager is more skillful than average, the expertise will show up in long-term past performance records in the form of high compounded rates of return. In addition, to the extent that a fund generates excessive expenses for its investors, either through annual expense fees, excessive trading costs, and/or explicit loads to buy or sell the fund's shares, the fund may under perform other funds long-term. Often, higher expenses charged to funds stem from inefficiency and/or the lack of economies of scale and scope (i.e., too few assets over which too many fixed expenses have to be spread), and, at some point, the return from additional trading and management effort does not offset the costs.

These hypotheses have been verified in empirical research that evaluates future returns as a function of the foregoing variables. For instance, empirical research does indicate that funds with good long-term past performance may be more likely to generate future good performance than funds with poor past performance. Performance is often measured by the total compounded rate of return over a long period of time like 4-10 years.

Funds that earned higher compounded rates of return relative to other funds that invest in that category of assets are more likely to do so in the future as well (although they are by no means assured of doing so).

Some studies have also found that funds which charge investors low annual expenses for managing the fund are more likely to provide investors with a higher net return after deducting those expenses. Annual expense ratios are generally compared to theexpense ratios of other funds that invest in that category of assets, and a low ratio would be one that is less than the average. For example, a stock fund with an expense ratio that is lower than the average for all stock funds would be low. Generally, a ratio less than 1% is considered to be fairly low for a stock fund, while a somewhat lower expense ratio would be expected for a bond fund. On the other hand, futures funds and hedge funds typically have extremely high expense ratios equal to 5% or more of assets (largely due to management incentive fees that often are set to take 20% of all profits), and many investors may choose to avoid these types of funds for this reason alone. A 1997 study by Collins and Mack indicates that a mutual fund family typically needs about $20 billion in assets to attain the economies of scale and scope to have the lowest expense ratios, and so investors may want to target only the largest mutual fund families. Some research also indicates that funds with low annual portfolio turnover are more likely to provide investors with higher net returns after deducting the frequently hidden transaction costs of their trading, although not all studies indicate a significant relationship. Like expense ratios, turnover ratios can be compared to the individual and average turnover ratios of other funds that invest into the same category of assets. Turnover ratios under 100% are often considered to be low.

Studies have found that no-load funds are more likely to generate higher net returns than load funds after deducting the sales fee from load fund returns. The load essentially represents compensation to the selling broker, financial planner, or other agent for the time spent helping the investor make investment decisions and choose a fund.

These findings imply that a simple and liquid means of diversifying into an optimal risky portfolio is to pick 4 open-end no-load funds: one that invests into stocks, one that invests into bonds, one that invests into real assets (such as real estate), and one that invests into foreign securities (such as foreign stocks and bonds). The funds would be selected based on the criteria of high compounded returns over a long time interval (like 5-10 years), low expenses, and low turnover, with all comparisons being made relative to other funds that concentrate in that category of assets (like comparing bond funds to other fixed-income funds, international stock funds to other international stock funds, etc.).

Without any knowledge of the relative attractiveness of the four investment categories, it is possible to assign naive equal weights of 25% to each of the 4 funds just to ensure diversification, or use the market weightings (to mimic the overall return on the market portfolio of all assets). However, many investors may prefer to conduct some of the tactical asset allocation analysis to determine the optimal weighting of each investment type in a risky portfolio.

Alternatively, a single no-load asset allocation fund that has good long-term performance, low expenses, and low turnover relative to other asset allocation funds can be chosen. An asset allocation fund typically invests into all 4 investment categories of investments according to the fund manager's own fundamental analysis of the relative attractiveness of each investment type (although many asset allocation funds do not invest a significant amount of money into real estate or other real assets). As a result, selection of an asset allocation fund would be all that investors need to do to construct their risky portfolio p (unless they need some additional real estate assets, which most individuals don't because they already have a large amount of money tied up in the house they are consuming). For instance, TIAA-CREF (1-800-223-1200) offers a no-load asset allocation fund with an initial minimum of only $250 (or $25 for investors agreeing to periodic deductions from their bank accounts) and with extremely low annual expenses of less than 0.50%.

Once investors have chosen optimal risky portfolios of mutual funds, they can then use the guidelines provided for determining the optimal allocation of wealth to that risky portfolio (or use the SIA PORTFOLIO software for a more in-depth analysis within the context of a total financial plan). The remaining amount would be put into risk-free assets. Often, as explained, money market funds are considered to be risk-free assets, so that investors may select a money market fund in order to round out their selection of risky funds to meet their risk-aversion needs.

In all cases, investors can invest into a much larger assortment of mutual funds (as well as other assets), if they are unable to choose a single asset allocation fund or 4 single category funds that are superior to all other risky investment opportunities. For instance, many investors select several stock funds, including some from specific industry sectors, perhaps one that concentrates into growth stocks (with low dividend yields), and one that concentrates into income stocks (with high dividend yields). Choice of specialized funds enables the investor to be more selective in the proportions and timing of investments into various sectors of a given category of asset (like more into growth stocks and biotech stocks when the investor feels that technology stocks are under priced).

In addition to using long-term performance, expenses, and